# UNIVERSITY PRESIDENTS AS MORAL LEADERS

## Smith-Richardson Foundation
## Forums on Presidential Leadership
### September 21–23; October 3–5; October 28–30, 2003
### Participants

John R. Alexander, President, Center for Creative Leadership
Lawrence S. Bacow, President, Tufts University
James F. Barker, President, Clemson University
Andrew K. Benton, President, Pepperdine University
Robert G. Bottoms, President, DePauw University
Molly Corbett Broad, President, University of North Carolina System
David G. Brown, Interim President, Georgia College and State University
Phillip L. Clay, Chancellor, Massachusetts Institute of Technology
G. Wayne Clough, President, Georgia Institute of Technology
Mary Sue Coleman, President, University of Michigan
Scott S. Cowen, President, Tulane University
John J. DeGioia, President, Georgetown University
Philip L. Dubois, President, University of Wyoming
Gregory C. Farrington, President, Lehigh University
Larry R. Faulkner, President, University of Texas at Austin
Marye Anne Fox, Chancellor, North Carolina State University
Pamela B. Gann, President, Claremont-McKenna College
E. Gordon Gee, Chancellor, Vanderbilt University
William C. Gordon, Provost, Wake Forest University
David C. Hardesty, President, West Virginia University
Jody Hassett, ABC News
Thomas K. Hearn Jr., President, Wake Forest University
Freeman H. Hrabowski III, President, University of Maryland, Baltimore
    County
William E. Kirwan, Chancellor, University System of Maryland
Dale T. Knobel, President, Denison University
Edward S. Malloy, President, University of Notre Dame
Harold L. Martin Sr., Chancellor, Winston-Salem State University
Cynthia D. McCauley, Faculty, Center for Creative Leadership
James C. Moeser, Chancellor, University of North Carolina at Chapel Hill
Larry E. Penley, President, Colorado State University
Kathleen M. Ponder, Faculty, Center for Creative Leadership
John R. Ryan, President, State University of New York—Maritime College
Steven B. Sample, President, University of Southern California
Pamela Shockley-Zalabak, Chancellor, University of Colorado at Colorado
    Springs
Graham B. Spanier, President, Pennsylvania State University
Charles W. Steger, President, Virginia Polytechnic Institute and State University
Timothy J. Sullivan, President, The College of William and Mary
Julianne Still Thrift, President, Salem College
Rebecca Winters, *Time* Magazine
Albert C. Yates, President Emeritus, Colorado State University

# UNIVERSITY PRESIDENTS AS MORAL LEADERS

Edited by David G. Brown

Foreword by
Thomas K. Hearn Jr. and John Alexander

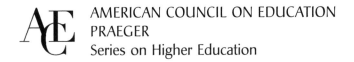

AMERICAN COUNCIL ON EDUCATION
PRAEGER
Series on Higher Education

Library of Congress Cataloging-in-Publication Data

University presidents as moral leaders / edited by David G. Brown ; foreword by
    Thomas K. Hearn Jr. and John Alexander.
        p.    cm.—(ACE/Praeger series on higher education)
    Includes bibliographical references and index.
    ISBN 0–275–98814–7 (alk. paper)
    1. College presidents—Professional ethics—United States.    2. Education,
Higher—Moral and ethical aspects—United States.    3. Leadership—United States.
I. Brown, David G.    II. Series.
LB2341.U59    2006
378.1'11—dc22            2005019266

British Library Cataloguing in Publication Data is available.

Library of Congress Catalog Card Number: 2005019266
ISBN: 0–275–98814–7

First published in 2006

Praeger Publishers, 88 Post Road West, Westport, CT 06881
An imprint of Greenwood Publishing Group, Inc.
www.praeger.com

Printed in the United States of America

The paper used in this book complies with the
Permanent Paper Standard issued by the National
Information Standards Organization (Z39.48-1984).

10 9 8 7 6 5 4 3 2 1

Understood generally as the process by which people unite to achieve common or shared purposes and projects, leadership is a sine qua non of successful collective endeavor. Groups may have good ideas, ample resources, and promising opportunities, but failure threatens unless and until the essential human resources are mobilized by effective leadership.

Thomas K. Hearn Jr.
President, Wake Forest University, 1983–2005
Chair, Board of Governors, Center for
Creative Leadership, 1996–

# CONTENTS

# FOREWORD

L eaders of today's American universities and colleges face daunting challenges as they seek to foster unity and set a direction in their own institutions and, simultaneously, to be moral exemplars who shape the thoughts and patterns throughout society. Like society, their institutions are by their very nature decentralized and resistant to authority. As a result, university presidents, chancellors, and other senior administrators must continually navigate a complex set of overlapping constituencies—from faculty, students, and alumni to donors, trustees, and legislators—to advance the educational mission of their institutions. In other words, these administrators are called upon to exercise outstanding leadership, both on campus and beyond. Their overall success in their roles—and surely the well-being of their institutions—depend in large part on how they respond to this call. Yet those seeking guidance on effective leadership will find that the resources that specifically address their concerns are surprisingly scarce.

It was with this need in mind that Wake Forest University and the Center for Creative Leadership (CCL) hosted the Smith-Richardson Forums on Effective University Leadership in the fall of 2003. Funded by the Smith-Richardson Foundation, this series of three forums brought together the leaders of thirty-six of the nation's leading universities and colleges for a period of reflection and debate. Their thoughtful presentations and exchanges were characterized by a remarkable candor, a willingness to think deeply about their successes and mistakes, and a desire to explore their most trying and rewarding moments, all in the spirit of aiding current and future leaders. The passion that these university leaders bring to their jobs, their sense of the vital role of higher education in a thriving democracy, and the moral imagination that their demanding roles require were all readily apparent. This book, also supported by the Smith-Richardson Foundation, is the fruit of these leaders' time together. It features a collection of essays that university presidents presented to their colleagues to spark discussion during the forums. Their choice of topics ran the gamut—from Mary Sue Coleman on the University of Michigan's legal battles in defense of affirmative action to Philip Dubois on the University of Wyoming's response to a series of high-profile tragedies involving students. Also included is a sampling of shorter responses to those essays from a panel of peers at each session.

We believe that, collectively, these stories offer a rich and unique resource for leaders as they contemplate and act on the matters of crisis, character, and community that are forever in play. These searching essays will help make today's leaders more effective through the concrete examples and hard-earned advice they provide. We hope, too, that they will assist up-and-coming leaders in preparing for the awesome responsibilities and possibilities that await them as senior leaders—and showcase for them approaches to leadership that will help ensure their success.

*Thomas K. Hearn Jr.*
*President, Wake Forest University*
*John Alexander*
*President, Center for Creative Leadership*
*August 2004*

# ABOUT THE CENTER FOR CREATIVE LEADERSHIP, WAKE FOREST UNIVERSITY, AND THE SMITH-RICHARDSON FOUNDATION

## THE CENTER FOR CREATIVE LEADERSHIP

The Center for Creative Leadership is a nonprofit educational institution with international reach. For more than three decades its mission has been to advance the understanding, practice, and development of leadership for the benefit of society worldwide. Center staff members conduct research, produce publications, and provide programs and assessment products to leaders and organizations in all sectors of society.

Headquartered in Greensboro, North Carolina, with locations in Colorado Springs, San Diego, Brussels, and Singapore, the Center annually serves leaders from more than 2,000 organizations—both public and private, including two-thirds of the Fortune 500. Each year, approximately 20,000 individuals participate in a Center program and 100,000 professionals complete a Center assessment. In 2003, *BusinessWeek*'s biennial special report on executive education ranked the Center first worldwide in leadership education for the third consecutive time.

## WAKE FOREST UNIVERSITY

A private, coeducational university in Winston-Salem, North Carolina, Wake Forest is recognized for its commitment to a liberal arts education, challenging academics, individualized teaching, small classes, an innovative use of technology, and its Division I athletic program. Wake Forest was ranked 27th among 248 national universities in the 2005 edition of *U.S. News & World Report*'s guide, "America's Best Colleges." Over half of Wake Forest's 4,000 undergraduate students graduate with credits from study abroad programs.

In addition to a small divinity school, Wake Forest's 2,000-plus graduate students are approximately evenly distributed among nationally ranked professional programs in law, medicine, management, and the arts and sciences.

## SMITH-RICHARDSON FOUNDATION

The mission of the Smith-Richardson Foundation is to contribute to important public debates and to help address serious public policy challenges facing the United States. The Foundation seeks to help ensure the vitality of U.S. social, economic, and governmental institutions. It also seeks to assist with the development of effective policies to compete internationally and advance U.S. interests and values abroad.

Based in Westport, Connecticut, through its domestic and international grant programs the Foundation supports research and policy projects on issues central to the strategic interests of the United States. The Foundation seeks to support research, writing, and analysis that inform the thinking of policy makers and the public. It also seeks opportunities to support the creation of innovative institutions and solutions that directly address issues in its areas of interest.

# Introduction

# CHAPTER 1

# The Presidential Forum

*David G. Brown*

H ow university presidents lead is an extremely important topic, for both the welfare of universities and for society. The Smith-Richardson Foundation gave Wake Forest University and the Center for Creative Leadership a grant to address the question of leadership in American universities. The forums were important opportunities for self-reflection and collaboration among colleague presidents.

Three groups of twelve effective presidents talked with each other about leadership. Thirty-six of America's busiest and most visible university presidents swapped and shared success stories and reflected upon the lessons they had learned on the job.

Each two-day forum session was catalyzed by three presidentially authored papers. The essayists started with a specific issue that he or she had faced—an issue that allowed the highlighting of leadership strategies and moral principles. They concluded with lessons learned. Three other presidents were asked to reflect on each essay from their own experiences. Throughout the forum, all participants joined in discussions.

Their objectives were threefold: (1) personal development, (2) advice or inspiration for other college and university leaders, and (3) enhancement of leadership talent in business and government. The intention from the outset was to publish a useful volume on how to lead in university-like organizations, organizations characterized by open, participatory decision making and multiple stakeholders.

## MORAL LEADERSHIP

This volume was to carry the fairly neutral, painfully expected, and rather boring title *Lessons Learned by Successful University Presidents*. This is a book rich with lessons learned. But the original title failed to capture the passion and idealism that shaped all conversation.

The essays and discussions reveal a compelling sense among all presidents that they share a crucial mission, a responsibility for the health of the national culture. All presidents believe that their calling to the presidency obligates them to illuminate and act upon the moral convictions and values of their institution.

These university presidents see their leadership responsibility extending beyond the university itself to the larger society. Universities provide the seed corn for innovations. They are the conscience of the culture. New social movements are often first manifest in universities. They are the canaries or lead indicators. Within universities are housed the opinions and expertise that provide self-correctives when majority culture is pursuing the wrong course. The presidents of universities therefore carry not only the responsibility for the welfare of their "own" institutions but also for advancing the general welfare of society.

The new title, *University Presidents as Moral Leaders*, grows directly from the tone of our conversations, as illustrated by the following quotations:

> "The challenges facing college and university presidents are not materially different from those in charge of any other large organization, but the responsibility for leading with virtue is greater because of the role that our institutions play in society. Even in an era of budget reductions and intensified competition from 'fast-food' education providers, higher education remains our society's conscience—institutions that are empowered to question and challenge, that are expected to instill values and character, and that are perceived as standing for more than the pursuit of a healthy bottom line."
>
> Albert Yates, President Emeritus, Colorado State University

> "Brains, beauty, wit, soaring eloquence or a single-digit handicap add up to nothing without an honesty that compels moral choice even under the hardest circumstances."
>
> Tim Sullivan, President, The College of William and Mary

> "Universities are utopian experiments, essentially, erected on the belief in the animate life of the mind that transcends skin color or gender or cultural origin or age or bodily ability. They hold up humanistic ideals, and a belief that humans have the potential to

overcome constraints of culture and time. . . . What you are doing contributes to the healing and repair of the world. I have invoked in several of my speeches the Jewish mystical concept of *tikkun olam*, which means to repair a world that is essentially broken and in need of our service and action to put it back together. I have always held that universities are ideal engines of that repair."

E. Gordon Gee, Chancellor, Vanderbilt University

"In our roles we are expected to demonstrate moral leadership. People look to college presidents to provide more leadership every day. As a matter of fact, this type of leadership in many ways defines the legendary college presidents who served in the twentieth century—Robert Maynard Hutchins, James Conant, and Clark Kerr. When we think about those presidents, we think about them in terms of their moral leadership. . . . It seems to me that all of us in our roles have to demonstrate more moral leadership."

Scott Cowen, President, Tulane University

"If this [hatred of gays] is going to change, it will begin on campuses because society grows from our campuses. . . . Ultimately the level of respect that society has for colleges and universities is going to be in direct proportion to their willingness to stand for humane values."

Gregory Farrington, President, Lehigh University

## CRISES PROVIDE OPPORTUNITIES

When asked to speak from an instance in their presidencies that could best reveal their leadership principles and strategies and styles, most chose a crisis—an event that, either voluntarily or involuntarily, dominated their time and energy for a considerable period of time.

Wyoming's President Dubois chose the Matthew Shepard incident and the simultaneous death of eight student-athletes in an automobile accident. Michigan's President Coleman wrote about the university's affirmative action case before the Supreme Court. Vanderbilt's Chancellor Gee focused on the university's renaming of Confederate Hall. Brit Kirwan chose Maryland's severe budget cut. Notre Dame's Edward Malloy reflected on the challenge of following legendary president Ted Hesburgh. In the telling of the stories of these seminal events, these presidents are able to teach us something about how and why they are successful in their leadership roles.

"It is during times of stress that both the need for leadership and the risk of failure are greatest. It is also true that such difficult times offer the greatest opportunities for change and progress. Such opportunities occur within most organizations once or twice a year—more if we are really unlucky—always unexpected and uninvited, but providing an invaluable window to communicate to the public what the institution stands for and what it values. At these times, the positive alignment of institutional will and courage is heightened and most are willing to accept leadership and direction. Such times should not be squandered by seeking only to restore the institution to its former self. These are times to reach as high as possible and make the institution better in significant and sustainable ways. At Colorado State University, periods of crisis have produced some of our most notable achievements and enduring changes."

Albert Yates, President Emeritus, Colorado State University

"I have come to appreciate the importance of the office I hold and its power for community-building at critical times."

Philip Dubois, President, University of Wyoming

"I have come to see my school as a kind of living organism that has a core that is solid and static and a surface that is dynamic and changing. The core is made up of the timeless stuff of character (fixed and tied to principles and values). The surface is made up of the stuff of change. It is constantly in motion, testing new ideas, embracing new ground. Both are vital. On most days the surface is the thing that is most revealed. In a time of crisis, it is the core that becomes evident."

James Barker, President, Clemson University

"My greatest crisis was the choice of Michael Sells' book, *Approaching the Qu'ran*, as the freshman reading assignment at UNC Chapel Hill in the fall of 2002, which prompted a lawsuit from the Family Policy Network, a Christian group that claimed that UNC was advocating Islam, and thus violating the establishment clause of the Constitution. The House of Representatives of the North Carolina General Assembly attached a proviso to the budget to disallow the use of state funds for any program or course that deals with a single religion unless all known religions were given equal treatment. And in response to this clear threat to academic freedom, the Board of Governors of the UNC System failed in an initial vote to endorse a resolution in support of academic freedom.

This crisis created, for me, an opportunity to put real flesh on the bones of the rhetoric I had articulated a year earlier in my State of the University Address about being a university with the courage of its convictions, about 'being a university that holds contemporary culture up to the critical light in the context of freedom.' I felt very much the presence of former Chancellor William Aycock and former UNC System President Bill Friday, both of whom had eloquently defended the university in the great speaker ban controversy of the 1960s. Once again, Chapel Hill was at the ramparts of academic and first amendment freedoms."

James Moeser, Chancellor, University of North Carolina at
Chapel Hill

"Out of crisis can come our most noble achievements and enduring changes."

David Hardesty, President, West Virginia University

"College presidents must link the actions growing from crisis with the basic institutional mission and fundamental societal values. College presidents have a special responsibility to use crises to reemphasize basic values and basic missions in the minds of all constituencies."

Julianne Thrift, President, Salem College

"After the days of media interviews and scrutiny in Washington, I returned to campus with several new tasks in front of me: the most immediate was to assemble a team to begin planning a new undergraduate admissions process that would be in compliance with the decisions. Another job was to begin to sort through the many requests to speak about the cases and their impact. As we had intended all along, these cases were going to continue to provide us with the opportunity to educate our campus and educate the public on the issues at stake and begin to heal some of the rifts that had developed on both sides of this important national issue [affirmative action]."

Mary Sue Coleman, President, University of Michigan

## THE PRESIDENCY

Throughout the essays and the six days of discussion, much was said about the office of the president, its conduct, and responsibilities. Tom Hearn, Graham Spanier, Edward Malloy, Charles Steger, and Mary Sue Coleman shared thoughts on presidential recruitment, selection, orientation, and transition.

Steve Sample and Al Yates suggest why the university is so, appropriately, hard to govern. Tom Hearn suggests that the university presidency is fundamentally a teaching role involving many of the same skills, plus some. Larry Penley, with many others, contemplates the role of the college president as priestly. Widely shared throughout all essays and comments is the idea that presidents can make a real difference. The quality of leadership matters.

"One of the most frequently asked questions, especially early on in my presidency, was 'What is it like to take over from a legend?'"
Edward Malloy, President, University of Notre Dame

"The very things that make a university stable—its myriad traditions and entrenched and tenured constituencies—are what make it so hard to govern."
Steve Sample, President, University of Southern California

"Change of an accepted paradigm is always difficult."
Marye Anne Fox, Chancellor, North Carolina State University

"As an organization resistant to the exercise of central authority, we nonetheless confront public requirements for accountability, and increasingly so, that demand leadership authority."
Tom Hearn, President, Wake Forest University

"One of the most critical attributes of an effective leader is to possess a clear set of ethical standards which can be communicated and understood."
Charles Steger, President, Virginia Polytechnic Institute
and State University

"Given the shared governance traditions on the campus, it was also clear that this [budget reallocation] could only occur with the active participation and collaboration of the Campus Senate."
William Kirwan, Chancellor, University System of Maryland

"The leader captures a reasonable probability about the future and uses the existing culture to bridge from where we are to where we might be."
Larry Penley, President, Colorado State University

"Here are some of the most important lessons I have learned: being passionate about my work; having an active presence both on and off campus; focusing on both the substantive and the symbolic; demonstrating genuine intellectual curiosity about issues (even when I am tired); focusing on the best ideas and helping to broaden others' thinking and to avoid parochialism; encouraging, even pushing, colleagues and myself to look in the mirror, focusing heavily on self-examination of our problem-solving efforts; encouraging ongoing interaction between the campus and effective external leaders; introducing best practices in academic and administrative areas that advance the institution's mission; showing appreciation for the ef-

forts and accomplishments of colleagues and students; and communicating priorities through deliberate use of both time and language."
Freeman Hrabowski, President, University of Maryland, Baltimore

## WAYS TO READ THIS BOOK

The impact of this volume is in the specific tales told, and reflected on, by the central figures (the presidents) in the stories. The first set of chapters, 2 through 20, relates to events and issues that captured the attention of the national media. Here the emphasis is on the events and issues. Thoughts about the presidency grow from the events and issues.

The starting point is reversed in Part II, chapters 21 through 27. Here the initial emphasis is on the presidency. Many smaller incidents are used to elaborate each point. If one can elevate these thoughts to theories, it is here that the "theory of the presidency" is considered.

For summaries, readers may consult Chapters 1, 28, and 29. In Chapter 28, perhaps the most useful chapter, two scholars from the Center for Creative Leadership place specific comments of forum participants in the context of leadership theory and the experiences of leaders in other sectors. Chapter 29 organizes many of the more poignant phrases emerging from the forums into eight lessons learned and ends with a comment on moral leadership.

In the spirit of "different strokes for different folks," readers are encouraged to start with the material they feel will interest and motivate them the most. The true justification for undertaking this effort rests with the good ideas and actions that grow from this stimulus. Perhaps that is what leadership is all about.

# Big Opportunities for Moral Leadership

# CHAPTER 2

## Carpetbaggery and Conflagration: Vanderbilt University Makes Enemies of Old Friends

*E. Gordon Gee*

### AN INSTANCE OF CHALLENGE

In 2002, Vanderbilt decided—meaning that our trustees, and a group of administrators, including myself, decided—to remove the word "Confederate" from the name of Confederate Memorial Hall, one of the residence halls on the campus of our education college. Although we could have guessed there would be a furor in some constituencies over our decision, we probably could not have anticipated its scope or volume. And I must admit that if I had not been guided by a carefully considered conviction that the university's decision was ethically correct, the furor, which included grotesque caricatures of me and threats to my life, would have left me shaken.

Confederate Hall's name had been an active issue on campus since at least 1988, when the hall was renovated without expunging the name, and the Student Government Association had voted just the year before the decision in support of changing the name of the building. Many African American students refused to step foot in the hall, which also served as a visible discouragement to many students (African American and otherwise) who toured Peabody's campus as they worked to discern which college they would attend. Many young people would choose to attend a university other than Vanderbilt, which already suffered from a long and well-earned reputation for lacking diversity. For many students from the northern United States, the name of the hall evoked bemusement at its quaintness, or befuddlement at why Vanderbilt would keep around something that was at best a dusty relic and at worst a painful reminder.

So, Vanderbilt decided that the name would have to be changed. The issue was not a burning, raging one but enough of a continued discomfort that we chose at last to do something about it. I have always believed that a university should align its symbols with its values. To designate a monument "Confederate" on a campus that wishes to welcome all people and that wishes to disseminate knowledge equally to all is counterproductive to that wish, to say the least.

The first and wildest shock at the news came from the members of the United Daughters of the Confederacy (UDC), a Southern heritage group, whose preceding members had contributed $50,000 in 1935 to build the dormitory, which ultimately cost $150,000. The UDC gave their support to Peabody College (which merged into Vanderbilt in 1979) because they wanted to instill in teachers of coming generations a Southern perspective on national and world events, and on condition that the UDC would approve the credentials and the pedigree of the young women who would receive room and board in Confederate Memorial Hall, and also on condition that the residence hall bear the name they had given it.

At the time the hall was built, the issue of its naming was not as conflicted. It was still fraught, but the constituencies that would have been caused pain by the name were not even allowed to enroll at Vanderbilt. We did not integrate until the 1960s, which is a polite way of saying that black people were not allowed to come to school here. Vanderbilt was very proud to be a Southern school, with all that comes with that designation (both good and nasty): proud of its civility and courtesy and grace, but also rather shameless about its treatment of minority presences. The conditions under which the UDC had given its donation were not out of keeping with this atmosphere.

Even though such a charge was problematic, the UDC felt it had some legal point about its initial investment and filed a suit against Vanderbilt to prevent the renaming of Confederate Memorial Hall. That case was decided in the university's favor on the thirtieth of September 2003.

Shortly after Vanderbilt's announcement and across the months to follow, my switchboard and my electronic mail and the switchboard and mail of Vice-Chancellor for Public Affairs Mike Schoenfeld were lit up, inundated, and flooded with angry messages excoriating Vanderbilt as a hotbed of political correctness (code for liberalism) and threatening to never again contribute to the school. Caricatures of Vice-Chancellor Schoenfeld and myself decorated Confederate web sites. But as in all things, the first scorch of interest and attention began to fade, and we anticipated a more peaceful winter.

But according to the law of unintended consequences, the Confederate Hall controversy would shoot forth a branch that was not entirely related to, but became indistinguishable from, the events surrounding the renaming of the hall in the minds of the Confederacy's most fervent living proponents. In December 2002, just as the hottest furor over the renaming of the hall was beginning to simmer down, Jonathan David Farley, a brilliant and volatile mathematics professor who ran for U.S. Representative on the Green Party ticket and is a self-styled hellraiser and enthusiastic editorialist, wrote a column for the *Tennessean's* Opinions page that suggested that rather than being lauded as heroes by any generations past, present, or future, Confederate veterans should have met traitors' fates at the end of a gibbet.

If you have any experience with the South, you can imagine the furor that ensued over this. Professor Farley, who was at the time a faculty member-in-residence, received threats on his life and went into hiding. The *Tennessean* fanned the flames of the story it had created by publishing angry letters to the editor and opinion columns by resident columnists accusing Vanderbilt of the worst forms of political correctness. I received a death threat and spent a day with campus police in my office. Ardent devotees of the Confederate cause demanded Farley's job as well as mine and that of Vice-Chancellor Schoenfeld. Eventually, I had to write an editorial piece (also published in the *Tennessean*) clarifying the meaning of academic freedom at a research university and defending Professor Farley's protected right to write and think whatever he believes. I would learn that while Vice-Chancellor Schoenfeld and I were busy covering Professor Farley's hellraising, by the way, he had accepted a position as visiting lecturer at MIT, so in essence we were left to clean up in his wake. I have been happier! But I knew that academic freedom is a right expressly protected within the world of the university, and as the representative of a university, I had the duty to defend that right and to clarify it for those who may misunderstand.

We are still going to clean the name off the hall. We are looking for stonecutters who can do this without damaging the building's edifice. We retain the hall's dedicatory plaque in its entryway, in recognition of those who did give financial support to Peabody during the Great Depression in the hopes that some future would happen.

The Confederate Hall controversy benefited Vanderbilt by forcing us to a crisis at which we had to clarify our moral stances and positions. After years now of controversy that sometimes crests and sometimes troughs, the affair has come to an anticlimactic end. In May 2005, a Tennessee Court of Appeals rejected the previous summary judgment on Vanderbilt's behalf. In July, we elected not to pursue the matter further, because Vanderbilt's resources need to be distributed in other directions. We are satisfied that we have made our discomfort and dissatisfaction with the inscription, and our disappointment with the court's decision, clear to the public. We have had to declare a moral victory and move on. The carving remains, but no longer receives any glory or energy from the university upon whose grounds it stands.

## CONCEPTS AND ISSUES

As I have already stated, I have always believed that a university's symbols should accord with its values, that they should not be in contradiction. Teaching aspects of history is one thing, but celebrating particular aspects is another, and the name of Confederate Memorial Hall amounted to a celebration of a movement in time that was contrary to the university's ideals of equality and compassion, a barrier to a kind and welcoming environment. Our campus should not allow itself to commemorate systems that are inconsistent with Vanderbilt's beliefs and ethos, to imply endorsement of a system that is at the very least offensive to so many people.

Universities are utopian experiments, essentially, erected on the belief in the animate life of the mind that transcends skin color, gender, cultural origin, age, or bodily ability. They hold up humanistic ideals and a belief that humans have the potential to overcome constraints of culture and time.

I mention pain, and in the South pain rides on both sides. I knew when I made my decision that many people whom I knew and cared about would be caused psychological pain by the removal of the hall's name, as people are to the removal of the Stars and Bars from state buildings. So, there was going to be pain either way: by keeping those symbols or by stripping them. Many Southerners do still have a sense of the South as being an occupied territory. Since this sense has not faded in 140 years, who knows if it ever will? How many generations (of any country) does it take for the pain of being vanquished to evaporate when one losing side has been overwhelmed and subsumed by a victor? When a side loses, it keeps losing chunks of its identity and slivers of its spirit every single day. I could sense in my opponents both a silent knowledge of this and a deep denial of it. From the tone of some of the Confederate correspondence, one might easily infer that there actually are people among

us who believe the South shall secede again to rise and that every pro-
pitiatory gesture made by some carpetbagger like myself fights this even-
tuality even further back into the realms of impossibility. I was not certain
exactly what better future those who disagreed with me dreamed would
come by keeping the name of the hall, but I do know that the decision
to revise that name caused a great deal of pain inside that constituency.

What administrators have to do in a situation such as this, ideally, is
to weigh one type of hurt over the other and figure out which loss is the
least costly to the university's spirit and to its ideals. I think that ignor-
ing the fact that African Americans used to be slaves in Tennessee and
that the name of Confederate Memorial Hall is a visual and aural reminder of this—a blunt and ever-threatening instrument—is much more
costly to Vanderbilt, morally and ethically. But in order to make such a
decision, I had to choose consciously not to give equal weight to the fact
that race is not the only source of discrimination or prejudice in our
country and that prejudice can also be economic and regional.

Movements of Southern heritage in their best and most ideal sense
(minus the racism that can break through) hope that the South will be
recognized for its own difference and diversity without prejudice, that
Southerners will not be represented in the mass culture as backward
hicks, that the South will be well-off materially and politically, and that
all power will not be in the hands of northern states that do not understand the issues of the South. I referred to myself as a carpetbagger above,
and one writer to the vice-chancellor did indeed mention carpetbagging
in his letter. A feeling of disenfranchisement, both economic and political, still pervades the hearts of some people here, and that feeling is what
makes their faces twist up in pain when they see the Confederate flag
being taken down or when they see the name of a hall being expurgated.

Universities increasingly have to operate no longer just on a regional
scale, but on a national and even a global scale. Every decision Vanderbilt makes must raise and sustain our acumen among our colleagues, or
no one will take us seriously. Allowing on our campus a building whose
very name gives offense to a cross-section of people from around the
world strongly reinforces the worst stereotypes of Vanderbilt as an institution trapped in a distant past. Vanderbilt cannot afford to appear "backward," and we therefore must balance the parts of our regional identity
that we can cultivate in order to maintain our distinction and charm with
our aspirations to be a global university that is respected by all peoples.
We cheer for Vanderbilt because it is a great Southern university: it
sprung from the soil and has its magnolias, and it brings distinction on
the South when people read about one of the university archaeologists

in the *New York Times* and think, Oh, I was wrong, the South is legitimate after all, and smart people *do* live there! But the price that Vanderbilt has to pay for that is a little stone polishing there and here, and
a little pain.

## REFLECTIONS AND LESSONS

In order to weather forces that would have your job—or even your
life—you need the courage that grounds you in the sense that what you
are doing is right. And I should clarify in this age of overly simplistic
demagoguery that "right" does not mean "self-righteous," but means simply that what you are doing contributes to the healing and repair of the
world. I have invoked in several of my speeches the Jewish mystical concept of *tikkun olam*, which means to repair a world that is essentially broken and in need of our service and action to put it back together. I have
always held that universities are ideal engines of that repair.

Keeping about a relic that maintains brokenness, that sustains sever-
ance, is not in service to healing. It puts nothing back together but rather
rends the world apart. The name of Confederate Memorial Hall has been
a harmful force, a polarizing force, that reminded black students of their
blackness and white students of their whiteness and made them all aware,
however barely conscious they might be of this awareness, of their differences from one another and of the historic circumstances that would set
their interests at odds. The name of the hall has been a threat, however
symbolic, to the integrity of the university's mission. Even while ac-
knowledging that Confederate sympathizers would feel pain over the
name's removal, I never could justify that the name merited preservation
simply because of its sentimental value to a politically invested faction.

One of the most powerful forces one can ever encounter as a leader of
any organization is resistance to change. I would submit that such resistance can be even greater surrounding an academic community, because
the people who belong to that particular community have involved their
identities and emotions with their idea of what that institution stands
for. What that institution means to them is bound up, for example, with
the alumni's own ideas of themselves as alumni, what experiential associations their degrees carry with them, and how their identities as alumni
signify within their larger conceptions of themselves.

A leader has to be sympathetic to this feeling, even if he or she is not
sympathetic to its particular manifestation. The people involved with any
organization want to feel as though they are involved with, and invested
in, a force that is ongoing and relevant. They do not want to feel as
though they are outdated or obsolete or old guard, that they are no longer

needed by the institution that has formed such a vital part of their self-identity. They dread the sense that their ideas are held in contempt and that they are without power and influence.

Knowing these things can help make a leader able to approach and respond to resistant factions in creative and compassionate ways, instead of viewing them as the wild-eyed fanatical opposition. In Vanderbilt's case, the Confederate alumni's desire for belonging became bound up with greater national forces of race and regional identity and sparked a conflagration that had to do with far more than the edifice of a single residence hall. The one regret I do have over this episode is our neglecting to tell the UDC directly of the decision as soon as it was made. They heard of the action from a reporter for the student newspaper, so not only were they offended by the change of the name itself, but they were also insulted by our insensitivity toward their concerns and their investment. I do believe that even if we had notified the UDC prior to making the announcement, they still would have raised a row and still would have filed a suit, but they would not have felt as though we treated them with contempt, and they might not have pursued legal action against us—or at least as aggressively or in exactly the same fashion as they did. We may have been able to undertake a more dialogic communication with them. We would not have alienated them to the extent that we did, and we would not have intensified the brokenness that already existed. We would have had good manners on our side and would have been able to act in the service of evolution without an utter disregard for our past. We may have had different results to show for it.

Even I have to admit that as Vanderbilt rises through the ranks as a world-class university, people will always think of it as a Southern university. But in order to bring distinction on the living South, in order to do the best credit to those who have supported this university through all its years of being, we have to give up a little here and there. We have to maintain our charm and our civility and our magnolia arboretum, but we also have to be willing to see what parts of our past might frighten away the best and brightest students whom we want to enroll here, whom we want to be a credit to us and to our great university. Vanderbilt has a role in the economic and cultural life of our region as it lives today, as it is vital and alive and moving into the future. The greatness of any body should lie in its present and future as well as, and even in spite of, its past. Much as we may grow attached to the traditions of an institution or to its artifacts, we have to recognize that a university is not a museum. We are a place of ideas, and we must live in response to the world, or we disable ourselves from relevance.

# CHAPTER

# Crises in Waiting: A Future Challenge for University Presidents

## A Response to Chancellor Gee's Essay

*Pamela B. Gann*

erek Bok's recent book, *Universities in the Marketplace: The Commercialization of Higher Education*, discusses an important set of issues about the efforts within the university to make a profit from teaching, research, and other campus activities. He attributes much of these challenges to the never ending desire of universities and their administrators and faculty for more resources. A cacophony of good ideas remains to be implemented if only there were more funds. This desire is matched by an increased level of opportunity to supply to the private sector the products and knowledge of higher education for significant sums of money. The aim of Bok's book is to note and discuss how commercialization risks the compromising of universities' basic core values and purposes and how universities should seek to protect those values.

Another significant type of commercialization, broadly defined, is the impact of fundraising and external relations activities on the university. In the quest for ever more resources, universities have never invested more time and attention to attracting the philanthropy of wealthy donors and the attention of public figures than they do now. One can easily see how gifts in particular shape an institution over time. They can impact which fields of knowledge grow at a particular institution, what is taught in the curriculum, the financial aid policies to compete for top students, and the size and prestige impact of buildings on a campus. Notwithstanding the best intentions of presidents and chief development officers, most of the really large gifts to a university remain highly restricted to a particular purpose. Presidents frequently note that too few of the revenues available to the university are really discretionary to shape the institution.

The purpose of this chapter, however, is not to speak directly to the institutional impact of wealthy donors and the restrictions on their gifts. It is, rather, to comment on another aspect of gifts and external relations activities, which is the extent to which philanthropy and efforts at external relations test the moral, ethical, and humanistic values that we expect of these institutions. Public confidence in higher education is generally very high, and well it hopefully remains, given all of the public support, direct and indirect, to universities and colleges (whether public or private). Nevertheless, one should not take that public confidence for granted. In a time of real crisis, those institutions that have conducted themselves in a way that is truest to core values are those that best weather their most difficult challenges.

The types of core values that I have in mind are nondiscrimination and respect for the opportunities and dignity of all human beings, and ethical and honest behavior. Let me provide some illustrations.

## RACE AND THE CORE VALUE OF NONDISCRIMINATION

Some of the most fundamental principles for which this country stands are equal opportunity and nondiscrimination, particularly as it pertains to race. We fought a civil war over these issues, and in 2004, we celebrate the fiftieth anniversary of *Brown v. Board of Education*, in which the United States Supreme Court overturned the "separate but equal" doctrine. Gordon Gee's paper, in Chapter 2, contains an elegant example of the problem. Vanderbilt University decided to remove the word "Confederate" from the name of its Confederate Memorial Hall. As he states: "I have always believed that a university's symbols should accord with its values, that they should not be in contradiction. . . . Our campus cannot allow itself to commemorate systems that are inconsistent with Vanderbilt's beliefs and ethos, to imply endorsement of a system that is at the very least offensive to so many people."

When we think about symbols, we must consider not only building names but scholarships and awards, traditional events, and venues for various university activities. Sensitivity levels should go very far down into the institution. What should one do about a major university award that has been given for decades but the person for whom it is named was clearly against equal rights based on race? This person's position would be totally unacceptable today as contrary to the university's core value of nondiscrimination. Does that mean that the award should be terminated?

What about the fact that a university regularly receives donations from a foundation funded from the private wealth of a real estate developer who included racially restricted covenants in all his residential developments after World War II? Of course, such covenants can no longer be enforced after the United States Supreme Court's decision in *Shelly v. Kraemer*, but the question remains about whether the appearance of the developer's name throughout a campus conflicts too much with the core value of nondiscrimination.

Related issues of prejudice pertain to the Holocaust period. The Mercedes-Benz Corporation is identified with Germany and the Holocaust and with the issue of whether it financially benefited from the war and slave labor. Faculty at Cambridge University and Oxford University raised questions about gifts from that corporation because of the concern over "tainted" wealth accumulation from one of the darkest periods of the twentieth century. Past treatment of persons on the basis of race and origin and reparations persist in this country, with respect to both the internment of Japanese Americans during World War II and the even larger issues of our period of legalized slavery. How long do such taints persist in society at large? How do you manage it in a university setting? Recently, President Ruth J. Simmons announced Brown University's Steering Committee on Slavery and Justice to pursue the investigation of the origins of Brown University in 1764, its early history, its role in and relationships to the difficult period of legal slavery in the United States, and how societies past and present deal with retrospective justice following human rights violations.

## BUSINESS ACTIVITY AND THE CORE VALUES OF ETHICAL AND HONEST BEHAVIOR

Much university philanthropy necessarily comes from wealthy donors who have acquired their resources through significant business activities. Not unsurprisingly, questions about the honesty and integrity of the activities by which that wealth was derived can arise well before a gift intention to the university, but also well after the gifts have been made. Again, several examples can help explain the point.

First, let me provide an example in which the source of the problem was known at the time of the gift. In 1995, the Cambridge University faculty voted on whether to accept a chaired professorship in international relations from the British American Tobacco Company, which was to honor its retiring CEO. Was it appropriate to accept funds from a company that had contributed so much to serious health problems? The majority of the faculty voted to accept the chair.

What about the situation in which the source of the funds seems perfectly fine at the time of the gift, but something later occurs that raises fundamental issues of honesty and integrity about the individual or the businesses with which the individual is associated? The Enron teaching award exists at the University of Houston. Does the university keep that named award? What about the Arthur Anderson Accounting Professorship? There are likely several of these around the United States.

In April 2002, A. Alfred Taubman was convicted of price fixing between the firm of which he was chairman, Sotheby's, and Christie's, both of which control most of the world's art auctions. He was sentenced to one year in prison and fined $7.5 million. Mr. Taubman is also a very wealthy individual and alumnus of the University of Michigan. His various large gifts to the university are reflected in many named areas of the university: the A. Alfred Taubman Health Care Center, University Hospital; the Taubman Medical Library; and the Taubman College of Architecture and Urban Planning. He has also made substantial gifts to Brown University, where there is located the A. Alfred Taubman Center for Public Policy and American Institutions.

A core university value is honesty and integrity in all of its own internal operations, in the manner with which it conducts its teaching and research, and in the values that it represents and teaches its students. How does one square these essential values with business-related philanthropy? Thorstein Veblen was concerned in his writings with the inappropriateness of business topics being taught at the university (see his *The Higher Learning in America: A Memorandum on the Conduct of Universities by Businessmen*, Chapter 7 [1918]). The faculty at Oxford University debated long and hard before accepting the appropriateness of a business school within the confines of that ancient and venerable institution. So, what now about the symbols of business-related philanthropy on a college campus, when it becomes associated with lapses in ethical and honest behavior? How different is this problem than the one confronted by Vanderbilt University over the name "Confederate Memorial Hall," which the university decided was antithetical to a core value of the university and that symbols do matter?

Some very few universities are responding to these sorts of questions by deciding not to take corporate naming gifts. That is one pristine way to handle the question with respect to the problem of corporate names, such as the Enron Teaching Award. Another formal policy approach, called "de-naming," is also being considered at some universities. Under such a policy, gift documents signed by the donor and the university would preserve the authority of the university to de-name a gift under specified subsequent circumstances.

## ASSOCIATIONS WITH (IN)FAMOUS PERSONS

Universities become involved and identified with persons in innumerable ways, and how they behave in these instances says a great deal about their pursuit of ethical and honest behavior. Of course, the facts are normally complex and often will engender criticism no matter what the university decides to do. A recent illustration concerns Harvard University and the bin Laden family, which includes Osama bin Laden, the most sought-after terrorist on the globe and the terrorist to whom the events of September 11, 2001, are attributed. The bin Laden family has given $2 million to Harvard for its Law School and Graduate School of Design. Although the family has disassociated itself from Osama bin Laden, and the university sees no connection between the sources of these funds and terrorism, the Cambridge City Council passed a resolution asking Harvard to forward all bin Laden family endowments to a fund for 9/11 victims. Harvard refused to follow the direction of this resolution but indicated that it would cease using the endowed funds if it found any explicit link with Osama bin Laden's terrorist organization. Harvard did set aside $1 million to establish a fund to educate the spouses and children of the 9/11 victims. It also removed the individual names of that year's bin Laden fellows from the Harvard web site out of security concerns. Readers will generally agree with these Harvard decisions, but the example shows some of the additional types of challenges that can occur with international external relations activities.

What does a university do when an alumnus becomes a famous or even iconic figure to some but is not necessarily representative of the university's values of honesty and integrity and academic freedom? One typical way in which this issue arises is in the consideration of candidates for an honorary degree. When Oxford University proposed in 1985 to award an honorary degree to Prime Minister Margaret Thatcher, an alumna of the university, the faculty turned down the proposal, not for basic honesty and integrity reasons, but rather for her government's lack of generosity in funding higher education and research.

Duke University confronted a controversial decision in 1954 when it considered the awarding of an honorary degree to Richard M. Nixon, a 1937 graduate of the Duke Law School. Then Vice President Nixon was identified with his prominent participation on the House Committee on

Un-American Activities, his campaign for the U.S. Senate, and his association generally with the McCarthy period. After several faculty meetings and process machinations, the recommendation managed never to come up to a direct faculty vote on the merits. Evidently, he was finally offered an honorary degree in 1961, but he turned it down.

These events were precursors to more substantial controversy in 1981 between the Duke administration and faculty over the subject of the location of the Richard M. Nixon Presidential Library. Of course, by this time President Nixon had experienced the impact of the Watergate scandals and had actually resigned from office. In the summer of 1981, Duke University President Terry Sanford had been in discussions with representatives of President Nixon about the possible location of the library on the Duke University campus. The subsequent controversy over this possibility was exacerbated by the fact that faculty only became aware of this discussion in the summer months and were told by President Sanford that a decision had to be made by late August, or the opportunity might be lost. It was surprising that such a politically astute leader would make such a fundamental mistake in dealing with faculty over an important and controversial topic, thus being perceived by the faculty as deliberately avoiding them and showing no respect for their role in university governance.

As a young faculty member at Duke, I attended the critical faculty meetings. These were the highest attended faculty meetings in my twenty-nine years in higher education. They possessed high drama, and even now, I and my former colleagues can remember the details of the debate. The arguments against President Sanford's keen interest in capturing the presidential library for Duke were straightforward: a presidential library is both a repository of important history materials (and typically scholars and universities welcome the repository of important papers in their libraries) and a memorial to the president. It was felt nearly impossible, given the ways in which presidential libraries are funded and operated, to secure enough assurances about the manner in which the memorial part of the library would be conducted and whether it would focus only on the more admirable parts of his presidency. Some expressed the viewpoint that they simply could not understand how under any circumstances Duke University could be associated with this presidential library and have any sort of permanent relationship with Richard Nixon, a dishonest and disgraced president who resigned from office and was pardoned by his successor from any prosecution of crimes, and who resigned from New York State bar membership (rather than confront an action for disbarment). In other words, it was simply wrong for

Duke University to be associated in any way with a person who did not exemplify the honesty and integrity expected of the university and its administration, faculty, students, and alumni.

Issues concerning the relationship of the Duke Law School and President Nixon even continued after his death, when I was Dean of the Duke Law School. He died on April 22, 1994, shortly prior to the Law School's graduation. A majority of the graduating students signed a petition that the Law School graduation ceremony include a moment of silence in memory of President Nixon, a graduate of the Law School. Of course, these students were mostly very young children at the time of the Watergate scandals and had not lived through this trying period in our presidential history. Nor did these graduating law students know that Nixon had resigned from the New York State Bar rather than confront a disbarment action. Yet, their parents would have lived through this history, and I knew that many of them would possess very strong personal opinions about President Nixon. The graduation exercises are intended to focus attention on the students and their achievements; they are not intended to bring into play a public debate about the merits of a deceased controversial leader's life. The Duke Law School faculty held a special meeting to consider the students' petition. I offered the following "Solomonic" solution to the faculty, which was accepted: there would be no public statements about President Nixon, nor would there be a moment of silence during the ceremony; an in-memoriam written statement about President Nixon would be inserted in the printed program. Of course, the story appeared in the press all over the country, including the *New York Times*. The Law School was blasted in every way, and I received mail from all over the country about our failure to honor a recently deceased president. I also received an e-mail from a parent of a graduating student that I will never forget: "If you had included a public moment of silence in my son's graduation ceremony, I would not have been able to attend the event." So Duke University could not remove itself from the controversy surrounding this graduate, even in death.

Issues surrounding the Law School's association with its famous alumnus continued for several years more, because the Law School owned a valuable portrait of President Nixon, created during the time of his presidency. The portrait had been taken down from the wall and put in storage during the charged late period of the Nixon presidency, in order to avoid further pranks (students had taken it down and secreted it above the ceiling tiles) or potential vandalism. Even in the 1990s, the mentioning of rehanging this portrait in the portrait gallery of the Law School raised significant controversy. My efforts to normalize the treatment of the portrait finally succeeded. We developed a policy that the portrait would be readily available on loan as well as hang in the Law School. It initially was placed on loan in the offices of Newt Gingrich, when he was Speaker of the House of Representatives, following which it was returned to the Law School where, in a dignified reception event, the portrait was unveiled for a second time and hung in the Law School itself, over twenty years after the Watergate incidents. It became a normal piece of portraiture again.

## UNIVERSITY RELATIONSHIPS AND THE RISK TO CORE VALUES

The challenges of moral and honest behavior go beyond that associated with wealthy donors, corporate donors, honorary degree recipients, and alumni who become public figures. Universities pursue elaborate methods of networking themselves through external relations and fundraising activities with politicians, numerous university advisory boards, alumni organizations, parents' organizations, numerous organizational partnerships, and adjunct faculty. Few, if any, of these relationships receive the vetting associated with the selection of a member of the university's Board of Trustees. Stop for a moment and ask yourself how many individual and institutional associations are present at your institution. What is your standard of care in vetting these associations? The answers are probably "a tremendous number of associations," and "pursued with very little vetting."

No one can anticipate whether any of these associations, from wealthy donors to honorary degree recipients to alumni in the public eye to members of advisory boards, will cause specific future challenges with respect to the university's core values of behaving ethically and honestly. Yet the likelihood is very high indeed. Our actions today will leave unknown problems for our successors. Knowing this, a university and its board should thoughtfully discuss these issues and try to determine whether better processes and policies ought to exist to protect the university from these risks and to also anticipate thoughtful and appropriate responses when these challenges actually arise.

Universities should pursue their missions with the highest standards of conduct with respect to core values. Universities are very much in the public eye, and much of their efficacy depends on it.

# CHAPTER 4

# Presidential Leadership in Time of Crisis

*Philip L. Dubois*

L
ike most university presidents, I spend a lot of my time communicating with internal and external constituents about the accomplishments of my institution. Whether addressing the local community service organization, meeting with the editorial board of a local newspaper, or issuing the annual State of the University address, my focus is on those things that are sources of institutional pride and public support: when our enrollments increase, when faculty or students win prestigious recognitions, when our budgets are enhanced by supportive legislators and the governor, when new buildings or renovation projects are completed, when alumni and friends contribute to our private fundraising success, when our research contracts grow, or when our athletic teams trounce the traditional rivals.

Most presidents, I would guess, are interested in leaving a legacy of accomplishments that will mark their tenure in office. They can only hope that, years after they are gone, others may look back and decide that his or her leadership as president helped the institution become stronger or defined it in new ways. Less likely to be remembered is how an institution or its president reacted in times of crisis unless, of course, the leadership provided during the crisis was misguided, mistaken, not apparent, or entirely absent. As one observer has noted, "while good deeds often go unnoticed, crises never do. This is because your stakeholders . . . are

Editor's note: An expanded version of this chapter is available at the University of Wyoming web site, http://www.uwyo.edu/News/shepard/PLD_book_chapter.htm.

measuring your conduct during the crisis. They know that a crisis does not *make* character—it *reveals* character."[1]

Notwithstanding the many points of pride I might cite during a presidency that marked the completion of my seventh year in April 2004, it is also the case that those seven years have been marked by a number of institutional and individual crises, notable by their number and scope:

- The death of a football player during spring practice in the third week of my first year as president (subsequently determined to be due, at least in part, to an enlarged spleen as a result of mononucleosis);

- The vicious beating and subsequent death in October 1998 of a gay University of Wyoming student, Matthew Shepard, a tragedy that drew national and international media attention;

- The local trial and sentencing of Mr. Shepard's assailants, events that occurred almost precisely one year after his murder, and which involved members of the faculty, staff, and student body as prospective jurors;

- The death of a student in the spring of my second year who barricaded himself in a study room on the twelfth floor of a campus residence hall and subsequently jumped to his death in full view of fellow students and residence hall staff;

- Multiple campus bomb scares in the aftermath of the Columbine High School mass murder, and the group exodus of African American student athletes from campus housing to local hotels when rumors circulated to the effect that the Columbine shootings may have been racially based in part and might stimulate copycat slayings;

- Campus reaction to the attacks of September 11, 2001, in New York City, Washington, D.C., and Pennsylvania;

- The simultaneous and instantaneous deaths, five days after September 11, of eight members of the men's cross-country and track teams in a head-on automobile accident on a highway south of Laramie. Investigation revealed that the accident was caused by an intoxicated UW student, headed in the opposite direction, who crossed the centerline and struck the vehicle containing the UW student-athletes.

- The death of a UW theatre and dance student from respiratory and cardiac arrest suffered during his participation in rehearsal on campus for an upcoming dance recital. Fellow students were unable to revive him from what turned out to have been an allergic reaction to aspirin.

Although the particular number, combination, and severity of events that have visited my tenure may be unusual, it is of course the case that most university and college presidents will, at one point or another, be faced with at least one significant institutional crisis. There are those who like to say that the job of a university president is, in fact, one long crisis interrupted by brief periods of normalcy. But, wags and pundits aside, "a crisis is not simply a bad day at the office."[2] It is often an event or series of events that bring virtually all "normal" university business to a halt and commands the full attention of the president and his or her senior officers for days, weeks, or longer. In the words of those who have studied crisis management in industrial settings, crises may manifest themselves "like a cobra" where the institution is taken by surprise. Others may manifest themselves "like a python," crushing the institution over time.[3] In the worst possible case, the crisis comes to be embedded in the public consciousness as the defining image of the institution.[4]

While the particular and peculiar circumstances of each crisis undoubtedly demand their own response, I hope it will be useful to use just two of the crises that have confronted the University of Wyoming to unearth a few useful lessons that may help other university leaders who come to face to face with such events.

For this purpose, I will focus on the two most significant crises faced by my institution during the past few years: the murder of gay UW student Matthew Shepard, and the accidental death of eight student-athletes (hereinafter referred to as "the Eight").[5] I begin with a fairly detailed description of each crisis, hoping that some readers will be able to benefit from seeing how we responded at the time. I then attempt some reflection on what we learned from each.

## THE MURDER OF MATTHEW SHEPARD

I was headed to a meeting at the student union on a beautiful October morning in 1998 when the vice president for student affairs, Jim Hurst, caught up alongside. He wanted me to know that campus police were reporting that a UW student, as yet unidentified, was in the emergency room of a Fort Collins, Colorado, hospital with severe head injuries from what appeared to be a vicious beating. I learned that the victim, Matthew Shepard, was a UW student and that there was a possibility that other students were involved in the attack. I asked my assistant to take the lieutenant's list of names and run a quick check against our Student Information System. We quickly confirmed that one of the women who would be charged as an accessory after the fact, Chastity Pasley, was a student who worked part-time in the student union. The two men who would be charged with the attack, Russell Henderson and Aaron McKinney, were not UW students and never had been, nor had the second young woman, Kristen Price, also to be accused as an accessory after the fact. We determined that Matt himself had just enrolled as a student for the first time in September, and we were barely a month into the semester. We quickly learned, through the student activities office, that Matt was a member of the campus Lesbian, Gay, Bisexual, and Transgendered Association (the LGBTA).

By fall 1998, Jim Hurst had been vice president for student affairs at the University of Wyoming for the better part of fifteen years. His calm, supportive, and empathetic demeanor—characteristic of his counseling psychology background—had endeared him to students, faculty, staff, and senior administrators. His was a couch most of us visited at one time or another. He was not prone to exaggeration, overstatement, or alarm. For these reasons, his words that afternoon on the doorstep of Old Main still remain vividly in my mind: "Phil, if Matt Shepard dies and this turns out to be a gay bashing, this could become the University of Wyoming's 'Kent State.'"

By Friday morning, the newspaper stories were out, and the lead article by the leading regional newspaper, the *Denver Post*, and the Associated Press erroneously reported that the victim and all of those accused were University of Wyoming students.

This was the beginning of the longest two weeks of my life. Because of the initial but erroneous media reports, we were immediately placed on the defensive trying to answer a question we surely could not answer: what had the university done—or not done—to foster in our students such hatred and violence toward one another? Over time, we were criticized for being "defensive" in attempting to correct misinformation.

By Friday afternoon, I had arranged to join the Albany County sheriff on the steps of the county courthouse to address the media gathering from around the region. At this point, while it was clear that Matthew was a gay man and had been out for some time, it was not at all clear that the crime had any hate-related elements to it. The facts were simply not known. A brief confidential conversation with the sheriff, just prior to my remarks at the microphone, suggested that the crime may have been motivated by robbery. When I directly posed to him the question of whether there were any elements to suggest that the assault was a gay bashing, he said that it would be unwise to so conclude until the investigation could be completed. With that rather limited information, I chose to direct my statement to the press (and our accompanying press release) solely to our concern for Matt and his family.

Almost as quickly as those statements were consumed by the media, we began receiving e-mails that my statement was completely inadequate; that I should have, at a minimum, suspended the accused students;

and that I should have taken immediate steps to correct the hateful environment at the university that had fostered attitudes such that students would attack a fellow student: "How can President Dubois sleep tonight," wrote one individual, "knowing that his leadership has resulted in the loss of a young mind, crushed beyond the ability to even sustain breathing at this time?"

By Saturday morning, it was clear that a massive outpouring of protest was beginning to develop. Whatever law enforcement may have been willing to say about the actual motivation behind the attack, that perspective was, by this point, irrelevant. The gay community, the larger community, and media from around the country had concluded that this was, indeed, a hate crime.

Initially, the protest was led largely by university students, and especially by UW minority students through the Multicultural Resource Center (MRC). The students came up with the idea of wearing symbolic yellow armbands with green circles—the yellow symbolizing antiviolence and the green circle representing international peace. Other student groups, most notably the student government and fraternity/sorority leadership, pitched in to assist in the mass production of the armbands. The armbands and a large yellow banner with large green circles were first seen that morning at the traditional homecoming parade, where a spontaneous mini parade of several hundred persons tagged onto the end of the usual array of antique cars, flatbed trailers, local bands, and homemade floats. Other banners denouncing hatred and violence, made by local citizens, lined the parade route.

I ordered a moment of silence at the afternoon football game where the players (and members of other athletic teams) had voted to put the yellow and green symbol on their helmets or on their uniforms; one could have heard a pin drop except for the sounds of people weeping quietly.

By Sunday, Matt's condition was being reported as grave; a candlelight vigil organized by the Catholic Newman Center was scheduled for that evening on the grounds of the center located immediately across the street from the university. Along with LGBTA leaders and the Newman Center pastor, I was asked to speak. Figuring that this was a teachable moment for my three children (at that time ages 15, 12, and 7), my wife and I brought the entire family. It was a powerful and moving ceremony, conducted under the watchful eye of the national media and reported on all of the major network morning shows on the next day.

By that time, however, the vigil was old news; Matt Shepard died Monday morning at approximately 1:00 A.M. (MST). At 3:00 A.M., a telephone call from a CBS radio reporter to my home awakened me with the news. He needed a quote for the morning drive-time show in New York. I asked his indulgence in allowing me to collect my thoughts. After a quick shower, I called him back, again expressing my condolences to the Shepard family and reassuring the New York caller that Laramie was like most small towns and large cities in America. Hate does not have a geographic bias; it could, and did, happen everywhere.

The circus had started. Ironically, it was the first day of the university's scheduled Gay Awareness Week. My Monday was spent fielding requests from television and radio media for interviews; the university's crisis management team assembled to plan a late-afternoon memorial ceremony that would be attended by hundreds in the full glare of the national media. I conversed with the governor about flag etiquette and received his acquiescence to lower campus flags to half-staff.

We also began receiving requests for information about where concerned citizens might send donations to support the Shepard family or to establish scholarships in Matt's name. A similar fund had already been established at the Poudre Valley Hospital, so, after listening to a lively debate among the crisis management team, I decided that we would redirect all donors to the Poudre Valley fund, with the message to be conveyed that our interest was in supporting the Shepard family until decisions could be made about how such funds might be best utilized.

I will leave it to others to explain why this particular murder of a gay man attracted the national attention that it did. As NBC anchor Tom Brokaw mentioned in his report on that Monday evening, there were over 8,800 hate crimes reported in America in the prior year. For some reason, this one was different. Suffice it to say that a number of powerful iconlike images cast across the nation during the first few days after Matt's attack and subsequent death drew national and ultimately international attention—the vulnerable and viciously beaten young gay man who was just over five feet tall and weighed just 100 pounds; the buck fence on a barren plain where his lifeless body was found; widely held stereotypes of what life in rural America must be like, particularly in a state nicknamed "The Cowboy State"; and the fact that Wyoming was one of just a few states that had failed to pass hate crimes legislation. Whatever the attraction, a small town with no television station and one daily newspaper that publishes less than two dozen pages daily, six days a week, was stunned by the arrival of network satellite trucks and correspondents camped on the lawn of the Albany County Courthouse representing all of the alphabet media (NBC, CBS, ABC, FOX, CNN) and Court TV.

Of course, television and radio were not the entire media story. Internet coverage and direct e-mail aimed at the campus administration and media staff allowed for repeated blows to be leveled at our collective gut. I opened my Tuesday morning e-mail to read the following:

> You and the straight people of Laramie and Wyoming are guilty of the death of Matthew Shepard just as the Germans who looked the other way are guilty of the deaths of their Jewish, Gypsy, and homosexual neighbors during the Holocaust. Unless and until the people of Laramie and Wyoming repent the sin of homophobia, your city and your state are no different than Auschwitz, no different than the killing fields of Cambodia. You have taught your children to hate their gay and lesbian brothers and sisters. Unless and until you acknowledge that Matthew Shepard's death is not a random occurrence, not just the work of a couple of random crazies, you have his blood on your hands. . . . Shame on you, President Dubois. Shame on Laramie. Shame on Wyoming.

People within the Laramie community were equally upset with the reportage of an Associated Press writer from New York who implied that the murder may have resulted from a socioeconomic split in Laramie that made possible the murder of a well-dressed, seemingly wealthy young man by two down-and-outers from "the other side of the tracks," where skinny stray dogs ran down dusty streets. I do not have space here to list everything the writer got wrong, but this article, printed in newspapers nationwide, helped reinforce the notion of Laramie as a biased cow town.

Media coverage only heightened as the day approached for the Shepard family funeral to be held in Casper, Wyoming, a two-and-a-half-hour drive north of Laramie. Enter stage far right—the Reverend Fred Phelps from Kansas's Westboro Baptist Church, an organization dedicated principally to the excoriation of homosexuals based on Phelps' literal reading of biblical passages. His Internet address (godhatesfags.com) says about all that needs to be known about him and his group. Phelps brought a small band of protesters to Shepard's funeral to "demonstrate" against Matt Shepard, his homosexual "lifestyle," and homosexuality generally. Although most people ignored Phelps on this intensely sad and snowy day, a few of Matt's younger friends and acquaintances chose to directly confront Phelps in verbal exchanges that, Phelps certainly knew, would become a clip on the evening news. Since Phelps had announced publicly his intention to bring his followers to Laramie, the university police chief was posted nearby as an observer so that we could know what to expect.

Back on campus, and with the concurrence of the Shepard family, I decided that we would hold a campus memorial service, just about two weeks to the day after the initial attack. During all of that previous week, the university's Counseling Center staff had been working overtime counseling students, staff, and faculty to deal with their personal grief and the trauma that had descended on the community. Faculty members had responded to the request I made through our chief academic affairs officer for the organization of small teach-ins on campus to address issues identified around broad themes related to the tragedy—prejudice, social justice, violence, and sexuality, among others. The university was in a unique position to help its students understand what had happened and why, and the faculty was simply spectacular in responding to the call for them to do so.

The memorial service, attended by a capacity crowd of 2,000 in the largest campus auditorium and covered by the local and regional media, was brief and dignified—psalms, a specially written poem, music from UW's multicultural chorus, and statements from representatives of LGBTA and the mayor. I used my then-expected "clean up" position to summarize what had happened and what I thought it meant for our community.[6] In my remarks I included a personal call for Wyoming to enact hate crimes legislation. Following a carefully worded disclaimer to indicate that the views I would express were mine alone and not those of the institution or the trustees, I expressed the view that it was time for Wyoming to live up to the promise of the state motto ("The Equality State") and to recognize in written law that we had a collective zero tolerance for hate, even if such a law would not have spared Matt Shepard his life or produced a more severe punishment for those accused of his murder.

I had hoped to awaken the next day to feel that the crisis of the past two weeks had past, but the front-page headlines of the morning paper and the story quoting my call for hate crime legislation reminded me that, notwithstanding my disclaimer of the prior evening, a university president is not allowed to have a personal opinion. This is surely true in most political environments, but it is magnified in Wyoming where the president of its only four-year institution of higher learning is perceived by many to be the second most visible public official, ranked only behind the governor. To some, it appeared that the president was trying to upstage if not embarrass the governor and the legislature on this specific issue.

Life returned to relative normal throughout the balance of the fall semester and throughout the spring, though my public relations staff and I continued to respond to what would be hundreds of media requests, e-mail messages, letters, and phone calls regarding Matthew's murder. Jury selection in March 1999 for the trial of Russell Henderson sparked the expected amount of angst among faculty, staff, and students concerned about how their classes and professional lives would be accommodated if they ended up serving on the jury for an extended period of time. The county attorney, frustrated during the jury selection process by large numbers of prospective jurors claiming personal conflicts or philosophical objections to the death penalty, asked me to issue a statement reminding members of the university community of their civic responsibilities. Although more than a bit put off by a request that seemed aimed only at university personnel and not the larger community, I agreed to issue a statement clarifying the policies we had in place to accommodate the needs of faculty, staff, or students selected for jury duty.

Reverend Phelps and his band of protestors showed up at the Albany County Courthouse to protest the first day of the trial, only to be surrounded in silent protest by a dozen LGBT students and friends dressed as angels, who raised enormous wings to block any view of him by the media or the passing public. That scene was repeated later in the day in front of the student union. The city mayor and I collaborated on a letter to the editor of the local and student newspapers suggesting that the best way to deal with Phelps' brand of hatred was to ignore it, to starve it with indifference. That tactic worked well, as we avoided any meaningful confrontations.

The community and the campus were spared a trial that spring, as Henderson agreed on the eve of the trial to enter a guilty plea in exchange for being spared the death penalty. Henderson's girlfriend, who had in December entered a guilty plea to being an accessory after the fact, was sentenced for her role. Aaron McKinney's girlfriend, who would later testify in his trial the following fall, ended up pleading to the misdemeanor offense of interference with a police officer. Much to our horror, the judge made a decision to push back McKinney's trial until fall; eventually, we would learn that jury selection would begin on the Monday following our scheduled fall homecoming—ironically, precisely one year after the events of the preceding year.

In the meantime, popular singer Elton John had requested an opportunity to perform a benefit concert on campus, a request we readily accepted. His sold-out June concert, conducted in the basketball arena, raised about $250,000 for a variety of John's favorite causes, including the initiation of a fund to create a distinguished chair in the Law School to be dedicated to social justice issues.[7]

The coincidence of McKinney's trial, the one-year anniversary of Matt's death, and UW's annual homecoming brought a surreal feeling to the weekend of October 8–10, 1999. It was again Gay Awareness Week.[8] The yellow and green symbols reemerged in the annual homecoming parade. A candlelight vigil, with many of the same participants from the Newman Center vigil of the year before, was held on campus just prior to a concert by folksingers Peter, Paul, and Mary. Those at the vigil were given an opportunity to sign a pledge of nonviolence on large boards erected on the campus quad and then to walk together to the concert. A powerful and moving performance by Peter, Paul, and Mary was punctuated by the onstage appearance of Dennis and Judy Shepard and the lighting of penlight candles throughout the 2,000-seat auditorium. A post-concert reception held at my home was an eclectic mix of members of my staff, invited special guests and university donors, Dennis and Judy Shepard, and leaders in the LGBTA.

Three weeks later, Aaron McKinney was convicted of two counts of felony murder, but acquitted of first-degree murder. Although the felony murder counts carried the possibility of the death penalty, a sentence bargain encouraged and supported by the Shepard family resulted in two consecutive life sentences. The crisis, at least as experienced by the university, was over.

## THE EIGHT

On Friday, September 14, 2001, UW conducted a campus memorial service for the victims of the terrorist attacks of September 11, a scene repeated on literally hundreds of university and college campuses that week. Like most Americans, I spent the weekend glued to my television and reading newspaper accounts of this national tragedy. Early Sunday morning, I received a call from the vice president for student affairs, Dr. Leellen Brigman, informing me that perhaps four UW students had been killed in an automobile accident shortly after midnight on the highway from Laramie to Fort Collins, Colorado. Details were sketchy, but fog may have been a factor.

Within two hours, the horrible details were known. Eight male students, ranging in age from 19 to 22, had been simultaneously killed when their Jeep Wagoneer, traveling northbound at a speed later estimated at 62 m.p.h., was struck virtually head-on by a southbound 1-ton Chevrolet pickup truck, later estimated to be traveling 76 m.p.h., on U.S. Highway 287 south of Laramie.

All eight victims were members of the UW cross-country and/or track teams and were en route back from a day in Fort Collins on a weekend when all competitive events had been cancelled as a result of September 11. The driver of the truck, 21-year-old Clinton Haskins, was also a UW student, a member of the rodeo team, and under arrest with a tested blood alcohol level of .16 several hours after the accident; Wyoming's limit was at that time .10. Haskins was also seriously injured and hospitalized with a lacerated liver, a bruised heart, and bruised lungs. Evidence at the scene showed that Haskins' truck had crossed the centerline to collide with the Jeep. Autopsy results for the driver of the Jeep later showed his blood alcohol level at 0.00.

By midday Sunday, the crisis management team was assembled, augmented this time with the athletics director and members of his staff, including the athletics' sports information coordinator. In addition to agreeing on the text of my public statement, we agreed to establish a web site where information about the victims could be posted and comments could be left by well-wishers, an idea we had taken from the experience of Oklahoma State University in dealing with the airplane crash that had taken the lives of students and staff associated with their basketball team.

I called the governor to tell him what we knew and to give him the names of the families affected. Five of the victims and five of the ten families affected were from Wyoming, a close-knit state once described by a former governor as "one small town with very long streets." State and campus flags were already at half-staff for the September 11 victims by direction of the president of the United States, but I let the governor know that I intended to keep the campus flags lowered until after all of the families had buried their sons. Cognizant of the public thrashing he had taken from the veterans' groups when the flag had been lowered for Matt Shepard, this was one of those situations where it was better for me to beg forgiveness than to ask permission.

Since the athletics director reported that student-athletes were hearing the news of the accident as they assembled back on campus at the end of the weekend and needed complete information and access to counseling, separate team meetings were arranged for all seventeen of UW's men's and women's intercollegiate teams later that afternoon. Plans were in formation for a candlelight vigil at the site of the "bucking horse and rider" statue near the athletic complex. Prior to the vigil, the athletic director and I assembled all of the coaches together to provide our own expressions of support and to detail the campus resources they could call on to assist their teams in dealing with the death of their eight friends.

A crowd estimated at from 700 to 2,000 assembled in a drizzling rain that evening for the candlelight vigil. Photographs of each of the eight young men had been set up on the grass around the bucking horse statue. Flowers and candles in large numbers began to appear, to be joined later in the week by cards and notes, running shoes, track uniforms, and other memorabilia brought by the families and passersby.

There is no way to describe the collective mood of those at the vigil. As one student quoted in the local newspaper observed, coming on the heels of the September 11 attacks and the campus memorial that previous Friday, the emotional environment was like "blackness on blackness." The vigil was led by the male and female captains of the cross-country team, who invited teammates or other friends of the victims to offer their personal reflections.

I had not prepared remarks, but I was prepared to give remarks. I told the students what I felt: in my 51 years up to that time, a tragedy had never hit me as hard as this one. Although the death of Matt Shepard was difficult in its own right, the death of eight was almost overwhelming. And with three children of my own in a state known to harbor the lethal combination of dangerous highways and alcohol abuse among its youth, it was not hard to picture myself in the posture of any of the ten sets of parents for the Eight. I urged the students to go home and call their parents. "Tell them you love them. If you have something unsaid to a brother or sister, say it." What I did not say, of course, was that I could also picture myself in the posture of the Haskins family, with a son badly injured in a hospital and likely to be facing eight charges of vehicular homicide. No one at the memorial had to say it, but everyone knew it—nine lives had been wasted that day.

The next morning I visited Clint Haskins in the local hospital. Although his injuries were significant, he was expected to recover fully. Surrounded by a handful of his friends, I spoke briefly with Clint and his mother, indicating that our student affairs staff would be available for any questions he might have relative to his classes or counseling he might desire. He was released later in the week and was able to make a personal appearance at a Friday bail hearing, which resulted in his release on a $100,000 bond and a requirement imposed by the judge that he continue attending university classes.

Since university personnel were not consulted by the judge concerning the conditions of Haskins' bail, we were unaware until some time later of the judge's requirement that Haskins continue attending classes. Following Haskins' release on bail and acting on the recommendation of both the chief academic officer and the student affairs staff, I called Haskins' father to suggest that Clint's temporary withdrawal from school might be in his best interest, particularly if other students were to confront him concerning the accident and its consequences. Moreover, if Haskins' presence were to be disruptive to the educational process of other students, I would have no choice but to issue a suspension. The Haskins family, then under the smothering advice of legal counsel, thanked me for my call but made no immediate decision. Later, Haskins would return to classes without incident.

In the days that followed, hundreds of expressions of condolence flooded into the university through telephone calls, letters, cards, and e-mails from sympathetic citizens, alumni, former teammates of the Eight, cross-country runners from other teams in UW's conference and around the country, and people connected with Oklahoma State University or Texas A&M who knew firsthand of the impact of such tragedies on campus communities. Contributions to a memorial fund established for the Eight mounted quickly, eventually reaching nearly $215,000.

In the immediate aftermath, there was a set of decisions to be made that were important, largely from a symbolic standpoint. A women's soccer home game, already rescheduled as a result of the September 11 attacks, was postponed again; so, too, was a women's volleyball home game. The student affairs staff followed suit, canceling all scheduled intramural competitions for the balance of the week.

We assigned the dean of students to serve as the primary university contact with the ten families. As the former director of UW's counseling center, Dr. Andrew Turner brought superb credentials and the appropriate temperament to this difficult task. We knew that the student-athletes and others in the community would expect a campus memorial service, but we did not want to have such a ceremony without the concurrence of the families, and we certainly could not have those discussions until the families had time to make their personal arrangements for the burial of their sons.

Funerals or memorial services for the Eight began on Tuesday, September 18, and were held daily through Friday night. Since it was logistically impossible to attend all eight funerals (two were out of state and one was in Canada), we used the crisis management team to ensure that we had appropriate university and athletic department representatives at each. A university flag accompanied the lead representative for each funeral and was to be delivered to the family. My wife Lisa and I attended

five of these heart-breaking services. The university airplane transported
the vice president for academic affairs and cross-country team representatives to the service held in Canada.

Prominently displayed by university personnel and student-athletes at
the funerals and around campus during that week were small decals containing a winged running shoe (modeled, I presume, on the winged foot
of Mercury) with the number 8 emblazoned on it. I later learned that the
winged foot had special meaning to the cross-country team members
who, before every meet, had recited a prayer that included the words
"give us wings so we can fly." These decals eventually found their way
onto the backs of the helmets of the football team and other athletic
team uniforms, as did the American flag in memory of the victims of September 11.

With the concurrence of all of the families, we arranged a campus memorial service for the following Tuesday, ensuring that the time and date
would make it possible for all of them to attend. Through the dean of
students, we conveyed our willingness for the university to pay all transportation and hotel expenses for the families if they required such financial assistance.

With instructions given to faculty that they should exercise liberal discretion in releasing students from classes to attend the memorial if they
wished and release time issued for staff, more than 3,500 crowded the
Arena-Auditorium for the service. Speakers included the governor,
coaches and team captains, the athletics director, and me. Several universities from the Mountain West Conference and one regional school
not associated with the MWC sent delegations of members from their
cross-country teams. Large photographs of each of the lost student-
athletes were displayed on either side of the podium; a candle in honor
of each was lit by a male and female member of UW athletics teams. A
celebratory video prepared by the Athletics Department staff, "Always a
Cowboy," was shown. A brass bell, symbolizing each athlete's last lap, was
rung eight times.

Lisa and I hosted a post-memorial reception and dinner at our home
for the members of the families and the coaching staff. Each family was
presented with a gift bag containing a copy of the celebratory videotape;
a framed photo of the candlelight vigil; a book containing all the e-mails,
notes, cards, and letters of sympathy we had received; and the memorial
service program.

The remaining members of the men's cross-country team, joined by
some redshirt freshmen who voluntarily gave up a year of eligibility and
middle distance runners recruited from the track team, returned to cross-

country competition in October. Drawing on the metaphor of the bucking bronco rider, the team captain observed that "cowboys always get back up."

Throughout the week of the funerals and thereafter for many months, public debate centered around the causes of the accident. The county attorney, seeking to buttress a vehicular homicide charge against Haskins, suggested at the bail hearing that the rodeo team in general and Haskins in particular had a history of alcohol abuse. Haskins had at least two previous citations off campus for underage consumption and, later investigation revealed, one on-campus citation during his freshman year in the university residence halls. Other organizations, including Mothers Against Drunk Driving, focused on the inadequacy of Wyoming's laws relative to driving while intoxicated.[9] Others, including the father of the driver of the Jeep, focused on the condition of the highway, a notoriously dangerous three-lane road that joins Laramie to Fort Collins.

Over the course of the next year, I corresponded frequently with the ten families of the Eight—to share copies of the videotape of the memorial service, to keep them posted on the status of the memorial fund, to solicit their ideas concerning its use and the dedication of a memorial to the boys, and to share other things that I thought might have meaning to them. These included copies of S. L. Price's sensitive *Sports Illustrated* article about the boys and pictures of the torch that a retired member of the UW staff had carried in their honor in the transmission of the Olympic torch through Cheyenne, Wyoming, on its way to the 2002 Salt Lake City Olympics.

By midspring, grief for some of the families had been transformed into anger, and the university became the target. Several of the families, who had obviously kept in contact among themselves, wondered aloud in letters to me personally, to Dean Turner, and to the newspapers why the university had allowed Haskins to remain enrolled in school, particularly after he entered a guilty plea in March in what appeared to be a negotiated arrangement with the county attorney. And as the weeks progressed closer to the May graduation date, several of the parents were angry that we were not only going to allow Haskins to receive his degree, but that we would permit him to participate in commencement exercises. As one pair of parents noted pointedly, instead of being able to return to campus to watch their son walk across the stage to receive his diploma, they would be returning to dedicate a memorial that owed its existence to Haskins' criminal behavior.

In letters to each of the ten sets of parents, I explained that I was not prepared to stop Haskins from attending class as long as he did not represent a disruption to the educational process. Moreover, since Haskins was not, in my view, a danger to the university community and the judge had not formally accepted a plea of guilty, I had no basis under our student conduct code to suspend or expel Haskins. As it turns out, the scheduled date for the plea agreement to be accepted by the judge and the sentencing was postponed until nearly two weeks following Haskins' scheduled graduation. Haskins would be allowed to graduate and, if he chose, to participate in commencement ceremonies. Privately, our dean of students worked with Haskins to encourage him not to participate in commencement. Haskins graduated, but he voluntarily chose to avoid commencement exercises. Two weeks later, in an emotional hearing attended by the families of the victims, Haskins' guilty plea was accepted. A young man, almost universally described by those who knew him as "reliable, decent, and polite," was sentenced by the judge to 14–20 years in the state prison; fines, court costs, and restitution of nearly $90,000; and 1,600 hours of community service.

On September 13, 2002—on the same weekend of the accident just a year earlier—all ten families and hundreds of onlookers joined us to dedicate a memorial garden for the Eight. We again covered the transportation and hotel costs of those family members requiring it. Eight granite boulders of various sizes harvested from the U.S. 287 right-of-way near the site of the accident were selected to form the core of the memorial, which also includes two benches, trees and flowers, and a bronze plaque with the silhouettes of eight runners under the words "Come Run with Me." I spoke, as did many of the same speakers from the memorial service of the year before, including coaches, representatives of the cross-country team, and the mother of one of the Eight. Members of the families were invited to tour the remodeled locker and team rooms for the cross-country and track teams, renovations that had been made possible by the funds donated after the accident.

## LEADING IN CRISIS: LESSONS LEARNED

Since the university is one of the world's most enduring institutions and because the range of potential crises is so great, I had presumed that published studies about academic leadership or the reflections of university presidents past would be filled with helpful guidance about leading under conditions of crisis. I was wrong. Apart from only a few passing references to the student unrest of the 1960s on American college campuses, neither those who have studied academic leadership nor those who have practiced it have considered the challenges of leading an institution under crisis conditions.[10]

Books aimed at the management of crises in corporate and industrial settings are a little more helpful, particularly with respect to dealing with issues related to the media and communications.[11] The value of crisis preparedness and having response plans in place prior to the arrival of a crisis also emerges from such volumes.[12] It would be unusual in my experience, however, for a public institution to have the resources necessary to fully identify and assess the range of potential crises and emergencies it might face.

With that said, the crises faced by the University of Wyoming suggest to me several lessons that might be of value to others who may find themselves similarly situated in the future:

**Lesson 1: When confronted by crisis, seek ways to ensure that your institution is not defined by the crisis itself, but by your response to it.** Both of the incidents that faced the University of Wyoming were, to say the least, emotionally wrenching for all involved. They differed in their particulars, to be sure. Unlike the death of the Eight, which was at its core simply a human tragedy without many downstream implications for the operation of the university or its reputation, the Matthew Shepard murder had significant political overtones and the potential to leave the public across the country with the impression that the university was insensitive to issues facing gay, lesbian, bisexual, and transgendered individuals.

In both instances, we certainly recognized the importance of distributing information from the university to the public on an ongoing basis during each crisis. But we also recognized early on that we could not fully control, dictate, or influence media reporting and the impressions resulting therefrom. Accordingly, as a matter of explicit direction that I gave to our staff through the crisis management team, our primary motivating factor in the management of each crisis was to provide maximum institutional support to the families of the victims. The academic literature on crisis management makes it clear that this approach is not only the right thing to do from a humanitarian standpoint, but will serve to minimize damage to the institution's reputation. "Above all, remember that a crisis is a human event. Do the right thing, especially in how you treat the people affected by the crisis. Even the most effective communications will not make your institution appear caring and competent if your actions are not."[13]

**Lesson 2: You cannot be prepared for every crisis, but you can be prepared.** As I suggested above and in the accompanying notes, I am skeptical that an institution such as mine can be prepared to deal with every conceivable adverse event that might confront it, whether the result of natural disasters, internal crises, or external events. Minimally, though, having in place a standing crisis management team turned out to be indispensable to UW's ability to manage each of these two major crises.

In our case, that group has a standing membership consisting of the president; the vice presidents of academic affairs, student affairs, and administration; the dean of students; the director of the Counseling Center; the director of university public relations; the director of the physical plant; and the chief of the campus police. That membership can and was augmented to meet the circumstances of each crisis.

**Lesson 3: Many media representatives are lazy; just plan for it.** Both crises involved misreporting by the media that could and should have been avoided. Fortunately, the university public relations staff did a tremendous job of monitoring newspaper and broadcast reports and seeking corrections whenever possible. Training senior members of my administration counted. The ability to appear nondefensive in response to the "when did you stop beating your spouse" question, to answer the question you wanted them to ask, and to deliver the answer in under fifteen seconds can make a tremendous difference in whether the message you want to appear on the evening news actually will do so.

The university public relations staff also actively sought out opportunities for me to meet with the most prominent media. You will never be able to stop reporters from trolling your campus or your community in search of the proverbial village idiot, and most times they will find him. As a result, it is advisable to take every opportunity you can to tell your institution's own story in your own words.

The university public relations staff also understood the impact of the Internet in ways that I did not, both in terms of the value of responding to individuals who chose to write to us and in posting information on the university web site that might be helpful. In the case of Matt Shepard, since the initial reports seemed to suggest that the attackers were students, we launched a comprehensive listing of the various diversity-related educational initiatives that the campus had already undertaken lest it be thought that we had been completely negligent in this area. In the case of the Eight, the web site not only helped convey information about the victims and the memorial services scheduled, but provided a place for grieving individuals to share their thoughts and feelings with the university and the families of the victims.

**Lesson 4: In times of a severe crisis, the president's voice matters, and it may be the only one that does.** Although university responses to many events are capably handled by a chief academic or student affairs officer or the university's public relations staff, both of the major UW crises convinced me that there is no substitute in times of community trauma for one comforting voice. And although every rule probably holds its own exception, that voice at a university must be the president's. Call it the Giuliani Effect, if you wish. For these moments in time, the president's values are the institution's values, and they cannot be conveyed with passion and meaning in a press release or by a press spokesperson. During times of crisis, the president may be not only the chief executive officer but also the mourner-in-chief.

**Lesson 5: Symbols matter, and so does substance.** I will leave it to those who understand how humans deal with severe trauma better than I to explain the importance of tangible symbols (such as the armbands and the winged running shoe), candlelight vigils, memorial ceremonies, concerts, and other activities to bring communities together in times of crisis and to help people deal with their emotional reactions. I believe, however, that each of the events was helpful.

At the same time, such moments cannot be allowed to obscure substantive issues or concerns that may emerge. This was certainly the case almost immediately after media attention focused on the attack on Matt Shepard. National media noted that Wyoming was one of the few states that, up to that time, had not enacted a hate crimes statute and did not have the full range of antidiscrimination statutes to protect homosexuals in housing, employment, and health care. National gay activist groups quickly noted that the university's official policies and procedures did not extend the same kind of access to university services and protections forbidding discrimination based on race, gender, religion, and national origin. The university's employer-paid benefits, including health, dental, and life insurance, were available only to married couples and did not extend to homosexual (or heterosexual) domestic partners. There was no mandatory diversity requirement in the university's curriculum or specific major or minor courses of study dedicated to gay and lesbian studies. And although there was an existing Multicultural Resource Center that served as a gathering place for ethnic minority (and white) students, there was no similar place to serve as a safe haven for LGBT students.

Some of the revelations relative to the university's policies and procedures were news to me but were relatively easy to address. Although the university had, for the better part of a decade, maintained a statement of nondiscrimination/antiharassment, which included sexual orientation, that requirement had never been formally incorporated in the large number of campus policies that contained nondiscrimination clauses of one sort or another. My subsequent proposal to the Board of Trustees to include the same list of ten prohibited bases of discrimination in all university regulations and policies was unanimously adopted, and almost without debate.[14]

There was then, and there remains to this day, no way for the university to independently address the extension of employer-paid benefits to domestic partners, heterosexual or homosexual. By statute, the university is a participant in the state of Wyoming's group health insurance system, which is funded and controlled through the state legislative process.

On the other hand, by administrative directive I was able to extend certain university-provided benefits to domestic partners, including access to UW's recreation, athletic, and housing services. And a campus policy on bereavement leave and sick leave that had been interpreted locally to apply only to traditional nuclear families was "reinterpreted" with the stroke of a presidential pen to include "all members of an immediate household."

We were also able to address the matter of space for the campus LGBT community through the creation of the Rainbow Resource Room, a small facility that contains a large number of purchased and donated educational materials on LGBT issues. That particular approach, modeled on the Multicultural Resource Center, permitted us to be responsive to the LGBT concern while avoiding the almost certain criticism that we were providing space to the "gay student group" but not to any of the other student groups on campus that have no place to call their own.

Finally, in response to the criticism that we had focused on symbolic palliatives to the exclusion of substantively dealing with LGBT and other human rights issues, we were successful in securing an anonymous private gift of $1 million to support diversity-related educational programming. When matched through the state's matching gift program, we were able to create a $2 million endowment for these programs. Included among these is the annual Matthew Shepard Symposium for Social Justice (http://outreach.uwyo.edu/conferences/justice/).

We certainly have a long way to go in addressing the substantive concerns of our LGBT faculty, staff, and students, but there can be no question that the crisis itself had the positive outcome of raising our awareness of just how far.

The substantive issues that arose as a result of the accident that took the Eight were not nearly as important but were still instructive. We developed a more stringent rodeo team policy on alcohol and drug use to bring it in line with the same policy used in intercollegiate athletics. Under the leadership of the vice president for student affairs, we also formed the "A-Team" to address the need for a community-wide approach to alcohol education and enforcement (http://uwadmnweb.uwyo.edu/AWARE/ATeam.htm).

**Lesson 6: Do not let the crisis override your principles, but do not let abstract principles get in the way either.** In any period of turmoil or emotional stress, it is easy to make decisions that are based on emotion rather than principle. My opportunity came with the arrival on campus of Reverend Phelps and his antihomosexual protesters during the trial of Russell Henderson. Not only was Phelps personally offensive to me and nearly everyone I knew, but he had peppered my office repeatedly with repulsive fax announcements that, as frequently as not, named me personally as part of what Phelps saw as a grand conspiracy to protect and pander to the homosexual community. When Phelps indicated that he planned to protest at the university, my initial reaction was not to allow anyone who had condemned me to hell to come onto my campus; if I had to invent a reason to justify his exclusion (e.g., being unable to ensure the safety of Phelps and his followers), I could get creative. Fortunately, sober second thoughts prevailed and we arranged a space we could secure for Phelps to protest, with armed officers posted nearby and on the surrounding rooftops. Our principled commitment to the First Amendment, academic freedom, and other central university values did not have to be sacrificed.

On the other hand, abstract principles may have to be tempered on occasion to deal with the circumstances of each crisis. In the late afternoon on the day after Matt Shepard's beaten body had been discovered and transported to the hospital in Fort Collins, my executive assistant alerted me to the organization of the candlelight vigil for Matt to be held on the following Sunday evening. The pastor of St. Paul's Newman Catholic Center, Father Roger Schmit, had called to see whether I would speak on behalf of the university. My immediate reaction was that I did not want to do that. It did not seem appropriate, at least at first blush, for the president of the state's only public university to participate in what I was sure would be a religiously oriented vigil. My assistant, who had learned that she could usually steer me straight once the venting was over, simply waited for the end of my powerful lecture on the separation of church and state, looked up from her desk at me, and said, "You need to be there; you really need to be there." I made the decision to attend and to speak; it was the right decision (see Lesson 4).

**Lesson 7: When facing a crisis, look to the institutions that have been there and done that—and, when possible, learn best practices before you need them.** Although the Matthew Shepard tragedy unfolded in a way that did not prompt us to look to any other institution for assistance, we benefited immensely from our colleagues at Oklahoma State University and Texas A&M University in dealing with the loss of the Eight. Both of those institutions had, within just the previous two years, suffered catastrophic losses of their own. Upon learning of the accident that claimed the Eight, both our public relations staff and our athletics staff contacted their counterparts at each institution to learn more about how they had dealt with the families, comforted students and other members of the campus community, responded to media inquiries, organized memorial services, and managed the large volume of public expressions of sympathy and condolence that came in from around the country. Although we had to make our own decisions about what approaches would best fit our campus and serve the families of the victims, the lessons learned by others who had previously faced awful times were immensely helpful to us.

**Lesson 8: You are not a superhero.** I am lucky to be one of those people who does not experience physical or emotional symptoms from the stress of the job as president. As my wife enjoys observing, I do not seem to feel the effects of criticism because I do not really care if anyone likes me—and that is a good thing because no one does. I have always tried to practice what one of my mentors told me early on in my administrative career: "If you like to have people like you, that's fine; if you *need* to have them like you, better get yourself a dog!"

But campus crises of the kind I have described here are, by definition, not the norm. They bring about strong emotions, not only on campus but within the university leadership. Unfortunately, the crisis may obscure your vision with respect to your own personal needs for counseling and support.

Parents always live with the haunting possibility that one of their children may die unexpectedly from an illness or an accident. Months after the Matthew Shepard tragedy, though, I discovered that I had developed an abiding sense of vulnerability with respect to my own children. However remote the chances that one of them might be kidnapped from a local bar and murdered, what should have remained buried within my brain kept popping up in my head. The normal worry of waiting up for a teenage son to return home from a Friday night party became, at least for a period of months, an agonizing fear.

The deaths of the Eight might have been expected to have the same effect, but what could have emerged in the aftermath as overpowering fear was simply overpowering sadness. The lasting effects of attending five funerals of promising young men within the space of four days left me (and those around me) completely exhausted and drained. Only after weeks of restless nights did it occur to me that the tragedy had had a much larger impact on me than I really understood.

The appropriate remedy for dealing with personal trauma and grief will undoubtedly vary from one individual to the other. Personal counseling may work for some. In my case, I might have been able to deal better with each crisis had I not let each crisis interfere with my regular exercise routine. I did so largely because I was afraid of how it would look to other members of the campus community to see the president in the campus gym walking on the treadmill and pumping iron in the midst of such horrific events.

In my case, I was also aided tremendously by the presence and support of my wife Lisa and our three children. Lisa was particularly insistent that we not spend time hunkered down in the house and that we find a way to spend some time together and with friends. Although such occasions inevitably led to conversations about each tragedy, they only forced me to articulate to Lisa and our friends what I was thinking and feeling anyway.

## EPILOGUE

As I complete my eighth year as the president of the University of Wyoming, I can look back with pride about the notable accomplishments of my institution, speak to the value I place on the wonderfully enriching set of personal and professional relationships developed here, and express continuing excitement and enthusiasm for my work.

I cannot say that I was glad to have had the opportunity to preside over the management of the various crises we have faced. But I can say that, as is the case with many of life's negative experiences, there have been some positive consequences. Certainly I feel that I am a stronger leader than I was before and, although others would be in a better position to judge than I, am perceived by my colleagues as such. I have come to appreciate the importance of the office I hold and its power for community building at critical times. And finally, more so than at any time previously, I understand the fragility of life and the power of university communities to deal with its unexpected loss.

## NOTES

1. Murphy, 2003, p. 36; italics in original.
2. Seymour and Moore, 2000, p. x.
3. Seymour and Moore, 2000, p. 28.
4. Murphy, 2003, p. 36. Commenting on what most observers would probably say is the most difficult crisis ever to confront an American university or college, Murphy observed that "for many Americans, the name 'Kent State' evokes images of a nation in conflict. A single crisis decades ago forever defined that institution as a symbol of civil outrage and government run amok."

5. Readers interested in materials related to the University of Wyoming's response to the murder of Matthew Shepard may wish to consult the university's resource web site: http://www.uwyo.edu/News/shepard/. See also Loffreds, 2000. There is no comparable set of materials related to "The Eight," but a poignant and powerful account can be found in S. L. Price's "Crossroad," in *Sports Illustrated* magazine (November 26, 2001, pp. 86–99).

6. The text of my remarks may be found on the University of Wyoming Matthew Shepard Resource Page at http://www.uwyo.edu/News/shepard.

7. Although Elton John's contribution of $50,000 to the fund initiated to establish a Law School chair was received, we were unable to generate additional interest in the concept to raise the $1.5 million required. Eventually, with the permission of John's foundation, we redirected these funds to join an anonymous $1 million gift to underwrite a variety of diversity-related initiatives, including support for the Rainbow Resource Room described later in this chapter.

8. In addition to the activities organized by LGBTA, the campus administration arranged for a photographic exhibition of LGBT young people, "The Shared Heart" offered by artist Adam Mastoon, to be displayed in UW's union art gallery. The theatre department offered its production of *Angels in America*.

9. In the 2002 legislative session, Wyoming enacted legislation reducing the blood alcohol limit for driving from .10 to .08.

10. In a volume packed with useful advice for presidents on nearly every conceivable topic related to university administration, former University of Texas President Peter T. Flawn makes only passing reference to the management of student protests, advising that the president should send a dean or vice president out to the front lines (Flawn, 1990, p. 15). Steve Sample's useful small volume on presidential leadership also makes only a small comment about the importance of the president in crisis management, principally to provide a "sense of security" to the campus community (Sample, 2002, pp. 75, 80). Addressing the challenges to presidents in the 1990s, Clark Kerr described them as a "mince pie" of issues, only two of which could be considered "crises"—the need to accommodate growing numbers of underrepresented students and some level of student unrest over issues such as the racial and gender composition of the faculty" (Kerr, 1994, pp. 115, 126–128). None of the other major volumes I consulted (Birnbaum, 1992; Bloustein, 1972; Budig, 2002; Crowley, 1994; Plante with Caret, 1990) mention the challenges of presidential leadership during crisis situations.

11. See, for instance, Seymour and Moore, 2000; Ogrizek and Guillery, 1999; Heath, 1998; and Nudell and Antokol, 1988. The crises typically dealt with in these books involve those with near-term and long-term potential damage to a company's reputation, including things like airplane crashes, oil spills, product safety problems, labor crises, economic boycotts, institutional scandals, disease outbreaks, and the like.

12. See Seymour and Moore, 2000, pp. 190–212; Ogrizek and Guillery, 1999, pp. 88–90.

13. Murphy, 2000, p. 37.

14. The University of Wyoming's nondiscrimination statements (applicable to admission, employment, and access to programs and services) now all include the same list of ten prohibited bases of discrimination: race, color, religion, sex, national origin, disability, age, veteran status, sexual orientation, and political belief.

## REFERENCES

Birnbaum, Robert. 1992. *How Academic Leadership Works: Understanding Success and Failure in the College Presidency.* San Francisco: Jossey-Bass.

Bloustein, Edward J. 1972. *The University and the Counterculture: Inaugural and Other Addresses by Edward J. Bloustein.* New Brunswick, NJ: Rutgers University Press.

Budig, Gene A. 2002. *A Game of Uncommon Skill.* Westport, CT: American Council on Education, Oryx Press, and the College Board.

Crowley, Joseph N. 1994. *No Equal in the World: An Interpretation of the Academic Presidency.* Reno: University of Nevada Press.

Flawn, Peter T. 1990. *A Primer for University Presidents: Managing the Modern University.* Austin: University of Texas Press.

Heath, Robert. 1998. *Crisis Management for Managers and Executives.* London: Financial Times Management.

Kerr, Clark. 1994. *Troubled Times for American Higher Education: The 1990s and Beyond.* New York: State University of New York Press.

Loffreda, Beth. 2000. *Losing Matt Shepard: Life and Politics in the Aftermath of Anti-Gay Murder.* New York: Columbia University Press.

Murphy, Sean K. 2003. "Crisis Management Demystified: Here's How to Prevent a Crisis from Ruining Your Institution's Reputation." *University Business* (February): 36–37.

Nudell, Mayer, and Norman Antokol. 1988. *The Handbook for Effective Emergency and Crisis Management.* Lexington, MA: Lexington Books, D.C. Heath and Company.

Ogrizek, Michel, and Jean Michel Guillery. 1999. *Communicating in Crisis: A Theoretical and Practical Guide to Crisis Management.* New York: Aldine de Gruyter.

Plant, Patricia R. 1990. *Myths and Realities of Academic Administration.* With Robert L. Caret. New York: American Council on Education, Macmillan.

Sample, Steven B. 2002. *The Contrarian's Guide to Leadership.* San Francisco: Jossey-Bass.

Seymour, Mike, and Simon Moore. 2000. *Effective Crisis Management: Worldwide Principles and Practice.* New York: Cassell.

# CHAPTER

## Moral Leadership
### A Response to President Dubois' Essay

*Scott S. Cowen*

Reading President Dubois' essay was therapeutic to this reader. Last week I had to speak at two memorial services for students we lost in the last two months. Reading the previous essay brought back to me all the crises we have had on our own campus. Phil Dubois is not alone. I appreciate that he has shared his situations so openly.

### CRISES AND LESSONS

In our way of life, crises define our universities and test their core values. Even though we think we prepare for these events, there is no way to prepare completely because by definition a crisis is something unexpected. I know I have had my share of crises in five and a half years at Tulane University, including the deaths of eight students and seven hurricanes. When you live in New Orleans and you are under sea level, when a hurricane comes it is always the time of crisis. These hurricanes have been particularly difficult for me because I was raised in the East and Midwest and had never seen a hurricane.

I have also had legislative threats in retaliation for actions of the faculty, including the governor of Louisiana coming out publicly and suggesting that people never give money to Tulane again because there is a group of faculty in the law school that supports environmental efforts. And last, and perhaps most distressing, are the personal attacks I and many of my board members received over the last few months as a consequence of our review of intercollegiate athletics.

So, on the basis of my experiences, I resonated with Dubois' eight les-sons. I teased out two other lessons for myself. Lesson 9, corollary to Dubois' Lesson 7, is *always do a post-audit of a crisis* and make sure you articulate lessons learned. After it is over, it is important to sit down and analyze how you could do it better the next time.

The tenth lesson, corollary to Dubois' Lesson 8, is *if you do make a mis-take, do not run away from it and do not ever repeat it.* We spend a lot of time talking about the mistakes we make and making sure we do not re-peat them. It is important to be honest in identifying them, not in plac-ing blame.

I think that openness, transparency, and candor are key attributes at the time of crisis. Dubois certainly witnessed those during his.

## ARCHETYPES OF LEADERSHIP

As I was reading Dubois' essay, I was thinking of something totally different from crises. I was thinking about different types of leadership we demonstrate, both in times of crises and stability. I actually went to the point of developing four archetypes of leadership. These archetypes are very simplistic, but they helped me think through what Dubois had done and to actually tease out some more general lessons for myself.

The archetypes I developed were first expressed in a book I wrote sev-eral years ago on change in higher education. One is that in our roles we are expected to demonstrate moral leadership. People look to college presidents to provide moral leadership every day. As a matter of fact, this type of leadership in many ways defines the legendary college presidents who served in the twentieth century—Robert Maynard Hutchins, James Conant, and Clark Kerr. When we think about those presidents, we think about them in terms of their moral leadership. Even though we are de-fined today by our moral leadership on our campuses, I feel that our moral leadership in the eye of the public has diminished significantly. Now that may be a provocative statement, but it is in fact something I believe very strongly.

I think Dubois showed extraordinary moral leadership, especially in the Shepard case where there was a moral issue at stake and he took a stand on it. It seems to me that all of us in our roles have to demonstrate more moral leadership. I fear that in the eyes of the public we are not taking that leadership. That got me thinking about Lee Bollinger (for-mer president of the University of Michigan) because Lee's leadership on diversity is probably the best example I can think of in recent decades where a university president showed extraordinary moral leadership that had an impact on society. Yet, it is a rare example. I am having a hard time thinking of others, at that scale. That is not to say that we have not provided visible moral leadership on our campuses. I fear that our universities are being more defined by commercialization and industrialization, rather than by moral leadership.

The second kind of leadership I began thinking about was intellectual leadership, where we champion ideas that lead to substantive, profound academic change in our institution. It is difficult to provide intellectual leadership when you lead a very large and complex major research university. Yet our ability to provide this type of leadership is what really gains credibility and sustained respect from our faculty. I ask myself every day, "to what extent are we providing intellectual leadership?" Are we guiding our colleagues through our ideas about how we can make the academic experience a more valuable and worthwhile experience for all those who are in our university?

In order to have intellectual leadership, it seems to me that we need a lot more time to think, write, teach, and reflect. One of the attributes of the presidency now is that we barely have any time to do those things. I think that, as a result, it may be that our ability to provide intellectual leadership is diminished. We are so busy managing that we do not have enough time to provide that type of leadership.

I also think it is a function of time in office. One of the things that has always amused me is to watch the careers of the presidents that have never stayed in a position for more than three or four years. I have always wondered how these presidents demonstrate intellectual leadership when they are never around long enough to actually see whether their ideas come to fruition. My sense is that you really see the depth and breadth of intellectual leadership in a presidency when that president is somewhere between his or her fifth and tenth year because it takes three to five years to get to the point where one can begin to have an impact. Intellectual leadership is something that has to be sustained over a long period of time. It is my feeling that perhaps we are not doing as much as we could in our positions to provide that intellectual leadership, yet I know how difficult that is.

The third type of leadership I began to think about is executive leadership or what I will call managerial leadership. This is the ability to manage large and complex organizations. Based on our managerial acumen, this leadership archetype is most valued now in higher education. People with managerial expertise are in demand. In my former life, I was dean of the school of management for fourteen years and a professor of finance and accounting. But I have been very concerned that universities are looking more for management or executive leadership, many times over-looking whether the person has sufficiently evidenced intellectual or moral leadership. It seems to me that executive leadership, absent moral and intellectual leadership, is not in the best interests of higher educa-tion. One of the reasons that I think we are seeing increasing commer-cialization is because of the more pervasive type of executive leadership. We are really managing these institutions, not leading them. This ar-chetype, in my mind, is not a bad archetype at all. It is only bad when not accompanied by other types of leadership within the institution.

The last leadership, and the most dangerous, is political leadership. We have to maneuver systems to get things done. I have been interested in one of our states that habitually puts former politicians in as university presidents. I chuckle at that. It may be that the state and those univer-sities will go on to bigger and better things. But it seems to me that that is a very frightening and dangerous form of leadership where our institu-tions are run as if they are strictly political systems in the absence of other kinds of leadership.

## CONCLUSION

I think what impressed me the most is how Dubois handled very dif-ficult situations at the time of crisis. It seems to me that he demonstrated all four types of leadership. He clearly exhibited moral leadership in his handling of the Matthew Shepard case when he made a statement about hate crimes and about intolerance. I do think that people look to presi-dents of institutions to take that type of stand. In terms of intellectual leadership, the fact that Dubois began to think about converting these into teachable moments, to find out what could be taken from these les-sons learned, to sustain them over time and integrate them into the fab-ric of what we do as an institution, to me was very, very important.

And clearly Dubois exercised extraordinary executive leadership. He had to manage the crisis at each twist and turn. Politically, he had to deal with the governor and other major constituencies.

As one former management professor to another college president, I would give Dubois an A+. But his essay also led me to wonder whether we, as university presidents, are more generally demonstrating these lead-ership models in our roles as president. I, for one, begin to worry about whether we are doing what we should be doing in the areas of moral and intellectual leadership, even though I am convinced that we are doing a fairly good job at executive leadership and political leadership.

# CHAPTER

# The Importance of Values and Principles
## A Response to President Dubois' Essay

*Gregory C. Farrington*

I, too, will compliment Phil Dubois' essay. It is not that it has all the answers, but it certainly is packed with questions. In thinking about the questions, you come up with your own answers along the way. I also came away feeling thankful that I was not the president of the University of Wyoming over the last several years.

## THE IRONY OF PLACE

Matthew Shepard's death has been seared into the consciousness of so many people, myself included. If his murder had taken place in a decaying section of a large city, it probably would never have risen to the level of a national event. Somehow you expect to encounter evil in certain surroundings, but not against a fence on the open and seemingly endless prairie of Wyoming. The image of his death is etched so clearly in my mind. From a distance it can be mistaken for that of a scarecrow. Close up, it is a crucifixion—the body of a young man killed simply for being who he was and living as he was created.

I must say that I had forgotten that Matthew Shepard was a student at the University of Wyoming. What I can never forget is the hatred that lay behind his murder. Somehow it still is acceptable in our society—and in many others as well—to hate people simply because they are gay. It still is acceptable to hate individuals simply because of what they are, so long as what they are is gay.

President Dubois mentioned that a group of veterans in Wyoming protested that the American flag had been lowered in honor of Matthew Shepard. I doubt they would have protested if the flag had been lowered for the eight white or black students killed in the unrelated automobile accident he described. But they did protest when the flag was lowered for a gay student.

This visceral prejudice must change. Change should begin on campuses because larger society grows from our campuses. I would hope that the leadership of all colleges and universities would be just as unambiguous and unwavering in their support of the rights of gay students as they are of black, or Asian, or Hispanic, or white students. Of course, it is not an easy stand to take.

## DIVERSITY AT LEHIGH

One year ago at Lehigh, the Lehigh leadership group and I created a statement entitled, "Achieving a More Diverse Lehigh," which dealt with all the issues one would expect. It is a very straightforward statement on the subject and importance of diversity, and we clearly included issues of gay and straight. Doing so also earned my campus and me a personal visit from Mr. Fred Phelps and followers from the Westboro Baptist Church in Topeka, Kansas, the same group that picketed Matthew Shepard's funeral in what was a seemingly inconceivable act of cruel disrespect to his family, friends, and community. The Phelps family brought to our little town of Bethlehem their engine of hate. Encountering them was an extraordinary experience.

Lehigh is much smaller than the University of Wyoming. If the state of Wyoming is just one small town with long streets, we are a small town with very short streets. Lehigh has about 6,000 students. It is possible to be personal in our environment in a way that is more difficult on a large campus. During my six years at Lehigh, which followed nineteen years in the much larger and urban world of the University of Pennsylvania, I have not had to endure crises anywhere nearly as large as those described by President Dubois, and for that I am thankful. However, in dealing with Lehigh's human crises, I have been impressed by what would seem to be a contradiction.

On one hand, it is remarkable to me how issues and events such as the horror of Matthew Shepard's death, or September 11th, or even simply rude graffiti on a dormitory door can bring out in a small number of people extraordinary feelings of hate. It is almost as if some people are waiting for a moment when they can hate and do so openly. Crises bring out the very worst in them.

More optimistically, I am also impressed—renewed—by just how many more people are capable of such extraordinary good when a crisis hits. So many students who would otherwise be lying on the green, tossing a football, or dreaming of what they are going to do that night suddenly bloom into empathetic and very human beings in the face of crisis. Their thoughts immediately are for others. Crises bring out the best in them.

## LESSONS

In moments of crisis—large and small—I have been impressed by the hunger of the campus community for clear leadership, and this includes students, faculty, and staff. What seems important to me is consistency, candor, and honesty, a bit of humility, visibility, and speed. When a crisis occurs, a president should be a visible leader, not hidden in an office. Nobody else can really serve the role. It may be tempting to say, "That's the job of the dean of students." But in an event of any kind of magnitude, there really is no substitute for the president in terms of setting the tone and stating clearly the values and principles that are involved. If the values and principles are not clear, the related tactical moves will lack coherence and be hollow.

I think it is critically important to *engage the community personally*. I remember the morning of 9/11 as clearly as if it were yesterday. We watched the horror unfold on television. Our campus leadership group assembled quickly and decided on the steps we would take right away. Then I said to the provost, "We're out of here." The two of us spent the rest of that day simply walking the campus, being visible, appearing in every dining hall, in virtually every building, walking, talking, and simply being very, very visible as real human beings. We really had nothing profound to say, but we were sending the message that even if the world in New York City had turned upside down in a horrific way, the campus world was still intact and students could count on its stability and support.

I think it is important to be *honest, candid, and human*. I can think of too many times when an attorney has said to me, "You can't say that." Well, folks, real people have pretty good sensors for legal-speak and they tune it out. If you talk like a lawyer, you just do not connect. People are a lot more understanding and forgiving if you are real.

Of course, the *Internet is such a powerful medium*. It has made everyone a publisher, and it has speeded up the communications clock enormously. One aspect of our crisis planning at Lehigh has been very careful thinking about our use of the Internet in all our communications strategies. How quickly can we get information to students? Who will send what to whom?

Right after 9/11 we had a particularly unpleasant event that had to do with the display of a flag on campus. Within the twenty minutes it took to fix the problem, the incident was spreading across the country on the Internet. By that evening, Lehigh began to be discussed on right-wing talk shows, based on very little that was real and a lot that was imaginary. We spent the next week responding as the story spread from radio station to radio station. Crazy stories spread fastest, and the Internet is a superhighway for misinformation, speculation, and plain old gossip. It can dominate your life so quickly and make it possible for others to set your agenda and put you on the defensive, within hours.

Let me add here a word about the board of trustees. Whenever a big event happens on campus, they are one of the first groups we inform. We contact them all by e-mail. We want them to have clear information as rapidly as possible because they are the contact points for a lot of other people. As we all know, well-informed boards can be very effective in blunting the spread of misinformation. They are definitely more effective when they know what is going on, and sometimes they are even quieter too.

Finally, I think it is very important for university leaders to *take strong and principled stands on issues that really matter.* This is an area in which I think universities and colleges have tended too much toward silence, for all sorts of rather obvious reasons: funding, the risk of offending alumni, and so forth. You know the list. When the Westboro Baptist Church came to Lehigh, a few alumni took it as their moment to contact me to support the Westboro views. It was not pleasant. But if we do not stand up and talk about issues that really count, who will? Ultimately, the level of respect that society has for colleges and universities will be in direct proportion to our role in standing publicly for principles that matter.

Far too often, our responsibility to respect the right of others to speak is interpreted to mean that we must remain silent, or perhaps taken as an excuse to remain silent. Far from it. Simply because others have the right to speak does not mean we must accept what they are saying and have no right to reply. If we are silent on big issues that really matter, we leave the definition of the debate to those who have other agendas.

Of course, in the end, our biggest impact is in influencing students. Each year I remind incoming students that Lehigh is a community, not a collection. Communities have values. We have values. Each student is free to express his or her opinions, but not all opinions are of equal merit. I tell them that from time to time we will remind them of those values. It is our obligation as educators to do so.

# CHAPTER

## Clemson and South Carolina's Confederate Flag Controversy
### A Response to President Dubois' Essay

*James F. Barker*

The work that Phil Dubois has presented and written is most impressive. The candor and self-reflections are qualities that are an inspiration to me. This essay has generated some thoughts.

Let me start by quoting two sentences: "[Y]our stakeholders . . . are measuring your conduct during the crisis; they know that a crisis does not *make* character—it *reveals* character."[1]

### CORE AND SURFACE

I have come to see my school as a kind of living organism that has a core that is solid and static and a surface that is dynamic and changing. The core is made up of the timeless stuff of character (fixed and tied to principles and values). The surface is made up of the stuff of change. It is constantly in motion, testing new ideas, embracing new ground. Both are vital. On most days, the surface is the thing that is most revealed. In a time of crisis, it is the core that becomes evident. I think all presidents themselves have a similar cross-section: character at the core, values at the core, and dynamic stuff at the surface.

What struck me in studying Dubois' essay was how important it is for these two cross-sections to be the same. If our core and surface are different from our schools' core and surface, it will be revealed in a crisis. The result will be a lack of authenticity and a lack of genuine communication and trust, and the crisis will likely expand.

## CHALLENGES FOR A PRESIDENT

In almost four years of service at my alma mater as president, I have not faced the intense challenges Dubois has faced. My contribution of an example is a bit more subtle, but hopefully helpful.

In 1999 as president-elect (two months prior to taking office), the South Carolina legislature was debating whether to remove the Confederate flag from the state house dome. The issue had divided our state. Feelings and emotions were as high as I had witnessed. I was asked to write an editorial for three state newspapers on my position on the issue. I realized that this would be my introduction to the very people I would soon visit in the general assembly to ask for support, budget improvements, and budget appropriations. Trying to write such an editorial in the middle of the night, I was determined to draw on my experience as an undergraduate at Clemson in the 1960s, when "Dixie" and the Confederate flag were removed from campus and how that act had changed Clemson in the most positive ways. I stopped just short of giving the state of South Carolina my advice, but I did draw conclusions for my school and posed the question of the implication for South Carolina. Further, I asked Clemson's faculty specializing in rhetoric to review my draft and provide their counsel.

Later, it became clear that more was needed, and I asked Clemson's basketball and football coaches to join me in a march from Charleston to Columbia to support the removal of the flag.

Lessons I learned: First, ask faculty experts for help. They are very wise and they want to be involved. Second, if the issue is vital, stand up and take whatever heat that comes.

It seems there is a kind of trust bank we have on each of our campuses. Every day, we, as presidents and chancellors, make deposits and withdrawals from this trust bank. The deposits are usually small in number and often small in size. We work hard to build our account. The withdrawals always seem to be large in number and size. The largest withdrawal comes with crisis, but Dubois has demonstrated that there can be deposits made in the trust bank during times of crisis.

Let me illustrate with one more example. We lost one of our female freshman students during the spring semester in a traffic accident. Alcohol was involved in the crash. A memorial service was held in our historic auditorium at the heart of campus. Several students spoke at this service. The conclusion of the service called for me to leave the auditorium and place a wreath on the plaza overlooking the central campus green, called Bowman Field. The Carillon rang one time for each year of her life and "Taps" was played (Clemson was a military school for its first sixty years). This central campus green was filled with sun worshippers, Frisbee players, football, and students playing with dogs. They were not dressed for a funeral. What happened when they realized our presence on the edge of this green was spontaneous and remarkable to me. As the bells rang, a wave spread across this green. The 400 or so half-dressed students froze. They stood. They told their dogs to heel. They removed their baseball caps and stood motionless facing us until the ceremony was complete. It was unplanned and unusual. It was a teachable moment and I was the student. I went immediately to my office and wrote a letter to the student newspaper, to communicate my gratitude and the gratitude of the lost student's family. A deposit was made in the trust bank by the students in a time of crisis.

## CREATIVE LEADERSHIP

I am an architect and I have spent a good portion of my career trying to understand creativity and how it can be applied to solving problems. This search and lessons must now be drawn on in my current service as president. I have few conclusions at this point about creative leadership, but I will share with you six points (these are probably points you have already learned):

1. There is wisdom in the counsel of many. I have found that if I engage people with expertise and experience and listen carefully, good things happen. I have found that asking those not normally asked is particularly helpful and significant.
2. Rowing and steering. Most people say leaders steer, but I have found that at the right time, I must also row.
3. Accountability. Genuine accountability is vital. I have a report card that is presented to the campus and the board of trustees every quarter, sharing progress or lack thereof in each of our ten-year goals.
4. I try not to take myself as seriously as others take me.
5. I thought I could do things quickly, but not substantively. I have found that I could do things substantively, but not quickly.
6. Finally, I have found that leadership is service—nothing more.

## NOTE

1. Sean K. Murphy, "Crisis Management Demystifield: Here's How to Prevent a Crisis from Ruining Your Institution's Reputation," *University Business*, February 2003, p. 36.

# CHAPTER

# Inaugural Transitions: The University of Michigan's Affirmative Action Case

*Mary Sue Coleman*

Preparing this essay has been a fascinating journey, particularly as I read of the challenges that other presidents have faced.

I would like to address an issue that we all have had to face, namely, the transition of leadership. As each of us has assumed the position of provost or president, we have had to cope with the predicament of continuing valuable programs and initiatives of our predecessor, while beginning to carve a new legacy and imprint our administration with its own identity.

Most of us have held administrative positions at multiple institutions. I have dealt with the dilemma of transition in four administrative positions at four universities.

But my experience of transitions at the Universities of North Carolina at Chapel Hill, New Mexico, and Iowa provided only a pale shadow of what the transition of my first year at the University of Michigan would be like. Let me mention, however, two cases that I confronted in those earlier transitional settings that helped to prepare me for the need to address complicated issues in a straightforward manner. One was an issue primarily external to the institution. The other was an issue internal to the academic environment.

In my first months as provost of the University of New Mexico, I had to resolve a case of sexual harassment that had developed into a major public issue, in which factions external to the institution were advocating opposite outcomes for the case. In resolving to terminate an administrator who had been found culpable of sexual harassment through our internal processes, the integrity of which I never doubted, I experienced the pressures of public opinion and public outrage to a degree I had never encountered previously. This provided an early experience with the highly politicized environment of public higher education in New Mexico, one of the more litigious environments in the United States. A number of lawsuits were filed against the University of New Mexico, and many of those were directed at the provost. From that incident, I learned that lawsuits come with the terrain and that having expertise and good judgment in the Office of the General Counsel is extremely important.

When I arrived at the University of Iowa, I faced an immediate challenge that was primarily internal. As the new president, I inherited a strategic plan that had been generated with great expense and effort by the faculty. However, it was clear to me that the very ambitious plan had been assembled without reference to available resources, which made it essentially impossible to implement. In addition, there were pending lawsuits that had been filed by faculty members whose programs had been eliminated as part of an earlier strategic plan.

As an institution, we needed to plan strategically. But all planning exercises are not necessarily focused strategically. I wanted to keep the campus focused on significant institutional issues, but within a new and more realistic plan that instituted selected campuswide metrics against which we could measure ourselves, the outcomes of which we could publish every year. The decisions that were made, of course, affected units at all levels. Extensive consultations—extending throughout the year—were needed in order to pull the regents, faculty, and staff onto the same page. This reorientation of prior planning, which had been undertaken in the context of a certain degree of faculty distrust of any planning exercise embraced by administrators, helped us to identify some very important institutional goals and, unexpectedly, to cope with a looming state fiscal crisis in the state of Iowa.

My final year at Iowa was marked by several terrible events—within the space of one month, an accidental fire destroyed our beloved campus symbol, the Old Capitol Dome, and one of the university's senior administrators was killed by his wife. These fateful events happened only two months after 9/11, when our campus, like the rest of our nation, was in a fragile state. Additionally, the economic downturn in Iowa caused the worst funding deficit in the history of the university. My most important objective during these stressful times was to maintain morale throughout the university community, and I worked toward that goal every day.

In fact, the earlier strategic planning exercise helped immensely to structure the discussions that had to take place in the face of unexpected fiscal duress. We had established clear consultative procedures, and we put them to good use. When we had to make cuts, the faculty knew that the president was not making decisions alone but along with administrators who were working together with senior faculty leadership, as we had been for some years.

## THE FRONT-BURNER ISSUES AT MICHIGAN

When I assumed the presidency at the University of Michigan, I believed that those earlier moments of transition would provide me with a foundation of experience for the new challenges I would face. I had no idea of the magnitude of the events that would assail our university in my first few months.

Foremost in my own mind, and perhaps in yours, were the lawsuits that had been filed against the university—one on the basis of the Law School admissions process and one on the undergraduate admissions policy. Each case was sitting at a different level of appeal in the federal courts. The Sixth Circuit Court of Appeals (the level just below the Supreme Court) had recently issued a decision in favor of our Law School case. It had not ruled on the undergraduate case, although the district court had upheld our policy in that case.

We were waiting to see if the United States Supreme Court was going to agree to hear one or both of our cases. Because we had won our cases at the lower levels, in some ways it would have been satisfactory to walk away with our victories—but our victories in the lower federal courts would not have resolved the many questions that had arisen nationwide over the past twenty-five years regarding the landmark *Bakke* decision, which appeared to allow the inclusion of race as one of many factors in admissions policy in universities around the country.

The admissions cases provided a particular challenge for me, as a biochemist. The previous president, Lee Bollinger, was a noted constitutional lawyer, and he had participated extensively in planning the university's legal defense on the cases. For an attorney, being involved in a landmark case on constitutional law is a highlight of one's career. I never imagined that it would also be the highlight of the career of this biochemist.

My senior staff agrees that I could probably have spent the entire first year of my presidency working on nothing except these cases. The amount of background material, the legal expertise required, and the work that went into becoming a national spokesperson on the issue of affirmative action was monumental.

As a scientist, I like to be able to both quantify and analyze data, so I recently asked for some data regarding the sheer bulk of materials that had accumulated over the course of the six years of our lawsuits. It was a bit staggering to get the final tally:

12 lateral file drawers of printed material

6 large boxes weighing a total of 300 pounds

103 binders of trial exhibits and other court documents

45 inches of expandable folders of amicus briefs

In physics, we learn that force equals mass times acceleration. In addition to the mass of the documentation that awaited me, we had the weight of the twenty-five years of interpretation of the *Bakke* decision and about 100 years of federal civil rights legislation. This mass of paper and time was about to receive the acceleration that only the U.S. Supreme Court could provide. In short, the force of this case alone was immense.

But I also found other forces poised to bear down on our university. In October, a student group decided to host the second annual Palestinian Solidarity Conference, and the weeks leading up to the event brought an unprecedented firestorm of outrage and criticism. Given our commitment to free expression, we affirmed the right of the students to host the meeting, as long as all events were open to all and all sides of the issues at stake could be heard. However, in the weeks leading up to the conference, my time was devoted to discussing this issue with regents, alumni, donors, community, and student groups, several of which had directly opposing views on the content and legitimacy of the conference. It was an exhausting but ultimately rewarding experience, since all views were heard and the safety of all participants was assured.

On another front, at the moment I was accepting the presidency of the University of Michigan in June 2002, the attorneys of the university were just learning of the magnitude of the scandal regarding former players in the basketball program. Of course, I knew that there had been an obstructed investigation into this matter. Two previous presidents had attempted to deal with this issue. But it was an unforeseen coincidence that exactly one day before I was named president, the indicted booster who was at the center of the controversy struck a plea bargain, creating two contrasting sets of headlines: my selection as president and documentation of the violations of NCAA regulations. It was a jarring note in what should have been at least a brief moment of a honeymoon period.

By November 2002, we had decided that we were going to self-impose severe penalties on the basketball program in response to our investigation of the decade-old transgressions of former players and coaches. I had to deliver a harsh message to our university community and our worldwide circle of ardent alumni and fans, all of whom were unaccustomed to such reprehensible behavior by athletes. To an overflowing room of sports reporters and media from around the country, I stood in front of a bank of cameras and declared November 13 to be a day of shame for the University of Michigan. We forfeited five years' worth of games and championships and removed ourselves from postseason play for 2003.

I braced myself for an onslaught of criticism from basketball fanatics. And of course, there were some bitter e-mail messages about the action we had taken. But I was quite surprised by the support that emanated from so many quarters about the honesty and transparency of our central admission—that the basketball team of that era had not played by the rules and that we therefore had to rewrite the history of that era. It was a hard call, but we decided that we as an institution had to take responsibility for the actions of those former players, even though they, the former coach, and former athletic director were no longer at our institution.

The tone of some of the critical e-mail messages clearly indicated that some of our fans strongly believed it was problematic to have female leadership at a university with major athletics programs. But those who were close to the case—our regents and senior administrators—have told me that they found themselves quite reassured by my level of understanding of the rules and governance structure of the National Collegiate Athletics Association. My extensive participation in the committee structure of the NCAA had provided me with a deep understanding of intercollegiate athletics. This was one of many instances when I was very grateful that I had served as president of another large research university before assuming the presidency at Michigan. Experience can be a gender-neutral teacher.

## THE SUPREME COURT GRANTS THE WRIT OF CERTIORARI

As we set aside the NCAA issues, awaiting our formal hearing before their Committee on Infractions, we turned our attention to the lawsuits. By mid-November, the Supreme Court had already announced it was going to hear a number of other cases, and there was considerable speculation about whether it would choose to hear our admissions cases. Multiple scenarios were contemplated.

As defendants, our position had been upheld in both cases, albeit in different courts. The Law School case had been decided in our favor in the U.S. Sixth Circuit Court of Appeals but had been appealed to the Supreme Court by the plaintiffs. The undergraduate case was still on appeal in the Sixth Circuit Court, but no decision had been rendered.

We knew that if the Supreme Court wanted to wait for the circuit court decisions on both cases, it could be several more years before the cases would reach the top court, because of widely reported dissention among the judges about judicial process that accompanied the Law School ruling.[1] If the Supreme Court had chosen to hear only the University of Michigan Law School case, we believed the full spectrum of admissions issues would not be addressed by this single decision and that higher education would be left in limbo for several more years. Given these possibilities, both sides requested certiorari before judgment, a highly unusual maneuver that would allow both cases to go before the Supreme Court at the same time, should the court decide to accept the cases.

The last day for setting the court calendar for hearings in 2003 was December 2, and we still had no word about our cases. But then, on that last day, the court announced that it would hear both cases. Suddenly, what had seemed so remote when I moved to Michigan became very real and immediate.

I began to see the implications for both my university and me personally as we entered this new stage and also to see how much was at stake for us. Indeed, over the next few months, I began to realize how much also was at stake for the history of civil rights in the United States. We now felt the full force of this situation—the mass of the cases multiplied by the acceleration of the Supreme Court process.

## WAITING FOR THE NEW PRESIDENT—THE BACKSTORY

Behind every presidential transition, of course, is a story that almost never gets told but that is very germane to this account. The untold story is the period of waiting at the University of Michigan for an announcement of a new president. Some new presidents, as you all know, like to import new senior staff and administrators, and some prefer to maintain as much continuity as possible. Often, the departure of a previous president automatically creates a number of senior-level vacancies, as current vice-presidents take this opportunity to explore other options.

At the University of Michigan, there was a nine-month period of an interim presidency before I assumed the position, which meant that the legal and communications teams knew they would potentially be working with three presidents within the space of one year's time.

I learned much later that the key attorneys and administrators involved in the cases were quite concerned about the level of commitment of any new president to a vigorous defense of the cases. They understood that the regents were seeking a president who would be willing to be a leader on the issue of affirmative action. However, levels of commitment certainly can vary—and they knew that whoever would be hired also would become the public spokesperson for affirmative action. Their concerns were various and significant, and even while they held these concerns, they had to move forward with the day-to-day management of the lawsuits.

## PREPARING FOR THE SUPREME COURT

At the time the university had been sued, several years earlier, it had committed not only to defending the cases, but to use the cases to promote a national dialogue on the issue of affirmative action. This dialogue intensified tremendously once the Supreme Court decided to hear both cases.

Although I had received a great deal of public attention as president of the University of Iowa, the intensity of national scrutiny on this issue required a significantly elevated level of awareness of the pressures of national media and their deadlines. I was extremely fortunate to find not only an expert legal team, led by Marvin Krislov, vice president and general counsel, but also an outstanding communications team, led by Lisa Rudgers, our vice president for communications. This group had excellent national media contacts, media experience, and a deep understanding of the requirements of reporters from various media outlets. Their relentless demands to think in advance about our reactions to various outcomes allowed me to learn how to shape our public presence on the substance of the cases. They instructed me, in this day of ten-second sound bites, on the best way to communicate extremely complex ideas as crisply as possible—but we also worked together on the best ways to discuss the issues in depth whenever necessary.

Their expertise in preparing me was valuable in my early months at Michigan, when we found ourselves surrounded by national broadcast and print media on the day following the announcement that the Supreme Court would hear our cases and on the day I am about to describe.

## THE (U.S.) PRESIDENT WEIGHS IN

Once we had received the Supreme Court announcement in December, our attention turned toward the executive branch of the government and to the question of whether President Bush would direct the Department of Justice to file an amicus brief on behalf of the plaintiffs in the cases.

You may recall that December 2002 was the period of the debacle surrounding Senator Trent Lott and the birthday celebration of Senator Strom Thurmond. Senator Lott's overt support for Senator Thurmond's 1948 presidential platform revived memories of past civil rights struggles and the divisive nature of some politics from that era. We speculated that the furor over this revival of pre-civil rights era values and the resurfacing of old wounds from the nation's segregationist past might oblige the executive branch to step back from any statement of opposition to affirmative action in college admissions.

However, on January 15, President Bush publicly declared that he had directed the Department of Justice to file a brief on behalf of the plaintiffs of the case. In making this announcement, he characterized the University of Michigan cases in a manner that shocked me. Although the president stated that he supported diversity as good educational practice (the legal argument on which the cases were based), he asserted that the University of Michigan had been using illegal quotas. In fact, he used the word "quota" four times in his brief five-minute statement. President Bush further implied that we used only two factors in our admissions decision: race and test scores, and that we weighted race more heavily.

I was scheduled to respond to his position on *Good Morning America* the next day. How should a university president answer a serious charge of illegal practices, issued by the sitting U.S. president, when those charges are unfounded?

In some respects, the fallacies of President Bush's statement provided us with a way to take the high road in responding while continuing to educate the public that we were not currently and had never used quotas. My staff and I quickly agreed that I should first, and rightly, praise President Bush for his support of diversity in the classroom but then express concern that he had misunderstood our admissions procedures. I also explained that we had no quotas and that we considered many factors in our admissions process—but that academic achievement was the most important consideration.

The various elements of my reaction allowed us to avoid direct confrontation with President Bush, while placing our most important message—the educational benefit of diversity for all students—squarely in front of the nation. The reaction we heard from around the country confirmed the wisdom of this approach. Our position was reasonable, and when we presented it, our rationale was easily comprehended.

## GATHERING THE BRIEFS

As soon as we knew that the Department of Justice would be filing a brief supporting the plaintiffs, our legal team and I shifted into high gear, speaking publicly and seeking support for our position. The strategy on providing amici curiae was simple. We wanted the court to hear from as wide a swath of society as possible, and we anticipated filings from civil rights, educational, and social organizations. But we needed an even broader voice in order to make our case, and we obtained exactly that support in the corporate world and especially from former military leaders—all of whom provided briefs and solicited additional briefs. Our original supporters sought briefs from even more corporate organizations, and we found the offers of support to be quite stunning. This unprecedented array of amici curiae briefs was going to be critical to our assertion that affirmative action in higher education had in fact become a cornerstone of the economic competitiveness and security of the nation.

These briefs had another effect on us that did not alter the legal proceedings but greatly affected our morale—we felt strong support from many public sectors, and that was a considerable factor in our own attitude toward the possible success of our case. I have heard from many legal experts since the decisions were issued that they believe that the University of Michigan strategy was brilliant in its conception and execution. Of course, it is far easier to say that in retrospect than it was to live through it at the time—even before I had arrived at the university, there had been pressure to broaden or change the strategy, but our legal and communications team remained focused on our original plan.

## ORAL ARGUMENTS

April 1, 2003, was the day on which the Supreme Court heard the oral arguments in our cases. Admission tickets to the public seats in the Court were extremely rare and almost impossible to obtain in advance, although as defendants, we had received a small, but insufficient, allocation. Our regents traveled to Washington with us; we gathered with many of our staunchest supporters the night before the arguments to celebrate and prepare ourselves for what we imagined would be a bruising and difficult two hours in front of the justices—one hour for each case.

On the morning of the arguments, long lines of hopeful Court observers and banks of reporters greeted us outside the Court several hours before the 10:00 A.M. start time. Three of our regents who are attorneys obtained tickets to the courtroom by taking advantage of a courtesy of the Court. They were sworn in that morning as members of the Supreme Court Bar, sponsored by other members of our legal team.

Some potential courtroom observers had camped on the steps of the Court the preceding night, in the hope of getting one of the fifty tickets that would be made available to the public. Busloads of student supporters and protesters from around the country also had assembled in front of the Court. Those of us from the university began to understand in a new and visceral way the historic significance of what was about to occur.

We knew what to expect in the arguments themselves—that the plaintiffs' lawyers would present their case, and that our lawyers would present ours, sequentially for each lawsuit. We knew that the justices would ask questions and that the dialogue among the justices could become quite contentious.

Little more than three minutes into the plaintiffs' initial presentation, the expected rhythm was interrupted by Justice O'Connor, who asked the plaintiffs' attorney a pointed question about the brief that had been filed by the former military leaders in support of our policies. Her initial interruption opened the path to a very lively two hours of questioning and debating among the justices and all the attorneys. The dialogue that emerged over those hours was so completely riveting that I was not at all aware of the passage of time.

We emerged from the Court heartened by what we had just experienced, believing that our attorneys had defended our policies well and that they had sustained their positions very well even against some withering questions. To our delight, thousands of supporters were waiting and cheering on the street in front of the steps of the Court, along with a phalanx of broadcast media and cameras. Part of our preparation had been for this moment, when there would be multiple and immediate demands for short and memorable statements about our impressions of what had happened in the courtroom. And fortunately, we were able to stay focused, even as we were facing the throng that reached far into the distance.

A wonderful moment for us occurred when a large assembly of our students and alumni started spontaneously singing "The Victors" (the Michigan fight song). To my amazement, all of us, including the regents, gathered to sing along with them—unfortunately, the Court staff almost immediately instructed us that such outbursts were inappropriate and encouraged us to move along. But that brief instant of camaraderie was so palpable that I will never forget it.

An extremely unusual aspect of this case also played into the public reaction when, for only the second time in its history, the Supreme Court issued an audiotape of the oral arguments (the other case had been the arguments regarding the 2000 presidential vote counting in Florida). These tapes were widely broadcast and allowed the public a rare glimpse inside the workings of the Court and the opportunity for the public to draw its own conclusions regarding the tone of the dialogue in the courtroom.

The waiting for the decisions now began. As always, the Court provided no indication about its schedule for a decision, and the docket for Spring 2003 was particularly heavy. Often, the Court would wait for the end of the term to issue significant decisions, and we expected to hear a decision in about two-and-a-half months, in early to mid-June.

## PREPARATION FOR THE DECISIONS

During the next few months while we waited for the decisions, we alternately enjoyed or endured over 200 substantive articles and essays about the cases, many of which speculated about the various outcomes. Waiting for an uncertain outcome would have been taxing in any circumstance, but the relentless publicity about the cases managed to heighten enormously the tension of this period. Although we disagreed with George Will's position on our cases, he did manage to summarize the waiting period nicely with his essay titled "High Noon for Diversity."[2] It was a "high noon" that lasted for over three months.

All the regular business of the university, including planning for a significant budget cut in our state appropriation, had to continue as usual, while we watched for signals from Washington.

Our communications and legal teams took full advantage of this interlude to accomplish two important tasks. First, they worked to prepare me to be the spokesperson in the days following the decision, whether we won both cases, lost both, or obtained a mixed decision. Second, they worked to prepare our campus community, particularly the students, to understand what a victory or defeat would mean and also to understand the need to thoroughly consider the legal substance of court decisions.

Our most grueling discussions focused on the scenario of a possible defeat in both cases. Because defeat in these cases would be so problematic on so many levels, we devoted the majority of our time to this possible outcome. I had to prepare for this possibility and to plan for the best ways to encourage the University of Michigan community to move forward, maintaining our commitment to diversity, even if we were denied access to the tool we believed was critical for this purpose.

As we prepared for a possible negative decision, my staff joined me in sessions in which they bombarded me with complex questions that might come up in every conceivable circumstance imaginable with reporters, students, alumni, and the public. We also readied ourselves for a positive outcome, focusing on key messages and themes, if we received decisions that would permit us to continue to use race as one of many factors in the admissions process.

For me, this was a challenging time because rumors about the decisions of the Court were swirling everywhere, and the daily pendulum swings of the press and broadcast media kept us keenly focused on a large array of possible outcomes. Try as we might not to be affected by reports that often had no basis in fact, we could not help but be buffeted by them.

## DECISION DAY

Although we could prepare for our statements and potential scenarios, the one unknown factor (aside from the decisions themselves) was the precise date on which the decisions would be announced. The Court had been issuing several decisions a week in early June, but we had no indication at all of the date we could expect to hear the outcome of the cases. We only knew the final decision date for the court term was scheduled for June 26.

Several months earlier, I had agreed to present a keynote address on June 23 to a bioengineering symposium at the National Institutes of Health in Bethesda, Maryland. I had warned the NIH that if we knew June 23 was to be the decision date, I might have to cancel my appearance to be on campus—but back in January when I made this commitment, we had even less a sense of the possible timing of the decision.

As June progressed, and we still had no decision, we vigorously debated whether to proceed with my keynote address at the NIH. All of our plans for the day of decision hinged on my being on campus to deal with the extensive media attention that we knew would occur.

Our communications team finally decided that it would be possible to put together a plan that would allow us to react from Washington, D.C., if the day of decision happened to be the same day as my keynote address. This was not a simple matter, because it meant having to maintain constant contact with a number of people in both locations. The NIH also graciously agreed to move my keynote address earlier in the morning, so that I could be at the court by 10:00 A.M. when the day's decisions would be announced. In retrospect, it was an extraordinarily fortunate coincidence for us, because I was in the city where the media outlets were located—the story certainly would have been reported in a different way if I had not been present.

Although I delivered the bioengineering keynote address in record time, I found myself trapped in transit in a construction zone outside the NIH, so I did not arrive at the Supreme Court in time to be admitted to the courtroom. At that point, we still did not know if our cases would be announced on that day.

I sat in the cafeteria of the Court while a member of our communications staff tried to find out what was happening upstairs. He found reporters running out of the pressroom on their way to file reports and managed to learn the first verdict, which he came to relate to me—a complete victory in the Law School case. I could not believe the wave of relief and joy that swept over me—and just a few minutes later, we had the results of our undergraduate case, which was a more mixed decision but which also clearly left the door open for a use of race as one of many factors in admissions processes.

We walked into the sunshine outside the Court to face every major media outlet in the country. That day, I owned those cases—so many others had contributed to the University of Michigan's effort, but I had taken the university over the finish line—and as I stepped up to the microphones, we began a new phase of the history of commitment to equality at the University of Michigan, and our nation began the next phase in its history of civil rights.

## SECOND BAPTIST CHURCH

After the days of media interviews and scrutiny in Washington, I returned to campus with several new tasks in front of me: the most immediate was to assemble a team to begin planning a new undergraduate admissions process that would be in compliance with the decisions. Another job was to begin to sort through the many requests to speak about the cases and their impact. As we had intended all along, these cases were going to continue to provide us with the opportunity to educate our campus and educate the public on the issues at stake and begin to heal some of the rifts that had developed on both sides of this important national issue.

I now have spoken about the cases to a number of very different audiences. But one that was most meaningful to me was a presentation and dialogue at a leading African American church in Ann Arbor, which provided me with the opportunity to address a minority community that had been so concerned about our policies and our handling of the cases. The evening I visited that church congregation, I was greatly touched by how deep the pride over this victory runs in the African American community but also at how deeply the pain of the past is still embedded. That event allowed the seemingly conflicting emotions of joy and sorrow to coexist in a way that was not contradictory. This community has heard many promises over the years and is completely aware that it is still waiting for and working toward solutions.

I had said all along that whatever the outcome of the cases, we would still have much work to do, and that evening at the Second Baptist Church was a vivid illustration of that reality. There were lifelong residents of Ann Arbor who said, "You've won the cases, but I'm yet to be convinced that you care."

We still have so much work to do and many miles to go on these issues. I find it distressing that our colleges and universities are often the first place that students of different races and ethnic backgrounds begin truly to encounter each other. I am deeply saddened that our K–12 educational system prepares too few minority students for success in higher education. And I regret that our institutions are not always hospitable places for all students. I hope that the hard work undertaken by so many people at the University of Michigan in defending its principles will give our nation the opportunity to reflect once again on what it means to welcome everyone in the American family to the opportunity to pursue educational achievement. We still have a great deal to accomplish in Michigan—as do other states. If we succeed, our democracy will be immeasurably strengthened.

I cannot pinpoint the moment when the cases made the transition from belonging to the administration of my predecessor to belonging to my administration. Like so many transitions, it occurred across a continuum of time in my first six months. I know the shift had happened before the day of the decisions, and that day underscored the realization. In the best of circumstances, the legacy we assume from our predecessors will become the basis for a new era that bears our own identity.

## NOTES

1. Charles Lane, "Judges Spar over Affirmative Action," *Washington Post*, June 7, 2003, p. A4.

2. George F. Will, "High Noon for Diversity," *Newsweek*, May 26, 2003, p. 76.

# CHAPTER

## Moral Leadership at DePauw
### A Response to President Coleman's Essay

*Robert G. Bottoms*

I f I were writing an essay to hand to people who are coming into college presidencies for the first time, I probably would not start with some of the lofty goals that we put into our inauguration speeches. Instead I would say, "Make sure you have a good lawyer." At DePauw seventeen years ago when I became president, we handled all of our legal affairs with a couple of volunteer lawyers on our board of trustees. They just did it out of their hip pocket and it did not cost anything. We now spend about $200,000 a year.

I would also say, "Learn how to deal with the press." When Dan Quayle, a DePauw graduate, was named as President Bush's running mate, our lake vacation suddenly ended. We headed home and prepared for the press barrage. Somehow, sometimes, in an unplanned way, we are thrust into the national spotlight. Suddenly, the *New York Times*, the *Cleveland Plain Dealer*, and the *Los Angeles Times* were ringing up people in Greencastle, Indiana, to find out who in the world this man was. I learned a lot about the press, and it was depressing in terms of the people I dealt with. I observed a lack of scruples and little knowledge of higher education. For example, there was one piece written saying that because the Quayle family had given so much money to the university, we were not releasing his transcript. So much for student privacy and the press's knowledge of the law.

Some of the stories that were written about Mr. Quayle treated DePauw as a frivolous place with a really small library. We did not have control. None of us would like to publicly denounce any of our alumni, but the college's image was being hurt. Learning to deal with the press is an essential lesson for college presidents.

We live in a world of ten-second sound bites. The second year or so I was president, I did an op-ed piece for the *New York Times*. The topic was student loans and proprietary schools: you will remember the debate. They printed my piece and by 10:00 the *Today Show* had called. We do not have a large press corps at our small liberal arts college. I called on a former journalism professor for coaching in preparation for my appearance. I thought he would rehearse with me the questions that Bryant Gumbel would ask. Instead, he said it did not make any difference what Gumbel asked. He advised me on the things to say.

He also coached me on vocabulary. He told me to quit using the term *proprietary school*. Nobody knows what a proprietary school is. We should call them trade schools. In this business of the ten-second sound bites, it is essential to use words that listeners recognize. That is somewhat contrary to the way that we have been trained. In philosophy, we wrote long papers and explored both sides of each issue. Dealing with the press and media is an essential, even if unfamiliar, part of the job.

So much for comments about the press. I would like to talk about the importance of race as an agenda item for presidents. Through three different organizations, I am involved with getting inner-city kids into college and putting this goal on the national agenda. I told Mary Sue Coleman earlier that one of the University of Michigan's alumni, Roger Wilkins, helped us design our program at DePauw. He was actually with us on campus while the University of Michigan case was before the Supreme Court.

This case, at least on our campus, opened a lot of the old wounds. People started discussing racial quotas. All of a sudden, as a result of this case, articles appeared in the campus newspaper. Were our minority students getting special treatment and were they worthy to be here? Were more qualified majority students being rejected in order to make room for less qualified minority students?

When I came into my presidency seventeen years ago, the job of educating the public was not on my agenda. The job of educating the board was not either. But both educational campaigns need to be high on the agenda of every president.

Two other comments about President Coleman's essay: I really appreciated her appearance at the black Baptist church. We are not trusted in the black community, no matter what we say. That needs to be improved. From our bully pulpits we must continue to address some of the racial issues.

We are models. Others are watching. Mr. Quayle, then sitting vice president, came back to his alma mater and gave a rousing anti-affirmative action speech. On the platform with Mr. Quayle, I was quite visible. Yet it was more than I could do to clap politely because he really worked the students into a frenzy. Later, I learned that the black community noticed that I did not quite clap, and they did see that as a political statement.

The last thing I will say about President Coleman's essay is that I appreciated her saying that she was prepared for a variety of choices. I think if I were talking to somebody just coming into the presidency who found him- or herself in one of these controversies with the press, that would be pretty good advice. It is easy for the right words to come to our lips when we win. It is more difficult when we are defeated.

In closing, I might say to this imaginary person who would like to be a president, "I can't remember a time when we operated in a more politically charged environment than we have now." My college has gotten itself crosswise with our heritage denomination, the United Methodist Church, because of our stand on insurance for same-sex couples and our balanced symposium discussing the issue of ordination of gays in the church. It is very political and it is escalating. In the South, we were labeled as that loser school in Indiana that was undermining the Christian faith of all Methodists. I have never received as much hate mail as I have because of this issue. That was not what I had in mind when I took this job.

Because we inevitably find ourselves involved in controversy, often regarding basic principles, it is essential that we own and understand a set of basic values that we act to preserve and enhance. That is leadership.

# The Importance of Ethical Standards: Reflections of a Candidate Chosen from the Inside

## A Response to President Coleman's Essay

*Charles W. Steger*

After reading President Coleman's essay, I reflected on what types of observations I might make that would add value to the discussion. Having spent the majority of my academic career at Virginia Tech, I thought to offer observations on the relative merits and disadvantages of being an insider as president. Is being an "inside" president better or worse than coming from the outside, assuming either would enter the position under reasonably normal circumstances? What have been the most critical tools for success?

There are some obvious assets associated with being chosen from within the institution. The good news is that you know everyone and they know you. The bad news is that you know everyone and they know you. Insiders frequently can enter the job with an already established political base, which we know often takes several years to build if one is from the outside. The in-depth knowledge of the institution has been gained over a period of years so that the evolutionary characteristics of the organization are also understood. As an insider, one has time to reflect on the types of needed changes for the university and, perhaps most importantly, the time to identify the change agents. When substantial change is undertaken, it is often valuable to have a familiar personality to manage the stress levels that always accompany restructuring and so forth.

Does the variety of experience an outsider brings offset the depth of knowledge possessed by the insider? Which is easier to obtain? Obviously, both have advantages, but one cannot look at the performance of the insider only after he or she has entered the job of president. Most individuals within an organization who would likely be named as president have had an opportunity to shape at least a portion of the organization while in other positions in the organization. For example, at Virginia Tech, I had an opportunity to play a major role in shaping the previous strategic plan. This has proven to be critically important for establishing new directions for the future.

One of the most challenging areas for any president is dealing with the athletic enterprise. Needless to say, athletics generates a great deal of publicity for the university. When in the midst of difficult times, critics have no hesitation in focusing their antagonism on you personally. In dealing with athletics, it is very important to be very clear and set the standards of behavior and performance early. Further, it is necessary to always be in a mode of proactive message management with the public. There are many groups trying to occupy the communication channels. Often you must go outside the traditional channels in communicating with your alumni base. A carefully prepared letter from the president can be very effective, particularly if there has been sufficient time to establish trust and understanding.

For an inside president, the presence of mentors from outside the organization is an extremely important asset. I have been very fortunate to know two business leaders with national and international reputations who willingly shared their broad life experience with me. Their support and insight have proved to be invaluable.

At the end of the day, whether a president is chosen from within the institution or from the outside, one of the most critical attributes of an effective leader is to possess a clear set of ethical standards that can be communicated and understood. This was never more evident than dealing with the issue of diversity on our campus in light of the Supreme Court considerations of the Michigan case. These are times in which the broad university community expects you to take a stand. It must be thoughtful and clear.

# CHAPTER 11

## Succeeding a Legend at the University of Notre Dame

*Edward S. Malloy*

### INTRODUCTION

I am now entering my sixteenth year as president of the University of Notre Dame. One of the most frequently asked questions I received, especially early on in my presidency, was "What is it like to take over from a legend?" This reference was to my immediate predecessor, Father Theodore M. Hesburgh, CSC, who was president of Notre Dame for thirty-five years. He was one of the most visible and highly regarded leaders in American higher education, and he also had a national and international reputation as a representative of presidents and popes. The implication of the question was that I was faced with an impossible task that any rational person would have tried to avoid. It might also have suggested that I was made of puny stuff in comparison to this distinguished figure.

Like all good questions, a proper answer requires a setting of context and then, from this vantage point in history, some retrospective and analysis. The intent of this chapter is not simply to offer a history of the succession at Notre Dame, but also to raise more theoretical questions about presidential succession and about the process by which boards of trustees take on this responsibility.

### THEODORE M. HESBURGH, CSC

Father Ted, as he likes to be called, became president of Notre Dame at the relatively young age of 35. He had completed a doctorate in systematic theology at Catholic University with a doctoral dissertation on the role of the laity in the church. When he returned to Notre Dame, he was active as executive vice president, chaplain to the married students, and otherwise right-hand man of then president Father John Cavanaugh, CSC. In those days, the university was owned by the congregation of Holy Cross, Indiana Province, and the congregation was entirely responsible for the appointment of presidents and other administrators. There was a lay board, which had advisory function but no determinative powers. By most accounts, it was clear that Father Hesburgh was slated to succeed Father Cavanaugh when he completed his term of service. According to church law, because the president of the university was also the local religious superior, there was a canonical restriction of six years of length for the president's term. This made the matter and timing of succession quite predictable.

In the fall of 1951, Ted Hesburgh began his formal term as president. Over the next thirty-five years, he transformed the life of the institution, with a particular emphasis on building academic quality and raising the standards in the hiring of faculty and in the preparation and credentialing for all members of the administration. He has said frequently that the two most dramatic changes in the life of the institution were (1) the transfer of formal responsibility for the institution from the congregation of Holy Cross to a predominantly lay board of trustees (with a complementary board of fellows) and (2) the initiation of coeducation after an inability to effect a merger with the neighboring all-female Saint Mary's College. During Father Hesburgh's multiple terms (he avoided the canonical restrictions in length of term by ceasing to be local superior), there were noteworthy developments in the physical plant and successful fundraising in building endowment and in the growth of the academic reputation of the institution.

Separate from the wonderful improvements in the internal realities of the institution, Father Hesburgh was also quite active in a wide variety of external forms of service. He served as the chair of the Civil Rights Commission during a tumultuous time, represented the Vatican in a number of international forums, chaired many of the higher education associations, and spoke out frequently on many of the most important public policy issues of the day. In response to the vital leadership that he provided, many universities awarded him honorary degrees (he presently holds the record for one individual for most honorary degrees in history), and received the Congressional Gold Medal. Suffice it to say that when he stepped down after thirty-five years of distinguished leadership, there was legitimate cause for concern for the well-being of the institution.

Could the momentum be sustained, and could Notre Dame find a leader who could step in without being intimidated?

## THE TRANSITION PROCESS

Like a number of religiously affiliated higher education institutions, particularly in the Catholic network, the presidency of the University of Notre Dame is restricted in the bylaws of the institution to a Holy Cross priest of the Indiana Province. This means that now into the future, the pool of potential applicants is much more limited than it would be in secular institutions of higher education, as well as many of the private institutions. The rationale for this restriction is that the founding religious community has a special role to play, and with sufficient numbers of well-prepared members, that continuity can better be assured and the distinctiveness of the institution can better be preserved on into the future. If at some point there were no qualified Holy Cross priest candidates, then I am sure that both the board and the community would assent to a change in the bylaws. However, such a change would be seen as a portentous break from the past and might also be seen as calling into question the institution's commitment to sustain its Catholic sense of mission and identity.

In order to facilitate the process of development of the next generation of leadership and to provide sufficient time for the board of trustees to become familiar with those considered to be candidates, five years before Father Hesburgh stepped down, a number of younger Holy Cross priests were invited to assume major leadership positions in the administration. I became vice president and associate provost, the fourth officer of the university and the number two academic officer; Father Bill Beauchamp, CSC, became executive assistant to the president and executive assistant to the executive vice president; and Father Dave Tyson, CSC, continued to serve as vice president of student affairs. Two other priests remained in their present positions. Over the course of the subsequent five years, those of us in the central administration were given multiple opportunities to serve in various representative bodies of the university, like the Officers' Group, the Provost Advisory Council, the Strategic Planning process, and the meetings of the board of trustees. At the same time, each of us had specific informal responsibilities for some part of the institution's life. Yearly performance was reviewed, not only by the president and those to whom we reported, but also by the leadership of the board of trustees.

Looking back, I believe that the time I spent in preparation in the central administration was invaluable. I was able to observe Father Hesburgh and the other officers in action. I was able to come to know a broad cross-section of the university community, faculty, staff, and students. And I was able to continue teaching, scholarship, and pastoral activity. The relationship among those of us who were considered candidates to succeed Father Hesburgh remained quite positive and healthy. There were no petty rivalries, and we enjoyed the sense of being involved in a complex and exciting enterprise in which we all believed.

About one and one-half years before the transition was due to take place after Father Hesburgh formally retired at the age of 70, the board of trustees constituted a search committee to review the candidates and to make a recommendation to the full board. Each of those who had been identified as candidates was interviewed, and so were our colleagues in the administration; a representative group of faculty, staff, and students; and various members of the board of trustees and the leadership of the Indiana Province. As is usual in these kinds of situations, I was asked to offer my views about the future of the institution, describe my leadership style, indicate what I learned during my years of service as a vice president, and otherwise give the nominating committee a better sense of my personal qualities and my potential for successful leadership. In November 1986, at the board of trustees' meeting, I was elected to be the sixteenth president of the university. I indicated at that time that I would invite Father Bill Beauchamp, one of the other candidates, to serve as executive vice president after I began my term of service. One of the other candidates, Father Dave Tyson, would stay on as vice president of student affairs. Since I did not formally assume the office until July 1, 1987, I had about nine months to prepare myself and to effect a successful transition. Ted Hesburgh was very gracious in welcoming my participation in any decisions that had implications for the future. At the same time, I was able to travel around and solicit counsel and advice from various presidents whom I respected and whom I thought would have helpful things to say.

Many presidents advised me not to redo the president's house the first year, since that had led to inauspicious beginnings for a few presidents; but I assured them that I intended to continue living in one of the student dormitories, so the advice was not relevant. One president advised me, very sagely, to make sure I got enough sleep since multiple audiences would be interpreting my physical appearance as a sign of whether the university was flourishing or not. Another president concentrated on the importance of the central team that reported directly to me since, as he described it, new presidents are prone to want to convey a sense of a lean and mean administration but may underestimate the significance of the direct assistance necessary to perform the task effectively.

I think I used the time well between November and July. Once I got past the congratulatory mode, I began to recognize what a daunting task the presidency of a modern university really is. I was comforted by the good team with whom I would be sharing primary responsibility for the well-being of the institution. The then chair of the board of trustees, Donald Keough, then president of the Coca-Cola Company, was also very supportive and encouraging.

I would summarize my overall condition of mind at the end of the transition period between when I was elected and when I took over as confident that I could get the job done but fully aware that I would need to develop my own administrative style with the officers and find appropriate ways of conveying to the broader campus and university community that I intended to build on the solid foundation that had been laid during the Hesburgh years.

## THE FIRST YEAR

Ted Hesburgh, along with his thirty-five-year executive vice president colleague, Ned Joyce, CSC, decided to spend the first year of my presidency on the road, so to speak. They took a recreational vehicle and together explored the range and beauty of the continental United States. Later they went on the Queen Elizabeth II on a world tour. In between, they took various side trips and jaunts of their own. Effectively, Ted and Ned left the campus for the year and gave me the freedom to make a fresh start without constant implicit or explicit efforts by others to solicit their judgments or opinions about how the new administration was doing. This extended travel time away meant that the campus community quickly got used to the new order of things and settled into customary routines.

In conversations with Ted Hesburgh before he left, I received a number of very important kernels of advice. He constantly encouraged me to be my own person and not to try in any way to imitate his style or set of issues. He told me to spend quality time with my mother (my father having died a year or two before), since he knew from his own experience that your parents would not be with you forever. He told me that he would never intrude on my presidential prerogatives and would only offer advice if it was solicited. He asked to have a role in some of the institutes and centers that he had helped establish by chairing the board of advisors, and I readily agreed to this. I also pledged that I would do everything I could to sustain these institutes and centers after he was no longer directly involved because I believed deeply in their sense of mission and their appropriateness as centers for public policy discussion of war and peace, civil and human rights, the environment, Latin America, and ecumenical scholarship in the Holy Land. My first year as president went amazingly quickly. Among other things, I decided not to teach my first year as president so that I could get a better feel for my distribution of time and the nature of my schedule. I also made decisions about various higher education associations to be involved in and not-for-profit organizations to which to offer my services and whatever leadership I might provide. Internally, I made some adjustments in the schedule and format of officer meetings and other forums of interaction with the central leadership group at the institution. I continued the tradition that I had established when I was in the provost office to meet individually with a cross-section of faculty each year and to get around to the various student residences for informal discussions. I also decided to celebrate Mass in as many residences and with other on-campus groups as I could so that I would have a rather full exposure by the end of each academic year.

Like most presidents, I quickly discovered that there is a huge difference between being an officer and presidential candidate and actually being the chief executive officer. In the end, you know that you are responsible for the whole institution's well-being and that you need to be flexible as issues arise and you become aware of crises and points of disagreement. I can honestly say that in my first year I never felt overwhelmed or disenchanted or totally flustered, but I did stumble a few times and came to a fuller realization of the limitations of the presidential office.

One dimension of the job that continues to be challenging even to this day is the regular decision making about how to apportion my time. This included the balance between on- and off-campus activity; time with faculty, staff, and students; fund-raising efforts; visits to local alumni clubs; and interactions with members of the board of trustees and the multiple advisory councils. In some sense, there is never enough time to get it all done. In the first year, I came to a fuller realization of the need to apportion my time according to the rhythm of the academic year.

A final consideration that became clear during the first year of my presidency was the importance of a sense of balance in my personal life with regard to prayer, recreation, reading and scholarly engagement, and sufficient rest and relaxation. I knew that I had to have a thick skin when it came to too much sensitivity to public or private criticism but, at the same time, sufficient humility to acknowledge when I had made mistakes and to attend to the aftermath.

By the time that Ted and Ned returned from their extended trips, I had finished my first year as president and things had gone reasonably well. I felt fully empowered to move on to pursue the specific challenges that our strategic plan highlighted and the ongoing responsibility for vision, effective communication, proper accountability structures, and openness to whatever opportunities the future might bring.

## FIFTEEN YEARS LATER

After fifteen years as president of Notre Dame, I feel like one of the gray beards in the profession. Many of our peer institutions have had three presidents during the same span of time. Some of my best friends whom I have come to know, particularly in presidential associations, have retired from the fray. In my present administration, none of the other officers was with me when I began. I have been through exhilarating moments, like the successful completion of two major fund-raising campaigns, which garnered more than $1.5 billion for the needs of the university. I have overseen the addition of many new facilities, the expansion in the size of the faculty, excellent evaluations of academic quality of the various degree programs of the university by outside evaluators, and several national championships in intercollegiate sports. Notre Dame continues to take seriously its distinctive mission as a Catholic university. The campus itself is attractive and safe and has become a real place of pilgrimage for many. We have become more fully coeducational, increased our international involvements, fostered healthier town-gown relations, and tried to cultivate a high priority for service learning and for responsible citizenship.

I have also dealt with our first major NCAA penalty, a tragic accident involving the members of the Notre Dame women's swim team, and the firing and hiring of coaches and athletic directors with high levels of public attention; I have been involved with extensive discussions vis-à-vis the relationship between the institutional Church and institutions of Catholic higher education, like Notre Dame; I have become embroiled in discussions about policy with regard to formal recognition of various groups on campus; and I have had to deal with a highly visible resignation of one of my central officers. This is not to speak of other consternating matters like the sexual abuse scandal in the Catholic Church, the proper role and function of intercollegiate athletics in university life, the balance between teaching and research, and the concern among alumni about the accessibility and affordability of a Notre Dame education for their offspring.

Despite the times that have been challenging and the lost sleep and the emotional and personal pressures, I can honestly say that I have felt blessed and privileged to have been given the opportunity to serve in this particular institution for so much of my adult life. I will leave it to future historians to make a definitive judgment about the so-called Malloy years at Notre Dame. I do believe that the transition from the Hesburgh years has been a smooth one and that much of what has been achieved has built in an organic way upon that which I inherited when I took over.

## CONCLUSIONS

I think that I can extract from the particularities of the Notre Dame experience of presidential transition certain lessons that might be applicable to other institutions of higher education and to those contemplating succeeding a legendary figure in the presidential role.

1. In situations in which there is a restricted pool of candidates for the presidential office, either because of the special history of the institution or because of its distinctive sense of mission, the explicit effort to prepare people for consideration for this responsibility is crucial. Since there are no formal degree requirements or prior courses to be taken, most presidents have prepared experientially by holding other leadership positions within the central administration of their own or some other institution. It is almost impossible to move from faculty member to president, or from business or professional leader to president. The period of preparation needs to be sufficient for the individual to learn firsthand from the experience of talented mentors and to develop a sense of confidence and purpose in an administrative role. I should add that during my time as president, I have made every effort to bring other Holy Cross religious into positions of leadership and responsibility so that they could constitute a core group of potential successors.

2. The time of transition between election and assuming the responsibility is a prime opportunity for putting together one's leadership team, soliciting advice from experienced presidents, interacting with the members of the board of trustees and other major constituencies, and reading in the literature about presidential leadership and about higher education. Many presidents-to-be have also participated in one of the leadership training programs at major institutions and/or convened with groups of individuals in the same position of transition. Whatever length of time might be involved in the period of transition, it is a precious moment,

both personally and institutionally, to maximize the potential for successful and smooth empowerment of the next leadership team.

3. The attitude and support of the outgoing president is crucial for the new president to be fully embraced by the broader university community. When a transition is precipitated by ill health, death, a scandal, financial insolvency, or some other major problem, it will be very difficult to achieve this goal. But otherwise, the outgoing president can play a pivotal role in fostering full receptivity to the new people in all that they might offer by way of energy and enthusiasm for the next phase of the university's history.

4. The leadership of the board of trustees and the other board members have a responsibility to do everything they can to help the new president and his or her team to succeed. The choice of a president is a responsibility that may be the most important one that the board exercises. Once the decision is made, the board must symbolically and really be seen as enthusiastic for and confident in its relationship to the new president and the new administration.

The Notre Dame experience of its last presidential succession had its own distinctive elements. But I hope this description of my participation within it might touch on the challenge that every institution of higher education faces as it seeks the quality of presidential leadership that it deserves and tries to ensure that the transition will go smoothly.

# CHAPTER

## Tell Them from the Beginning
### A Response to President Malloy's Essay

*Lawrence S. Bacow*

Sixteen years sounds like an eternity. We are really talking about beginnings. I came to Tufts under very different circumstances. I had been an MIT faculty member for twenty-four years and was eventually recruited in complete confidence. My name did not surface until the day my appointment was announced. One of the challenges of a very confidential search was that I could not have the kinds of conversations with faculty and students and staff that one really wants to have to understand the new environment. You reach a point where you jump out of the airplane, you pull on the ripcord, and you hope a parachute is attached to it. In my case, I did not find any huge surprises.

How do you begin, especially when you are unknown and new to the institution? Everybody is trying to figure out who you are and what you stand for. I got some very good advice from a CEO in the corporate sector, Alex Trotman (former chairman of Ford Motor Company). He warned me. He said, "Since people are going to be reading entrails, trying to decide who you are, tell them and tell them right from the beginning! Tell them what makes you tick, what you care about, what your values are. Look for opportunities to do that!" That proved to be excellent advice.

As luck would have it, I was presented with this opportunity on 9/11 just a week and a half into my presidency. Even the darkest clouds have their silver lining. Not only did it give me the opportunity to speak to the community (knowing that they were listening and listening carefully); it also gave me the opportunity to observe the people around me under pressure. This was a team that I inherited. I could see how my chief lieutenants handled the situation.

I was given some other good advice by Jill Conway, former president of Smith: "Everyone's going to be whispering in your ear, telling you that you've got to solve this problem, or that problem. This person is good, keep him! This person is terrible, get rid of him! You're not going to know what discount rate to apply to each of these pronouncements. Draw your own conclusions based upon what you see." It sounds so obvious when you say it. But different people will have different agendas. Some people will have been underutilized and others will have been overutilized or outlived their welcome.

One of the things I did when I set about letting people know who I was and what I cared about was to be as explicit as possible about both some of the challenges and opportunities that *we* confronted. I tried to say quite clearly to the faculty that any academic institution that had to rely on its president for all its good ideas was a university in trouble. I expected them to be part of this process.

I did not have six months, but I had two months. I used those two months to go around and talk with people within the university. I made a point to go to their offices. (I was astonished to hear how many people said, "This is the first time the university president has been in this building.") I asked everybody the same question: "You have three wishes to make Tufts a better place. What are they? And you can't just say 'more resources.' We're going to do that anyway, and it's not a terribly interesting task simply to relax a budget constraint. What are the other things you'd like to be done?"

I heard some very good suggestions about things, it turned out, that were very easy to do, and to do very quickly. This at least demonstrated to people that somebody was listening, that somebody was paying attention, that somebody was actually going to try and do something.

I say all this recognizing that I have not done everything right. I have made my mistakes, and I continue to make them. But, as I say to the faculty, the challenge is to make only new mistakes. It is okay to make mistakes as long as you learn from them.

I think about these beginnings, about the birth of a new baby, about airplanes taking off. I am a sailor. One of the most dangerous portions of any passage is leaving the harbor. It is actually safer once you get off shore. There are fewer things to run into.

Beginnings are really, really important. How we plan them, how we transition, how we reveal our deeper moral convictions, is key.

# CHAPTER

# Fitting Leadership Types to the Task at Hand
## A Response to President Malloy's Essay

*Andrew K. Benton*

I am honored to be a participant in this forum, and I am further honored to be a respondent to President Malloy's essay. I suspect that many years hence someone will be speaking about "succeeding a legend" and it will be Edward Malloy about whom the compliment is offered.

My own observations grow from intimate involvement in three presidential transitions at Pepperdine. Aside from the usual concerns about having a lawyer as a college president, my own transition was remarkably smooth. I served as executive vice president for nine years under my friend and predecessor, which has allowed me to treat budgeting, planning, personnel, board relations, and similarly nettlesome matters as near-second nature. I also served a stint as chief development officer and so those skills were in reasonable shape. My focus in the first three years of my service has been on students, faculty, and critical external relations. What a gift that has been in many, many respects.

I tend to view institutional development in chapters, and as a consequence, I tend to see the need to fit leadership types to the task at hand. Not unlike the view taken by Straus and Howe in analyzing the cycles of American archetypes, I do think that college presidents often need to be what their predecessors chose not to be.

Pepperdine University is similar to Notre Dame in that our president must, as a matter of bylaw provision, be an active member of our faith heritage. Thus, it is incumbent upon me during my tenure, to keep an eye out for those who may succeed me someday. (In fact, I keep a very close eye on them!) Some leaders in higher education take the position that a sitting president does not need to accept that assignment. I disagree and feel that talent development for all positions is an important task. I happen to love the institution that I serve, and I owe it a bright future, whatever that may mean.

If I could take my future successor aside and offer some all-purpose coaching today, I would offer these five observations:

**1. Learn how to inspire confidence and then be confident.** Be sincere but not too humble. Draw people close, but do not let them find hubris when they get there. To be successful in this position, people must trust me not only for what I decide but how I decide. I choose my confidants and advisors very carefully, and at the end of the day, I make my own final decisions. I would have to say that the worst mistakes I have made were when I did not follow my own instincts.

**2. If you have shortcomings in your training or experience, take care of that now.** Indeed, a college presidency is not a very convenient time for on-the-job training. I do not think it is possible to have too much experience, and so I have purposely surrounded myself with a senior team that, for the most part, approaches problem solving in ways very different than I do. Despite working in higher education now for nearly thirty years, that multidisciplinary approach helps make up for my many seemingly incurable weaknesses.

**3. If you do not like people, you will not like fund-raising.** If you do not like fund-raising, you will not like being a college president—at least not for very long. A consulting team, telling me earnestly that they "know how lonely it can be," approached me. I told them, "Actually, I *pray* for loneliness sometimes!" I simply do not need any more friends—unless, of course, they are very wealthy. I would tell my successor that they better love people and many different types of them.

**4. Obtain a clear vision for where you want to go and how you want to get there.** Developing that at the last minute will seem insincere, at best. What the Cheshire cat told Alice was right: If you do not know where you are going, any which way will do. There are many acceptable styles of leadership; indecision is not one of the good ones.

**5. Prepare to lead in your own way and in your own style.** To do otherwise will not be genuine. The campus community will forgive almost anything except a lack of honesty in your relationship with them. The best way to be defined by your strengths is to lead from them, I think.

Probably the question I heard the most in my first three years after following my own "legend" was, "So, how is it going?" I never knew what to say. It was a question that was a little like a Venetian approaching a Florentine centuries ago and saying, "So, Guido, how goes the Renaissance?" I believe I am making a difference—each day—but progress is sometimes hard to measure precisely.

I take comfort from something Winston Churchill is reported to have said: "History will be kind to me, for I intend to write it." There is a lot to be said for writing one's own history.

At the opening of our new science facility [in 2002], one of our visiting scientists said, "If it works, it is a discovery; if it doesn't, it was an experiment." I wish you "discovery" in your own leadership experiences.

# CHAPTER 14

## Leadership Transitions at Private Liberal Arts Colleges
### A Response to President Malloy's Essay

*Dale T. Knobel*

Wow!" I said to myself, as Father Malloy described the presidential succession process at Notre Dame. "What a thoughtful and humane way to select and prepare a president! To know the pool of candidates, to give leading prospects a trial run in senior administration at the institution, to have the luxury of extended consultation between the outbound president and his successor. Amazing! Those things simply don't happen at most of our schools."

While few institutions, I suspect, can replicate the Notre Dame process, I have come to appreciate that the gap is widest for those of us at exclusively undergraduate colleges. At least at the research university—the setting in which I had all of my experience as a professor and more than half of my experience as an academic administrator—the institution has the possibility of grooming internal candidates through deanships and a host of vice presidencies and directorships. By the same token, individuals have the opportunity to explore leadership at progressive levels of responsibility. But at most liberal arts colleges, there are precious few opportunities to conduct a try-out before making a decision to consider an internal candidate for a college presidency. By the same token, there are few chances for individuals to assess for themselves how they might enjoy leadership or how they might grow in it. At my institution, beyond the provost and other vice presidents, there is an associate provost, a faculty member who is a part-time director of the honors program, and a dean who works with first-year student programs. Chairing a department is thought to be rotational, something that every tenured professor takes on in turn for a few years. Most department chairs utterly reject the notion that they are "management." This condition, almost unavoidable at undergraduate colleges, has costs. The college never gets to see its own people grow and take on larger responsibilities. At the same time, individuals contemplating college leadership have a hard time assessing their own skills and interests. It is no surprise, then, that men and women in leadership in undergraduate colleges so often arrive after experiences in large universities, where they have worked through a series of jobs of increasing responsibility.

President Malloy appropriately reminded us of the effects of the "Wooden Factor" in college and university leadership succession. Coined for the legendary college basketball coach, whose shadow and campus presence made it difficult for anyone who attempted to follow him in the post, the Wooden Factor is something that we have all seen in operation at the presidential level. In fact, this seems like an apt example of how often institutions do not learn from one another. An ex-president who is moved down the hall into a chancellorship or emeritus post with ill-defined responsibilities rarely seems to have a positive effect on his or her successor. Yet colleges and universities large and small keep trying to make it work. This may be a case where the uniqueness of our institutions leads us astray. We admit that it has not worked elsewhere, but we believe it is going to work here. How little attention we pay to good practice in higher education!

For the new—and, for that matter, continuing—college president, one of the most important issues is time. How does one preserve time for self? How does one use time effectively on the job? At undergraduate institutions, the very access that all constituencies have to the president that makes them wonderful, intimate places also provides the biggest challenge. In short, the good news is that everyone can make a claim on your time, and the bad news is that everyone can make a claim on your time. Sometimes I worry that the system in higher education leadership pays a premium not for deep and thoughtful decisions but rather for how many decisions can be made fast without making an egregious mistake. We are asked to react to so many things on our campuses. It concerns me that this can lead to a very defensive approach to decision making. If motivated by "how do I avoid making a mistake?," one can go pretty far wrong in a hurry. I once met a president who, when complimenting her staff at the end of the year, reported "We didn't make a big mistake this year." That is sad. And it can result from making decisions quickly rather than thoughtfully in the face of pressure.

Many of us believe that when arriving as new leaders to a campus, one of the best things we can do is get out and visit faculty and leading staff in their offices. We all understand the power of seeing people on their own turf. Clearly, this is something that is most possible at relatively smaller institutions. I found such a practice incredibly valuable when I first came to Denison. But I also realize that I have created a monster. My faculty is turning over rapidly as a wave of retirements reaches us. In my sixth year, about a third of the faculty is new since I arrived, and I have not done nearly as good a job keeping up with visiting the new faculty in their offices as I did in getting around to faculty in my first year (which, of course, I could do before other activities crowded the agenda). Yet, I have created an expectation and lore that the continuing faculty have passed on to new colleagues. Now I find myself with a substantial backlog of new, unvisited faculty. As soon as possible, I am going to try to get out and see those people too. Even the best ideas need to be refreshed from time to time. This is one I need to refresh.

# CHAPTER

# Virtue and Leadership: Good Leaders Must First Be Good People

*Albert C. Yates*

C lara Lovett, president emerita of Northern Arizona University, be-
moaned the "dumbing down" of the college presidency, recalling
the golden age of such academic leaders as Clark Kerr and
Theodore Hesburgh, and decrying a system that too often "screens out
potential intellectual and educational leaders in favor of men and women
who look, speak, and act like candidates for political office."[1]

Certainly, these words ring painfully true for many college presidents
who spend their mornings grappling with state legislatures and their
evenings courting alumni and donors. There no longer seems much time
for thoughtful discussion about deeply held philosophical ideals, for reflection on the role of the university in society, or for the sorts of interactions with students and faculty that drew many of us to higher education
in the first place. Still, I would suggest that this is not a trend limited to
the academy. The role of the college president today increasingly paral-
lels that of leadership in any large organization, demanding not only academic and administrative credentials but media savvy, political awareness,
business acumen, strategic prowess, and enormous stamina. We live in a
time when our country and our system of higher education cry out for
leadership; yet good people of passion and ability shrink from the call, un-
willing to risk the all-consuming demands of the job and disheartened by
the ruthlessness and meanness that so often define contemporary public
roles. Any examination of leadership, therefore, cannot be divorced from
the times, nor can university leadership be examined outside of the context of the larger society in which our institutions exist.

One cannot help but be frustrated by "leadership" as it now seems to be practiced in our country, by the general lack of decorum among those who set our nation's example. Television commentators rub their hands with glee over every potential scandal, no matter how insignificant. Politicians act as if bipartisanship were the moral equivalent of crossing the River Styx. Corporations have adopted polite euphemisms like "down-sizing" to separate their operations from the people who compose them. In so many ways, we are reminded, daily, that virtue and leadership are too often at odds, as if one is incompatible with the other. The *New York Times* has provided a dramatic illustration of this, demonstrating what transpires when leadership becomes more about the pursuit of power and prestige than about making good choices. Reporter Jayson Blair was exposed for having manufactured sources and stories out of his imagination. And while his misdeeds are now well-known, the far more serious question is how some of the news industry's most prestigious leaders could not only sanction but reward such behavior. The experience of the *Times*'s leaders is far more telling than that of Blair himself. Blair's editors did not set out to deceive; they were not engaged in any sort of conspiracy—they had no malevolent plan, nor were they grossly incompetent. Instead, they allowed themselves to become distracted from their responsibilities by the pursuit of prestigious prizes and an overwhelming competitive spirit. What transpired was simply the result of small daily decisions, choices made, problems overlooked, questions that went unasked and unanswered, egos allowed to run unchecked, and leaders who permitted flattery to overwhelm their judgment. As one *Times* reporter commented, "It was pretty evident . . . that a sense of decency was either taken for granted or lost in the rush to pursue news with that high competitive metabolism rate."[2] And all of this led over time to a lowering of standards and to an overall failure of leadership at one of the most trusted and respected organizations in the world.

So, what does all of this mean for higher education? The challenges facing college and university presidents are not materially different from those in charge of any other large organization, but the responsibility for leading with virtue is greater because of the role that our institutions play in society. Even in an era of budget reductions and intensified competition from "fast-food" education providers, higher education remains our society's conscience—institutions that are empowered to question and challenge, that are expected to instill values and character, and that are perceived as standing for more than the pursuit of a healthy bottom line.

One of the greatest challenges facing higher education today is to help our students understand the vital link between leadership and those values that sustain a democratic society—to nurture an understanding of what it means to lead and to lead responsibly.

Leadership is more than a combination of boundless energy and missionary zeal. A true leader is neither fanatic nor bully nor prophet. A leader is someone who has a vision of what the world ought to be and a desire to help turn dreams into reality. A leader is one who knows the geography of her or his own interior, who relies not on trendy techniques or cute catch-phrases to make decisions but on the values that compose her or his very core. We expect our leaders to have a glimpse of the future, of a time and place better than now. We expect them to coalesce and focus our concerns and dreams and inspire us to action in pursuit of this collective vision. But more important, we want to trust our leaders, to have faith in them, to be assured of their virtue and know they will make the right choices. Viewed in this way, virtue really becomes the basis of trust and, thus, of leadership.

To me, virtue is not at all complicated—it is the embodiment of what is good and right in human life, the embrace and exercise of values that teach us how to be better people. The choice of values we hold dear, like the style of leadership we employ, is an intensely personal act. I doubt there is a unique set of values that defines virtue, but my own list would include truth and integrity, competence and commitment, and, above all, compassion. And here is why.

I include truth because without it achieving intellectual equilibrium seems virtually impossible. Rationalizing to avoid the truth is one of the easiest things we do. How often do we lie to ourselves to bring comfort in our isolation, selfishness, and cynicism? Truth, it seems, is our only viable bridge to reality.

Integrity is surely our most precious commodity. It is the quality that allows us to remain steadfast in our convictions, to resist the temptations of power, status, and money. It is the voice of conscience, the inner compass that allows us to steer a steady and true course.

Through competence we assure our usefulness—to ourselves and others. Competence is an acknowledgment that one of our most important duties as human beings is first to determine and then to cultivate our abilities. I believe all of us incur a special debt to the world from the simple act of being: we owe our best efforts to humanity simply because we are a part of it.

Commitment is not just duty or obligation or responsibility. It instills a reason to be, a passion for life. Commitment, in whatever form, expresses an unwillingness to lead a mediocre, half-lived life.

Perhaps our most uniquely human quality is compassion. Moving toward a better world seems to require at least two critical ingredients: an acceptance of those things about ourselves and others that we or they cannot change; and a recognition that "reverence for life" is not merely a noble phrase, but a necessity for survival. The root of compassion is a willingness to suffer with others. It is a willingness to take on not guilt but the responsibility that comes with being human. It is a recognition that we are, indeed, our brothers' keepers.

Virtue, it seems, derives from the interplay of all these values—how they function together. On their own, they do not amount to much. Lacking integrity and truth, committed and competent criminals are in great supply. Lacking compassion, subjective truth becomes the rationale for much evil. Commitment on its own may lead to fanaticism. Compassion alone can lead to helplessness and despair. Even integrity, without these other values, can be reduced to rigidity and narrow-mindedness. But taken together, these values can lead one toward virtue—each depends on another and only together are they complete. And such values derive their greatest power when applied not merely to the individual but to the individual in society.

Of course, we can have leadership—even effective leadership—without virtue, and we often do. Virtue is not something you earn along with your college diploma or buy with a Visa card. Highly intelligent people will not automatically choose "good over evil." But virtue enhances the probability that leadership will be effective and good. Virtue allows one to take the high ground; to transcend the petty, the routine, and the mundane; to fight the urge to succumb to temptations of power, status, or money; and to pursue a true course for collective good. I can think of few challenges where this is more true—and more important—than in leadership of our colleges and universities. So, how can we, as individuals and presidents, define and foster the kind of leadership that inspires confidence and assures success? Warren Bennis has written extensively on the subject of leadership, and he tells us it is not easy "to learn to be a leader":

> There is no simple formula . . . that leads inexorably to successful leadership. Instead, it is a deeply human process, full of trial and error, victories and defeats, timing and happenstance, intuition and insight. Books can help you understand what's going on, but for those who are ready, most of the learning takes place during the experience itself.[3]

I agree with Bennis that so much of what we can learn about the true nature of leadership must come from the pain and risks of personal experience. Yet at the same time, the fundamental essence of our choices and our actions will reflect our values and perspectives—our own individual understanding of what it means to "do the right thing." Stated more directly, good leaders must first be good people.

For more than twenty-five years, I have been keeping mental notes about things I think I have learned from personal experience about the nature of leadership. Ten years ago, I started to write what I call "My List: Assertions on Organizational Leadership." This list has now grown to forty assertions—and it changes occasionally, in keeping with my own sense of understanding and maturity. Some of these statements describe relationships to people, some are crucial to organizational progress and harmony, and others presume to provide advice directly to leaders. From this list, I would like to isolate six points that seem particularly relevant to the challenges of leaders in complex organizations. Each assertion carries its own story and recalls for me a special experience that has shaped my own understanding of leadership.

But first, why do leaders fail? For years, I have been intrigued and puzzled by this question. And here I do not include the incompetent or the ill prepared. My query is directed toward the perils of those thoughtful, intelligent, imaginative, and insightful leaders, knowledgeable in the art of successful leadership. There are many from this group, national figures and others, who end their careers by resigning in disgrace, who are ushered out with fanfare or simply disappear, never again to be heard from—or worse, remembered. Such sorry events are invariably preceded by signs of impending failure: a dean who readily takes credit for all positive events but points fingers and assigns blame for failures; the CEO who continues to muscle through a decision long after all others have observed the folly of his original choice; the president who discounts the dignity of even a single individual, whether janitor or Nobel Prize winner; the supervisor who has not yet learned to say "good job" or "thank you"; the colleague or friend who finds fault in just about everything; and the list goes on. Are there ways to avoid failure and improve the odds of success? Perhaps. That, for me, has been the purpose of my list. Each observation on the list has grown out of a personal experience, and the following points seem particularly relevant for this forum:

**1. Leaders must forego the luxuries of pessimism, cynicism, negativism, irresponsibility, and, at times, independence.**

Nearly thirty years ago, shortly after accepting my first administrative position, my chemistry colleagues held a gathering to celebrate my change in status and to wish me well. We were a close-knit group and often found excuses to come together socially. Over time, I have come to observe, with few exceptions, that chemists are highly opinionated, hold strong views on virtually every topic, and possess a ready willingness to share their insights with all who will listen; I, as a chemist, am no exception. At my celebration party, as usual, it became my turn to offer a recitation on politics, our wretched university administration, or the sorry state of the departmental budget, and, as usual, I expected to be challenged, dismissed, or ignored. To my surprise, the room fell silent, and everyone listened as I began to speak, nodding in agreement and smiling approvingly. Feeling encouraged, I began to embellish and take risks. "For once," I thought, "they appreciate my wit, intellect, and persuasive oratory." And then, suddenly, truth sank in. Their attention, deference, and courtesy had little to do with me or with what I was saying. A week earlier, my remarks would surely have been rebutted or, more likely, simply ignored. But now, I had been given elevated stature, and my comments—as tired, mundane, or outrageous as ever—were likewise accorded special status. What could this mean?

Since that time thirty years ago, I have noted this reaction of individuals and audiences thousands of times. And I have learned from these experiences that people in positions of power, authority, and responsibility incur an awesome obligation to others—an obligation that must be acknowledged and accommodated. When you are a leader, your constituents depend on you in ways they do not depend on others; they see you differently and listen to you more intently and completely. The people who look to you for leadership believe what you say, even if you do not entirely believe it yourself. Your moods become their moods; your uncertainties become their uncertainties. And so, as leaders, we relinquish a portion of our discretion; we may no longer embrace or exhibit the qualities of sadness, cynicism, or pessimism that have the power to damage our organizations or the people within them. As leaders, we must believe in the future and its possibilities—or no one else will.

Each of us has our own image of a leader; we have deeply held beliefs about the comportment and behavior of our teachers, doctors, college presidents, and others who seek our trust and loyalty. In spite of our temporary move toward individual isolation, we remain a people who generally harbor great respect and affection for our nation's institutions and the stewards to whom we commit their care. And we are disappointed, often unforgiving, when our expected images are betrayed. In other words, leaders are and must be held to a higher standard—an observation surely worth remembering.

**2. Great institutions are seldom built by giant leaps, but rather by small steps taken consistently in the same direction. And progress is faster if one first effects common understandings of culture and values.**

Throughout much of the 1980s, as executive vice president and provost at Washington State University, I spent a great deal of mental energy worrying about planning and decision-making processes that could "guarantee" institutional improvements in quality, stature, and responsiveness to the needs of all clientele. When my daughter was born in 1988, I made a request of the board of regents for paternity leave; it was granted, and I became the first father at WSU to be formally granted such leave—which was conditioned, however, on my using any extra time to do research on strategic planning. During this period, I read much of the work of noted authors and theorists on leadership, organizational management and behavior, strategic planning, and the structure and culture of successful organizations. From this period of study and reflection, I uncovered what seemed a critical ingredient of consistent organizational movement and success. My readings revealed that there are only a few organizations, IBM and Microsoft among them, that achieve greatness by huge leaps forward, and those rare few do so because they are fortunate to introduce a new order of things. Most other stellar organizations—profit, nonprofit, public, and private—reached their lofty status slowly, over long periods marked by steady and consistent progress. This observation led me to the question: is it possible to design a management and/or leadership strategy that will ensure steady and consistent progress?

Consider the example of a four-man sculling team. If each member of the team executes his or her task in flawless harmony with the others, progress is faster and along a precisely determined channel. Universities are diverse places and, in fulfilling their mission, welcome discord, controversy, and dissent, believing that the path to truth and discovery can never truly be scripted. But there are some aspects of the university, like other organizational entities, where harmony does produce success. What happens, for example, when a university community has strongly held common views about such matters as institutional vision, values, priorities, culture, operating philosophy, and so on? When such common understandings are strongly embraced throughout the university by faculty and staff, they determine the outcome of thousands of daily decisions made across the institution. Common understandings produce solutions and directions that are faithful to institutional aspirations and most often lead to enhanced productivity and steady and consistent progress.

The central task of the leader, then, is the creation of an environment of common understandings of a shared vision. In addition to greater assurance of progress (there are no guarantees), there are significant correlative benefits, including greater confidence in the delegation of authority to lower levels, a greatly enhanced sense of community and purpose, and a strengthened foundation of trust and open communication.

The "Common Understandings" planning project, initiated at Washington State University and later transported to Colorado State University, has, I believe, served both institutions well. At Colorado State, it has been the driver of our current status as the institution of choice for Colorado resident students, enrolling and graduating more in-state students than any other four-year campus in Colorado. It has also guided our efforts over the past decade as we have achieved record levels of research funding, private giving, and legislative support; as we have revamped and strengthened our undergraduate core curriculum; as we have brought about a physical transformation of our campus; and much more.

**3. Communication must be open, honest, direct, and frequent. Versatility in communication is a skill worth developing.**

First, I think it is critical always to remind ourselves that listening may be the most important part of communication. And the truly skilled have even learned to listen while talking. Good communication, including listening, is necessary to build trust—and trust is the basis for moving, in concert, toward commonly held goals. Building trust demands that those of you in leadership roles make the effort to develop empathy with all affected stakeholders, to walk in their shoes as you would in your own.

On becoming president of Colorado State in 1990, I joined a campus with a significant history of achievement and a wealth of positive attributes. But it was also a campus experiencing the consequences of numerous changes in leadership in the president's office over a dozen years. Phrases that described campus relationships at that time were "polarization between faculty and administrators," "absence of trust," "independent silos," and "a pervasive sense of on-campus isolation." The Faculty Council complained bitterly about salaries falling behind those of peer institutions and privately accused the administration of hiding resources and directing them toward nonacademic priorities. This complex of concerns was clearly symptomatic of a near-complete breakdown in communication across all levels and in all directions. There was little hope of getting to the real business of the university until a way was found to restore trust and to begin to build community.

Within a couple of weeks, I made two promises to the faculty: First, I promised that future salary increases would be sufficient to make progress annually in closing the gap between Colorado State and its peers. We kept our promise to the faculty and funded salary increases through a combination of new revenues and internal reallocation of resources. Second, I promised to create an open budgeting process where faculty representatives to the University Budget Committee would have full and unrestricted access to all financial data available to the administration. I also emphasized that real shared governance implied and demanded full accountability by all—faculty and administrators alike. These two promises were honored meticulously and did much to restore trust and set the stage for broad institutional progress. These actions were quickly followed by a wide range of communications initiatives that sought to engage faculty, staff, and students in the life of the university. These included regularly scheduled events on and off campus, walkabouts, lunches in student dining halls, special events for retired faculty and staff, open and frequent dialogues with faculty and student groups, and, it seems, every conceivable gathering in all possible venues involving all constituent groups. Written communication in the form of a periodic President's Letter, statewide op-ed pieces, press releases, and direct mailings to alumni and friends became an indispensable way of informing our many publics about institutional values, priorities, and policies.

The object of good leadership is to move an organization from one place to a better place and, in the end, to feel good about the chosen path. Sustainable progress, however, is unlikely to occur without the trust and commitment of all stakeholders. How can this occur? We all want to be close to our leaders, know that they see and hear us, speak to us as individuals, and understand our pain, our fears, and our dreams. For the leader, this means developing a special resonance with each of the many people and groups important to the success of the organization. It means truly understanding and embracing the history, culture, and perspectives of these diverse groups, as the basis of empathy for their concerns and aspirations. It means talking to people, all people, on their terms as individuals and in their "language," developing comfort in inner city and rural communities, corporate boardrooms, communities of color, across all income and social strata, and with media and legislatures. When the leader begins to hear whispers that "She's one of us—she understands us," the connection has been made. The challenge, then, is to continue to nourish the relationship and never to betray it, even unwittingly. This is all hard work, but for the leader who can muster this true and sincere brand of versatility in communication, the rewards are well worth the effort.

**4. Diversity in people and ideas is a cornerstone of organizational strength.**

On June 8, 2003, in the wake of the U.S. Supreme Court's ruling on the University of Michigan's affirmative action programs, the following headline appeared on the front page of the *Denver Post*: "[Governor] Owens Slams Race as Factor." The editorial page proclaimed, "Diversity Still a Hot Topic on College Campuses." The same headlines could have been written in 1970 or 1990; how much have we progressed? The following paragraphs are taken from my 1995 State of the University Address and seem as timely today as then:

> [O]ur mettle as a community has faced no greater test in recent years than that posed today by the ongoing divisive debate surrounding affirmative action. We all have been aware of what is happening nationwide around this issue—of the charged rhetoric that serves to demonize those on either side. It is an environment that attempts to pit fairness against quality, as if the balance of the two were an impossible ideal. . . .
>
> A national debate such as this one has the potential to cause much damage, to create divisions and wounds that take generations to heal. And sadly—amid all the oratorical warfare—it seems we have forgotten why affirmative action was created in the first place: to give all people, regardless of race, gender or ethnicity, the opportunity to participate in a meaningful way in the wealth and opportunities our society has to offer—to enjoy the same rewards for hard work and a good, fulfilling life that are enjoyed by the majority population. Quite simply, the goal is to give all people the opportunity to live life with dignity. That simple goal seems to have been forgotten in the zeal to roll back affirmative action and achieve political advantage.
>
> How important is diversity to a university? Diversity, in its myriad forms, is as essential to the university as books and classrooms. Without diversity of people, ideas, perspectives, cultures, lifestyles and more, achievement of the university's mission is impossible. Without diversity, pursuit of objective truth becomes a hollow, inaccessible abstraction. Without diversity, the university does not reflect society and thus cannot relate to society. Without diversity, our efforts to criticize and judge our world have no basis, no foundation. In other words, without diversity, there can be no university!

This was an important statement for our university and has been referenced countless times since it appeared in 1995. But the convictions that lie beneath those words guided the hands and hearts of our community long before that. One of my early experiences at Colorado State offers an example. In 1991, after tiring of the conflicting, though honest, reports from vice presidents and others about the climate our campus offered to students of color, I decided to create a structure that removed buffers and allowed me to see the university directly through the eyes of our students. This structure took the form of a group called the President's Multicultural Student Advisory Committee; it reported directly to me and was staffed by the president's office. The group has usually numbered about thirty students, chosen through an application process and comprising mostly students of color, although it is open to all. At each meeting, I reiterate the role of the group and my expectations for it, which are simple: I want to be able to see the university through a student's eyes. When there are problems, I want to be able to call on students for help in crafting solutions and in putting these solutions into action. More than anything else, we want all our students to have a great experience at Colorado State—and these meetings give me a chance to tell this group, directly, that I value and care about them. True passion—as conveyed through thoughtful language and behaviors—is a critical aspect of leadership. When a leader lacks passion or conveys an artificial or even blind enthusiasm for an issue, it will be noticed and it will undermine the trust that people have for that leader. As well, the president is the keeper of the culture, and his or her influence should neither be underestimated nor used inappropriately. That is why, when meeting with groups such as this advisory committee, there can be no proxy, no stand-in for the president. These students sense my passion for their concerns, and they believe me, and because they do, they build a true connection to the university and become our ambassadors, both within and outside the institution.

In the early 1990s, around the time this group first came together, campuses around the country were wrestling with the idea of building black and Hispanic houses or "cultural centers," allowing students to isolate themselves in the name of comfort and cementing their cultural identity. But at Colorado State, we realized that if we were to do that, we would confound the reason all our students are here—to learn, to gain skills, and to develop the capacity to deal with whatever the world throws at them. To have access to all our country has to offer, students of color have to at least be bicultural, to understand and be able to cope with the majority culture as well as their own. To isolate them takes away their opportunity to develop those skills. And so, while it is important to provide new students with a safe haven, a refuge in which they can feel comfortable and at home during their transition to college life, it is equally important to push them out after a time and encourage them to become fully engaged and a part of the greater community.

At Colorado State in the early 1990s, we had a series of advocacy offices situated in disparate locations around campus, and the members of the Multicultural Student Advisory Committee argued that if we could bring these offices together in a central location, increasing their accessibility and availability to the entire campus community, ultimately all our students would benefit. So, at the urging of the student committee, we built an addition to the Lory Student Center and found a way to create new and enriched spaces. The students developed the idea, I became its champion, and together we were able to make it happen. The result has been a wonderful addition to our institution and has promoted overall pride in the campus and community.

The value of surrounding oneself with a diverse group of people cannot be overstated. As presidents and CEOs, we want to make the best possible decisions for our organizations, take maximum advantage of opportunities, solve problems, and relieve pressures in the best way we can. I have not yet found that one person who has the knowledge, the experience, and the resources that will always lead inexorably to the right solution. When different talents and insights are brought to bear on a problem, we increase our odds of making the best choice for the institution. If I surrounded myself only with people who looked like me, thought like me, and behaved like me, I might add to my personal comfort and security but would add no substantial value to the institution; under such circumstances, one plus one, plus one, et cetera, can only ever be equal to one. Diversity provides the possibility, at least, of synergy.

Many well-meaning presidents and CEOs may subconsciously start to feel threatened by the young vice president who is energetic, ambitious, articulate, and talented. This is a trap in which many good leaders are ensnared, but one has to ask, If you deserve to be the president, why should you worry about such things? Do your institutions a favor and hire people of good character, support them well, and let them excel. It works.

**5. Genuine humility keeps one's feet firmly planted. And true humility consists of at least two main ingredients: An awareness that any aspect of one's life can collapse in an instant—and sincere gratitude it has not.**

All of us, no matter our role or occupation, can be lulled into believing our own press—fancying ourselves to be better and more important than we actually are. Those in positions of leadership can fall prey to flattery, to the conviction that they alone have the right answers or, in the worst possible case, that they are above the law and the rules do not apply to them. Regrettably, people in positions of power and authority are quite susceptible to such temptations, as news headlines remind us all too frequently. How can we avoid becoming so divorced from reality that we allow ourselves to stray down this wayward path? We need, in this world, a perspective that allows us to be grounded and have our feet firmly planted. Our worlds can change unexpectedly and in an instant . . . as bad as things are, they can always be worse.

For me, this awareness was accentuated following the birth of my youngest daughter, Sadie. Sadie was born twelve weeks premature, and her tiny, fragile body endured more trauma in the first months of life than most of us will confront in a lifetime—heart surgery, infections, retinopathy of prematurity, intravenous feedings, and more. During the long weeks of her hospitalization, I remember feeling afraid to answer the telephone, fearing the phone call that would end it all, change my life, rob me of the child we loved and had wanted and planned for. Thinking back, I can still feel the sense of helplessness, desperation, and unending anxiety—all of which were a conscious recognition that I, who was so used to being in charge, had absolutely no control over something that meant more to me than my own life.

Sadie lived, and today at age 8, she is healthy, whole, beautiful, and smart with the brightest smile imaginable. And as for me, I continue each day to feel grateful and truly blessed. I am also changed. The experience made me more patient, more tolerant, more understanding, and a bit less certain. I learned the real value of such phrases as "thank you," "great job," and "you made a difference."

While I do not recommend that everyone come to this realization through the same route, understanding our own inability to control all the forces around us is important to good leadership. Certainly, it reveals our dependence on others for the success of our own efforts. But what about those times when we get airborne—and we will. How do we know it, and what can we do about it? These may be the most important questions of any in these pages. Because the problem is purely personal and often emotion-laden, the solution is not within us as the affected party. Consequently, in my experience, it has been critical to have people in my life and close by, those who cared enough about me to tell me the truth, even when I did not want to hear it and even when I might be hurt by it. There are not very many people who are willing to tell a CEO that he is "full of it," so leaders who seek balance must also seek ways to encourage their trusted lieutenants to summon the courage and will to be candid and truthful about such delicate but crucial matters. Our lives balance, at times, on precariously high wires, and we need to cherish those people who consistently help guide us back to the safety of solid ground.

**6. Seek always to turn adversity to advantage; look for the silver lining, the ray of hope and opportunity.**

Why is this so important? It is during times of stress that both the need for leadership and the risk of failure are greatest. It is also true that such difficult times offer the greatest opportunities for change and progress.

Such opportunities occur within most organizations once or twice a year—more if we are really unlucky—always unexpected and uninvited, but providing an invaluable window to communicate to the public what the institution stands for and what are it values. At these times, the positive alignment of institutional will and courage is heightened and most are willing to accept leadership and direction. Such times should not be squandered by seeking only to restore the institution to its former self. These are times to reach as high as possible and make the institution better in significant and sustainable ways. At Colorado State University, periods of crisis have produced some of our most notable achievements and enduring changes. A few offered in sparing detail can illustrate the point:

*Illustration #1*. In 1992, an atmosphere of fear and intimidation in the Colorado State football program led to the firing of the popular head coach. The decision angered many alumni and fans, to the point where my family and I received death threats and torrents of hate mail. Still, I knew that any other decision would have been a betrayal of the institution's values and the trust placed in me as its president. And more than that, I was bound by the dictates of my conscience: it was the right thing to do. To have the courage of one's convictions is a prerequisite for effective leadership. I was not prepared, though, for the newspaper treatment of these events. Some vocal sports reporters and commentators sided with the coach, castigated me, and reported opinion as if it were fact. Newspapers pressed the story, kept it alive, embellished it, and used it as a basis for a raft of feature articles. The incident became surreal, nightmarish, and interminable. The "play" ended when several of the most celebrated football players called a press conference and described a football program more disturbing than anything even I had suggested. I observed, as well, the emotional investment and stridency of alumni and fans, and I noted how quickly many people—vice presidents, colleagues, even people I had thought were my friends—tried to distance themselves from me, doubted that my presidency would survive the crisis, and moved rapidly to avoid casting their lot with mine. It was a lonely time, and I must admit I could, in hindsight, have handled some things better.

But these events allowed our campus to make a significant statement about the role of the student-athlete and the relationship of athletics to the greater university. They also sparked in me a resolve to create an athletic program that would be a source of institutional pride, built on the best notions of integrity, fair play, and an emphasis on athletes as students first. In the eleven years since those dark days of 1992, our football program has won its conference championship six times, participated in seven bowl games, and is viewed by many nationwide as a model program. As a postscript, it was an important, though troubling, reminder that relationships are often little more than veneer for people in positions of authority, and those who stand beside us in times of crisis deserve our deepest gratitude and respect.

*Illustration #2.* In summer 1993, a group of skinheads attacked an African American high school student in downtown Fort Collins, during a time when the student was in our town to participate in a precollegiate program on the Colorado State campus. Rather than simply bemoaning the callousness of those who could perpetrate such an act, the community of Fort Collins, with leadership from the university, seized the opportunity to rally and pledge openly and loudly its commitment to eliminate discrimination. The resulting campus–community partnership has led to wide-ranging efforts, including a vibrant celebration each year of the Martin Luther King holiday and enhanced community support services for people who find themselves confronting racism and intolerance. In part because of this galvanized spirit of community, Colorado State has experienced record enrollment of students of color in each of the last six years. And many would now say we have become a warm and inviting place for all who come to work and study here.

*Illustration #3.* The Fort Collins flood of 1997 devastated the Colorado State campus and resulted in physical damage estimated at approximately $140 million. People in our community died during the disaster. On our campus, faculty saw their offices, along with years of their work, washed away. Library books were swept from the shelves, turning up blocks away in the street. Entire buildings became uninhabitable overnight.

And all of this occurred only a handful of weeks before school was scheduled to begin. It was, without question, the most devastating experience our campus has endured, and we easily could have lapsed into an era of self-pity and doubt. But the obligations of leadership were clear: We knew that while we could repair buildings and fix computers, the human psyche is much more fragile. If we did not tend to people and treat them well, we could lose forever our most precious asset and any physical recovery would be a hollow victory. And so, as an institution, we pledged to do everything possible to make people whole: to restock personal libraries, to make faculty spaces better than ever, and to create a fund managed by faculty to cover faculty losses. We vowed that classes would start on schedule and that we would rebuild our institution to make it better than it had ever been before. And we succeeded. From this tragedy, the university has been able to create a strong and ongoing sense of unity and community. What is more, the campus is now much better in all dimensions—stronger academic and service programs, a more pleasing physical environment, and a deeper sense of mission and purpose..

*Illustration #4.* As at every college and university in the country, the 2001 World Trade Center bombing caused considerable angst and fear on campus. Students, many of whom were too young to have had any real experience with war and the loss that results, questioned how such a thing could have happened and whether such acts of terrorism could somehow be prevented in the future. While feelings and emotions about 9/11 were still quite raw, the chancellor of the University of Denver and I talked about how our campuses together might channel this questioning spirit into an opportunity to engage our campuses and the statewide community in a compelling discussion about our nation and its role in the world. The result was a joint effort, "Bridges to the Future: American History & Values in Light of Sept. 11th," a yearlong series of programs, discussions, and activities that focused on the values we profess as a nation and how those play out in our practices and politics. Through "Bridges," we were able to direct some of the fear and frustration of 9/11 into a renewed sense of civic commitment and responsibility, a spirit that will continue to serve and inspire our state for some time to come.

## CONCLUSION

From each of these crises, our institution was able to emerge stronger and better than it had been before. Why? During a crisis, cynicism, dissent, and resistance are muted or in full retreat. There is, as well, a resolve and unity of purpose that inspire concerted action. At few times can one match the unique opportunity of deft and skillful leadership to harness and direct the shared values that bind and unify a campus community.

Unfortunately, there is no tried and true recipe for successful leadership, no magic formula to make the outcome certain. Still, as each of my examples illustrates, successful leadership involves seizing every opportunity to teach, to listen, and to learn from those with whom we interact. And I also know this: if the pursuit of virtue guides the hands and hearts of those we choose as our leaders, the road ahead holds great promise. Stated once more, good leaders must first be good people. In the end, it really is as simple as that.

As I noted at the beginning of this essay, the climate for contemporary leadership is more combative, more complex, and at times more frustrating than any of us would wish. Clearly, the challenges of leading any large, diverse organization are great, and the personal and professional demands placed on today's leaders are daunting. But in the end, leadership offers unparalleled rewards to those who accept the call. In committing these thoughts to paper, I have had an opportunity during the last days of my presidency to reflect on the past thirteen years—the pleasure and hard work that have helped to bring about a transformation in our campus and its sense of mission and identity. And two of leadership's greatest rewards seem particularly clear to me now: It is a privilege to have the opportunity to be involved in something important and lasting; and it is an honor to be in a position to have an impact on the lives of other people. I am most grateful for both opportunities.

## NOTES

1. Clara M. Lovett, "The Dumbing Down of College Presidents," *The Chronicle of Higher Education*, April 5, 2002.

2. Jacques Steinberg, "Bill Keller, Columnist, Is Selected as the *Times*'s Executive Editor," *New York Times*, July 15, 2003, pp. A1, A16.

3. Warren Bennis and Burt Nanus, *Leaders: The Strategies for Taking Charge* (New York: Harper and Row, 1985), p. 223.

# CHAPTER

## The Importance of Personal Values
### A Response to President Yates' Essay

*William C. Gordon*

As I was reading Al Yates' essay, I was reminded of a statement once made by General Norman Schwartzkopf concerning his view of leadership. To paraphrase his words, "Leadership is a potent combination of strategy and character. But, if you must be without one, be without strategy." Clearly this statement was not intended to minimize the importance of strategic thinking as a component of leadership. Nor does it imply that the learning of certain skills and the development of certain talents are unimportant in the preparation of leaders. However, what this statement does make explicit is that at its core, effective leadership almost always depends on the personal qualities, the personal values, and even the character of those who seek to lead. This, of course, is the very same point that Al Yates makes so eloquently in his essay.

There are several issues raised in Al's presentation that deserve comment, but there are two aspects of the essay that I found particularly interesting. The first is that he was actually willing to use words like "goodness" and "virtue" to describe the essential characteristics of great leaders. These are words that most of us avoid using, particularly when we are commenting on our own qualifications or on the qualifications of our colleagues. These are, after all, words that are difficult to define and states that are difficult to assess. In addition, since most of us are fully aware of our own personal failings, we hesitate to speak as if we are authorities on what it takes to be virtuous or good. Still, today, when there are so many accounts of failed presidencies and failed leadership efforts that seem to be tied in one way or another to matters of virtue, it is probably worthwhile for us to begin to call these essential qualities by their real names, at least when we are talking about leadership in more conceptual or abstract terms.

A second point that I appreciated in this essay was that Al made the effort to define virtue from his own perspective. In his view, virtue is a willingness to embrace and to live by a set of values that includes truth, integrity, competence, commitment, and, above all, compassion. He provides this list of values not so much to convince us that this is the one true list, but to give us a concrete idea of those values and behaviors that he feels are most commonly associated with virtue and, thus, with good leadership. Moreover, it is really this exercise of trying to define virtue that is more important in this case than how it is defined.

As university administrators, we continually seek to recruit students, faculty, staff, and other administrators who have leadership potential, and one of our primary responsibilities is to develop the leadership capabilities of those on our campuses. However, in order to carry out these responsibilities effectively, it is important for us to know what to look for in the people we recruit, and what values we should reinforce within our campus communities. If personal qualities such as virtue really are critical to the conduct of leadership, then it is important that we be able to define these qualities in ways that will allow us to identify them more consistently. That, I think, is the reason Al encourages us to struggle with the question of what it means to be a person of goodness and virtue.

Finally, in giving us his own definition of virtue, Al is careful to say that this is his own definition and that others might well include different values than those he lists. So with that permission, let me suggest one addition to his list. Actually, what I would suggest is not really a value in the strictest sense; it is more a motive or a predisposition that seems to be associated with such values as truth, integrity, competence, commitment, and compassion. What I suggest as one component of virtue and as one contributor to good leadership is the genuine desire to serve others as opposed to serving oneself.

In August 2003, I had the opportunity to attend a leadership forum for student leaders on our campus sponsored by our president, Tom Hearn. The keynote speaker at that event was Tim Auman, Wake Forest's newly appointed chaplain. As it happened, Tim's remarks to the students focused on the distinction between what he called "celebrity leaders," who seek leadership because of the limelight, the status, and the personal benefits associated with such positions, and "servant leaders," who are drawn to leadership positions because of a genuine interest in serving an institution and its people. He did allow that in certain situations, celebrity leaders can lead effectively, particularly when their own personal agendas happen to coincide with the goals of their institutions. However, he argued that it is servant leaders who tend to be more effective, particularly over the longer term.

The examples of leadership Tim talked about in his presentation suggested several ways in which a service orientation might contribute to leadership effectiveness. First, those who desire to serve an institution normally exhibit that desire because they have an affinity and a respect for the institution's core values and principles. As a result, the vision they create for the institution tends to reflect the values of the institution and its people, making that vision more realistic and more attractive to a broader constituency.

Second, servant leaders are often drawn to an institution because of a respect for, a confidence in, or positive feelings about the people within that institution. This increases the likelihood that a servant leader will focus more on the support and development of the institution's people. It makes it more likely that he or she will engage people more fully in decision making and in the process of shaping an institution's future. It even raises the likelihood that a leader will be more prone to share the credit for institutional successes with all those who have really played a role in those successes.

Still another advantage for servant leaders is that their decisions are more likely to be driven by institutional rather than personal concerns. This removes the conflicts of interest many leaders experience, and it makes it much easier to defend and carry through with decisions that have been made.

In effect, some of the very same values Al Yates talks about in his essay—compassion, commitment, and integrity—are the values that most often define those who lead out of a desire to serve. It is not clear whether a service orientation grows out of these core values or whether effective leaders manifest these values because of their service orientation. However, this quality of desiring to serve might well be a quality to look for as we seek to identify leaders for our campuses or as we seek to develop the leadership capabilities of those in our campus communities.

# CHAPTER 17

# Vision, Transparency, and Passion
## A Response to President Yates' Essay

*David C. Hardesty*

I think it vital for those of us "immersed in the day-to-day activity of taking people from one place to another," as Dr. Yates would say, to share our experiences. Howard Gardner said that telling stories is one of the most effective tools for a leader. Dr. Yates' reflections on his own experiences made his essay especially insightful for other leaders.

We learn about leadership both through a vast literature that includes theoretical reviews, case studies, and biographies and through our daily experiences. As we accumulate experiences, our readings become more meaningful.

In this essay, I respond to Dr. Yates by using both my experiences and the insights of others gained through reading.

All of my remarks are predicated on strong agreement with the axiom of his essay, and that is that leaders must first be good people. Like the Golden Rule, the simplicity gives Dr. Yates' theme timeless strength. It has been my experience that trust and integrity are among the most admired traits of leaders. Virtue, however defined and perceived, goes a long way to getting leaders over rough spots in the road. I can think of many examples where leaders have made mistakes, have misspoken, or have even taken a few misguided steps. Where those leaders have had the confidence of their constituents, they have been largely excused for temporarily failing to meet expectations—for being human. What is not excused, and what can rightfully destroy credibility, is a perceived breach of trust or lack of integrity.

Against this backdrop, Dr. Yates teases out a number of lessons—a few of which I want to underscore.

First, I want to lift up Dr. Yates' assertion that leaders need to have an understanding of their environment, a vision for where we ought to go and, most of all, integrity in their decision making.

In recent years, I have been thinking a lot about the term "transparency" in connection with leadership. I agree with Dr. Yates that in a large complex organization like a university, the traits of integrity, competence, commitment, and compassion are evidenced, or not, by the actions and the words of its leaders. I think organizations easily sense when a leader is inconsistent in his or her commitment, or when the leader's integrity seems dependent on convenience.

Law judges render opinions. The reasons for their decisions provide the moral support undergirding the rule of law. Leaders also make decisions daily, and I think that the reasons for those decisions should be as obvious as the judge's reasoning. In fact, the reasoning of the leader should be so obvious as to give clear guidance to other members of the leadership team and constituencies that their own decisions clearly align with the organization's previously announced mission, vision, values, goals, and objectives.

To the degree that everyone in an organization is a leader, and I believe this is especially true in higher education, it is important to be transparent—absolutely clear—about what you value and what you expect. Dr. Yates makes this point as well by positing that progress is accelerated when a leader is able to affect a common understanding of culture and values.

I became president of West Virginia University a little over eight years ago. It is not important to detail the environment I observed, other than to say I left little doubt among the university's constituents about what the core value of the institution would be: student-centeredness. The simplicity of this value made it robust enough to serve as a common denominator for decision making across campus. I later expanded the value to one of being "other-centered," which had added relevance for our hospitals and extension service. The point was that we had to be outwardly focused on those we serve: students, patients, research partners, 4-H members, and the many others who depend on a land-grant university like WVU. By giving the decision-making process this kind of centrifugal force, the values, mission, and goals of the organization more easily aligned and the rewards came back in spades.

Second, Dr. Yates causes us to reflect on change at different points in his essay. Society changes—it inevitably changes. In many respects, what we do is accommodate societal change on our campuses. We actually model changes and should do so constantly. There are very few institutions (the church and government come to mind) that are as interactive with society as are universities. We are usually the first to understand the implication of significant events, such as the dawn of the Internet, the launching of the genome project, or the war in Iraq. For this reason, what happens on campuses is often a reflection of and a facilitator for what will happen next in society. This certainly presents the opportunity for those of us in higher education to help bring about the changes we clearly see as needed in society.

As Dr. Yates shared through stories, a leader will need the courage to persevere, especially when the need for change is not readily supported. This courage can come from unexpected sources—a letter, a friend, a book, or a family member. One of the most memorable examples in my experiences occurred several years ago when I proposed putting faculty in the residence halls to serve as academic mentors for our freshmen. As you might expect, there was some initial skepticism from those who did not believe the role of a university extended outside the classroom. During a faculty meeting where I was fielding criticisms for the proposal, I asked how many in the room had sons or daughters attending WVU. Only a few hands went up. I asked how many had sons or daughters in the residence halls. One hand remained up, and that faculty member said, "Implement this plan as fast as you can." Today, the resident faculty leader program is one of the hallmarks of our campus. That faculty member helped give me the courage to persevere.

Of course, leaders do not always have the opportunity to set forth methodically a case of change. I am reminded of John F. Kennedy's response when a little boy asked him how he got to be a hero. He simply said, "Son, they shot my boat out from under me." Dr. Yates suggests that out of crisis can come our most notable achievements and enduring changes.

I think it is helpful to distinguish between what causes insights about what needs to be done on the one hand, and how we actually get things done on the other. The onset of a crisis can help us see our needs clearly. But planning how to respond is equally as important as the recognition of the need to change. Often, the decisions will be real-time, made without the benefit of complete information. Remember, General Eisenhower said the first thing he had to do when the troops hit the beach at Normandy was to throw out some of their plans. But they would not have reached the beach without a plan. As leadership scholars Heifetz and Linsky say, "A plan is today's best guess. Tomorrow you discover the unanticipated effects of today's actions and adjust."[1] I believe that Dr. Yates would remind us that while plans may change dramatically, the integrity of leaders and the values on which they base decisions should not.

Third, I echo Dr. Yates' strong commitment to diversity—expressed in both his words and his deeds. Dr. Yates asserted that "The value of surrounding oneself with a diverse group of people cannot be overstated. . . . When different talents and insights are brought to bear on a problem, we increase our odds of making the best choice for the institution." Different insights and talents are rooted in one's learning style. Similarly, Howard Gardner asserts that there are seven intelligences and that none of us possesses them equally.[2]

About seven years ago, our provost requested that all of us on our leadership team be tested for leadership proclivities and talents. We took a leadership style inventory developed by Bernice McCarthy.[3] What we found was that our leadership team was in fact diverse, not only in color and background but also in our approaches to problems. We expect our provost to ask for data, because he is highly analytical. We have others who simply shout, "Let's go! Let's at least try this," without really thinking through the practicalities. We also confirmed that once we decide where we want to go, we have some who are best at actually getting the tasks done. We even have dreamers among us.

Most importantly, we found that we need all of our distinct "voices" in the room to best address critical issues. We try to remember this in the hiring process. For this reason, at the beginning of every search, we do not say that we are simply going to replace the person who has retired or left the campus. We ask rather, "How shall we redefine this job now that we have the opportunity to do so? What kind of leadership qualities does the team need now?"

Fourth, in talking about humility, I think Dr. Yates is advising us to recognize the limitations of our own abilities as leaders. We cannot fix everything and must rely on the contributions of others, especially those that simply ground us in the gravity of our own flaws. To this point articulated well by Dr. Yates, I would like to add an insight from Ronald Heifetz and Marty Linsky's book entitled *Leadership on the Line*. I was so impressed with this book that our university cosponsored a statewide forum on leadership and used various chapters of the book as the topics for breakout sessions. The authors differentiate between technical and adaptive problems. Technical problems are those that can be readily resolved. Leadership on technical problems is derived from expertise. If our facilities do not meet our needs, we generally know what to do.

Adaptive problems are different. They require cultural change that people will often perceive as imposing a loss. Resolution requires engaging people in the process, communicating, consensus building, lifting up values, addressing the organizational culture, setting clear goals—all the faculties expected of a leader. A department's culture is not centered on students. This is an adaptive problem that will require fundamental changes within the culture of the organization.

Heifetz and Linsky suggest that some of a leader's biggest failures are caused by treating an adaptive problem as a technical problem. Perhaps too often, leaders fail to differentiate when they should use authority or rely on the authority of others and when they should use their facilitation skills. I think this relates to the humility that Dr. Yates advises will serve us well.

I want to add my own spin to Dr. Yates' encouragement that things can always get worse. A former law partner of mine said to me after I lost a case, "Dave, things are never as bad as they seem or as good as they seem." I have repeated this same life lesson to myself too many times to count, and it has both lifted me up and kept me grounded. It reminds me not to get too down or too confident.

Lastly, I want to end by amplifying Dr. Yates' theme of passion—the fire in the belly for what we do. Passion, which I believe is beyond commitment, gives us stamina.

Dr. Yates reminds us that "in the end, leadership offers unparalleled rewards to those who accept the call." I am at a university because I experienced the transformational education of three universities and have been associated in supporting one of them all of my adult life. As a result, my wife and I, both of whom are graduates of our institution, feel a strong passion for doing the very best job we can. We also feel humbled by the extent to which others depend on us. In the end, we have come to know that we are simply common people trying to do the common-sense thing in a position of uncommon responsibility.

Mark Twain, in *Life on the Mississippi*, writes about the importance of reminding each other of the passion that first drew us to our field. He remembered his early days as a riverboat captain and how exhilarating it was to be on the river, experiencing the beautiful elements of nature on the mighty Mississippi: the ripples in the water glistening under the sunset, the canopy of branches lining the bend. Later in his life, however, he came to regard the eddies in the water, the onset of darkness, and the branches over the river as constant threats to his boat. He dreaded these sights. He had forgotten what drew him to the river in the first place: his love for the work.

Many of us have been in higher education for a long time and have been presidents for many years. I still get as excited for new student orientation and commencement as I did my first year. I still jump at the chance to recruit a student or write a reference for one of my former students. I still cherish the times I get to talk to alumni who share stories of campus and their successes in life. We all feel run down from time to time, and every person has days when responsibilities overshadow one's spirit. But I encourage all of us to remember why we came to the river in the first place. We came to positions of leadership because higher education transforms lives, and in doing so, it has made America a great nation and a better place.

## NOTES

1. Ronald A. Heifetz and Marty Linsky, *Leadership on the Line: Staying Alive through the Dangers of Leading* (Boston, MA: Harvard Business School Press, 2002), p. 73.

2. More information about Howard Gardner's theory of multiple intelligences is available at http://www.howardgardner.com/.

3. More information about the Bernice McCarthy Inventory is available at http://www.aboutlearning.com/.

# CHAPTER

# Moral Leadership: Promoting High Achievement among Minority Students in Science

*Freeman H. Hrabowski III*

I am now in my thirteenth year as president, following the strong leadership of my predecessor and mentor, the late Michael Hooker, who helped establish minority student achievement as a high priority for the campus. During these years, our campus climate has shifted dramatically from one that routinely included black student protests to one that now celebrates high academic achievement among all of our students, including African Americans.

This essay focuses on my leadership experience working to increase the number of underrepresented minorities who excel in science and engineering.

Our challenge was great. Thirteen years ago, few African American students succeeded in science and engineering. Their grade point averages were slightly below 2.0, compared with 2.5 for whites and Asians. Admittedly, many of these students lacked the background needed to succeed—not simply in terms of high school grades, but also in study habits, attitudes about course work, and a willingness to accept advice about balancing school work, outside interests, and part-time employment.

With strong faculty leadership and generous support from Baltimore philanthropists Robert and Jane Meyerhoff, who were particularly interested in addressing the academic plight of young African American men, we launched the Meyerhoff Scholars Program in 1988. Collectively, the program's components created an environment that continually challenges and supports students, from their pre-freshman summer through graduation and beyond. Program components are the substance of the initiative: (1) recruiting top minority students in math and science, culminating in an on-campus selection weekend involving faculty, staff, and student peers; (2) providing a summer bridge program that includes math, science, and humanities coursework, training in analytic problem solving, group study, and social and cultural events; (3) offering comprehensive merit scholarship support and making continued support contingent on maintaining at least a B average in a science, mathematics, or engineering major; (4) actively involving faculty in recruiting, teaching, and mentoring the Meyerhoff students; (5) emphasizing strong programmatic values, including outstanding academic achievement, study groups, collegiality, and preparation for graduate or professional school; (6) involving the Meyerhoff students in sustained, substantive summer research experiences; (7) encouraging all students to take advantage of departmental and university tutoring resources in order to optimize course performance; (8) providing academic advising and personal counseling; (9) ensuring the university administration's active involvement and support and soliciting strong public support; (10) linking the Meyerhoff Scholars with mentors from professional and academic science and engineering fields; (11) encouraging a strong sense of community among the students (staff regularly conduct group meetings with students, and students live in the same residence halls during their freshman year); (12) involving the students' parents and other relatives who can be supportive; and (13) continuously evaluating and documenting program outcomes (e.g., studies funded by the Sloan Foundation and the National Science Foundation).[1]

By all measures, the program's positive outcomes are striking. Approximately 600 competitively selected undergraduates have enrolled since the first class of 19 Meyerhoff Scholars began the program in the fall of 1989. Since the first group of graduates in 1993, nearly 400 Meyerhoff students have earned degrees in science and engineering disciplines, with 85 percent matriculating into graduate and professional programs at institutions nationwide. Approximately 20 have earned MD/PhDs, 40 have earned MDs, and 40 have completed graduate engineering degrees. As of fall 2004, approximately 200 students were enrolled in the program. In 1999, the University of Maryland, Baltimore County, ranked first in the nation in the number of undergraduate biochemistry degrees awarded to African Americans, producing nearly one-third of the national total. It also ranked second in the number of undergraduate biochemistry degrees awarded to minority students in general, and fourth in the number of undergraduate biochemistry degrees awarded.[2] Most important, the program's graduates are part of a pipeline of minority and female doctors of philosophy, doctors of medicine, and MD/PhDs. Our evaluation also shows that graduates of the program are nearly twice as likely to persist and graduate in a science and engineering discipline than their student peers who declined offers of admission to the program and chose instead to enroll at other universities.

## LESSONS IN LEADERSHIP

From this gratifying experience several lessons emerge.

**1. Involve the top leadership.** It is easy to tell how important an issue is to a campus by looking to see who "the players" are and who takes ownership of addressing the issue. To what extent are the president, provost, and appropriate deans, chairs, and faculty involved? These and other senior campus leaders have instrumental roles to play in creating a healthy institutional environment that promotes the high academic achievement of all students, including minorities. From everyday actions to symbolic gestures, the president and others can set the tone for the campus climate, providing and demonstrating their strong commitment in visible ways.

**2. Build trust and confidence; focus on principles and values most important to the campus.** Get to know many of the faculty and their research interests, the academic challenges facing different groups of students, and people's perceptions of one another. Equally important, faculty, students, and staff came to know me and my passion for excellence; my own research interest in increasing the numbers of students, especially minorities and women, in science and engineering; and my strong belief that universities are responsible for helping students grow both intellectually and personally. I also knew that in order to build trust and confidence, my messages needed to reflect honesty, fairness, and consistency, and that the difficult decisions we had to make needed to be based on widely accepted principles reflecting the university's mission and values. It was imperative, for example, that when we made the difficult decision to eliminate our graduate program in African American Studies in response to externally imposed budget cuts, people knew that my motives were honorable and that the decision reflected the fact that we simply lacked sufficient resources to be all things to all people and to be excellent in all areas. Given our research strengths in science, engineering, and public policy, certain programs were clearly a better fit than others in the light of severe budget constraints.

**3. Identify allies among leading faculty and influential administrators who can be supportive of change.** We looked to leading faculty and influential administrators who would take ownership of the changes. We involved them in ongoing informal discussions about possible strategies, practices, and approaches to changing attitudes and raising expectations of all constituents. For example, at the time, the new chair of our chemistry department, who had been a professor in the medical school at Johns Hopkins University, honestly believed in the potential of talented minority students to succeed in science, and she was very helpful in focusing on strategies to improve their performance and that of all undergraduates. In my interactions with her and other leading faculty, I learned the importance of striking a balance between showing my strong interest in academic issues and the need to have faculty at the forefront of discussions and resulting actions.

**4. Aggressively and strategically pursue external partnerships and funding, appealing to both the public and private sectors in order to augment institutional resources.** It is essential to cultivate effective public and private partnerships. There is no substitute for providing entrepreneurial leadership, and in order to do so, the institution must clearly understand its mission, its strategic strengths and programmatic niches, its capacity, the broader community's needs, and the interdependent environment in which it operates. Most important, perhaps, is the institutional attitude or mindset.

**5. Recruit and support faculty and administrators of color, or who are women, to reflect the diversity of the student population.** We have focused on these objectives and were among a small number of universities to receive both a multimillion dollar advance grant from the National Science Foundation, in recognition of our strengths in preparing women in science and engineering, and a major grant through NSF's Alliances for Graduate Education and the Professoriate Program (AGEP) to prepare more minority doctors of philosophy in science.

**6. Take the lead in talking about the growing diversity on our campuses.** Recognizing the need to discuss challenging issues is often the first step in providing leadership; facilitating substantive discussions with fellow administrators, faculty, and students is critical. It has been important for me to show an interest in minority science and engineering student performance by being present at activities, raising questions, and talking about the issue's significance. More recently, we have been focusing greater attention on supporting women faculty in science and engineering disciplines and increasing participation of women in these fields (as well as that of domestic Americans of all races). We have found that what we have done to increase minority participation has proven helpful in addressing issues involving women faculty and students. We have been collecting and discussing data on representation of women students and faculty by department and conducting focus groups to learn more about their perspectives on instruction, academic support, and research opportunities.

**7. Visit other campuses to learn from other effective models.** I had the opportunity to speak at the tenth anniversary of Georgia Tech's Focus Program, designed to recruit outstanding minority science and engineering graduate students. On the basis of that model, my campus developed a similar initiative several years ago, the Horizons Program, which has been very effective in substantially increasing our minority graduate enrollment. Wayne Clough has provided both strong presidential leadership and a highly successful minority graduate recruitment model at Georgia Tech.

**8. Emphasize the importance of helping minority students, particularly those in their first year (freshmen, transfers, and new graduate students), to feel welcome on the campus and to become engaged.** This area, in particular, reflects the change in campus culture that has occurred over the past decade. In fact, our success in sensitizing the campus to the needs of first-year minority students has paid dividends for all first-year students, whose initial experiences both inside and outside the classroom are much more closely monitored by faculty and staff. First-year retention rates are strong for both white and minority students, with minority students actually enjoying slightly higher rates.

**9. Encourage faculty and staff—minority and majority—to talk about issues involving minority students and to interact with the students beyond the classroom.** I have found that in healthier campus cultures, people talk honestly about difficult issues, including race and academic performance, countering unhealthy resistance to change. Campuses with healthy cultures also find time to celebrate the successes of minority students and faculty. For example, we have celebrated the publication of faculty–student teams' research findings in refereed science journals by framing enlarged reproductions of the journal covers and displaying them and pictures of the teams throughout the campus. Some of our most highly regarded science faculty work closely in their labs with minority students, not only mentoring these students and helping them prepare for graduate school and research careers, but also serving as influential models for their faculty peers.

Regarding campus culture, I recently gave an address at another institution's fall opening session for faculty and staff. The president had arranged for a group of students, including minorities, to talk with faculty and staff about their experiences on that campus. Some students talked about how isolated they had felt at the beginning of their freshman year and how close they had come to leaving because they did not think they could fit in or succeed. However, what was especially encouraging about the students' experiences was that many of them could point to an individual faculty or staff member who had been critical to their success because the individual had established a personal relationship with them. The significance of this session was that the students were given the opportunity to talk about their experiences (and they made suggestions about how to help other students on the campus) and, most important, that faculty and administrators heard new perspectives on this critical topic. The key point is that the campus' senior leadership understood that everyone—faculty, staff, and students—needed to hear these students firsthand. Ideally, we also need to hear from those students who are not successful, including their perspectives and suggestions for improving their academic experience.

It may sound obvious, but it is important that presidents and other campus leaders take the time to understand the experiences of minorities (students and faculty) on the campus. (One of the lessons we have learned is that what works for minority students also tends to work for students in general.) Presidents also should consider language they can use to create high expectations for minority students and to encourage these students to become engaged on the campus. It is critical, too, for presidents and other leaders to be vocal about encouraging faculty and staff to work with minority students to ensure that they get the appropriate academic and personal support they need in order to be challenged.

Talking about the perspectives of minority students can be a sensitive matter. Even among high-achieving African American students, I found that they often had been encouraged by others to think of themselves as victims. In fact, one of the comments I most often heard when I arrived on campus in 1987 was that "this is a racist place." My colleagues and I worked closely with these students to change this mindset and to let them know how much was expected of them academically. In fact, in conversations with these students, I finally began to respond that we will find prejudice wherever we go and that they needed to understand that despite factors beyond their control—racism, discrimination, low expectations by some in society—they can control their own destiny and thus beat the odds. My suggestion to these students over and over was that nothing takes the place of hard work and knowledge and that even if someone on campus held stereotypical negative perceptions of them, that person would ultimately come to respect them if they were able to do the academic work. I felt comfortable assuring these students that the vast majority of people on the campus wanted them to succeed.

## FINAL THOUGHTS

So, based on my own experiences and observations, what practices have I found to be most helpful as a leader? Here are some of the most important lessons I have learned: being passionate about my work; having an active presence both on and off campus; focusing on both the substantive and the symbolic; demonstrating genuine intellectual curiosity about issues (even when I am tired); focusing on the best ideas and helping to broaden others' thinking and to avoid parochialism; encouraging, even pushing, colleagues and myself to look in the mirror, focusing heavily on self-examination of our problem-solving efforts; encouraging ongoing interaction between the campus and effective external leaders; introducing best practices in academic and administrative areas that advance the institution's mission; showing appreciation for the efforts and accomplishments of colleagues and students; and communicating priorities through deliberate use of both time and language.

I often read and talk about literature on leadership to gain other perspectives on why what we are doing is, or is not, working. For example, in *What Leaders Really Do,* John Kotter emphasizes several strategies we have found applicable—the importance of creating a sense of urgency, developing and broadly communicating one's vision, and taking time to talk with people to ask questions, cajole, and persuade—helping others to take ownership of an issue.[3]

Finally, in *Geeks and Geezers: How Era, Values, and Defining Moments Shape Leaders,* Bennis and Thomas emphasize, above all, the importance of leaders being passionate about what they do.[4] The geeks are outstanding American leaders under twenty-five years old, and the geezers are leaders seventy years of age and older. What the authors discover is that "every one of the geezers who continues to play a leadership role has one quality of overriding importance: neoteny. The dictionary defines neoteny . . . as 'the retention of youthful qualities by adults.' Neoteny is more than retaining a youthful appearance, although that is often part of it. Neoteny is the retention of all those wonderful qualities that we associate with youth: curiosity, playfulness, eagerness, fearlessness, warmth, energy. . . . Our geezers have remained much like our geeks— open, willing to take risks, hungry for knowledge and experience, courageous, eager to see what the new day brings. Neoteny is a metaphor for the quality—the gift—that keeps the fortunate of whatever age focused on all the marvelous undiscovered things to come."[5] Though my colleagues and I are not quite geezers, we have been successful largely because of just this attitude.

## NOTES

1. K. Maton, F. Hrabowski, and C. Schmitt, "African American College Students Excelling in the Sciences: College and Postcollege Outcomes in the Meyerhoff Scholars Program," *Journal of Research in Science Teaching* 37, no. 7 (2000): 629–654.

2. American Society of Biochemistry and Molecular Biology, "Graduation Survey," *ASBMS News* (January–February 2000). In 1999, UMBC awarded twenty-one of the sixty-seven undergraduate biochemistry degrees earned by African Americans in the nation. It also awarded forty-five undergraduate biochemistry degrees to minority students, the second highest number nationally, and seventy-two undergraduate biochemistry degrees overall, the fourth highest number (tied with Yale).

3. John P. Kotter, *What Leaders Really Do* (Boston: Harvard Business School Press, 1999).

4. Warren G. Bennis and Robert J. Thomas, *Geeks and Geezers: How Era, Values, and Defining Moments Shape Leaders* (Boston: Harvard University School Press, 2002).

5. Ibid., p. 20.

# CHAPTER

# Building Trust for Enduring Change
## A Response to President Hrabowski's Essay

*Pamela Shockley-Zalabak*

I am always inspired when I listen to Freeman Hrabowski and the passion he brings to challenges that matter. This is my second opportunity to learn about his efforts to promote high achievement among minority students in science. I am particularly appreciative of the way he describes leading change during troubled times. His essay reminds me how important it is to understand the presidency as both role and process.

In squarely addressing the need for achievement in the sciences among minority students (and all students for that matter), Freeman Hrabowski was tackling a complex issue that could make a substantial difference in individual lives and in supporting the core values of his institution. In so doing, I think he stimulates all of us to ask ourselves a key question: "Are we moving on the issues that will make a real difference?" He encourages us to think about our individual roles in stimulating change and also to think about the broad processes necessary to align institutional practices with needed change and core values.

History, research, experience, and conventional wisdom all teach us that sustained large-scale change is hard. I like what President Hrabowski says about ownership of change, "It is easy to tell how important an issue is to a campus by looking to see who 'the players' are and who takes ownership of addressing the issue." Certainly ownership of the major changes President Hrabowski envisioned was key in his role as president and to long-term success. But as he suggests, it takes more than that. Ownership has to translate into building a climate of organizational trust that sustains change efforts over long periods of time. This is what I characterize as the process of the presidency. How do we envision our own role in addressing challenging issues, and then how do we use our role to stimulate processes that make a difference? Our role and institutional processes are not the same thing. Our personal integrity and trustworthiness do not automatically translate into organizational trust necessary to stimulate productive change.

Earlier in this volume, several contributors talked about the importance of personal integrity, moral character, and trustworthiness as critical for leadership. I do not discount that and I certainly agree. But I do believe, as President Hrabowski's story illustrates, that personal characteristics and integrity are necessary but insufficient to generate a climate, a culture, and an imperative to work on challenging issues necessitating change. That is where the people and practices of the institution become the process of the presidency. It becomes our individual responsibility (role) to think and act to generate personal trust. But it is also our responsibility to contribute to a sense of organizational trust necessary to meet significant challenges. This is where we engage diverse constituencies, institutional practices, policies, values, visions, and political realities.

This notion of organizational trust is somewhat illusive to be sure. However, a growing body of research (and I have had the privilege of contributing to some of this work) suggests that institutions where trust levels are high are better able to respond to an ever-changing landscape, whether it is a crisis, unexpected adversity, or new opportunities. In thinking about President Hrabowski's experience I want to focus on what I believe (supported by practical experience and research) are key considerations in building organizational trust necessary to support a climate and culture for productive change. They involve but are not limited to five key practices and processes: competence, consistency, concern, openness and honesty, and identification.

## COMPETENCE

How does the president exhibit competence? Scott Cowen talked about moral, intellectual, executive, and political leadership. It is all of that and more. It is the people we hire, the people we fire, the technical aspects of the job, and the visions we contribute to setting. It is more than being individually competent. It is a subtle but important perception that we as a collective are moving in worthy and attainable directions. We cannot trust an institution that cannot support and attain its values and vision.

## CONSISTENCY

Change, crisis, and adversity bring uncertainty. Uncertainty can generate resistance to change, yield negative outcomes, or stimulate needed creativity. Consistency during uncertainty can contribute to organizational trust necessary to support productive change. Do we consistently examine and communicate how the change fits with the basic values of the institution? Do we consistently demonstrate the difference between our principles supporting change and the practices that need to change? And is that consistency demonstrated from others involved with the change? In some ways, consistency becomes constancy in our organizational commitment to change. Consistency should not be confused with requiring false agreement but rather should demonstrate a constancy of purpose so that even those who disagree come to trust that change will occur.

## CONCERN

How does the leadership of the change exhibit concern for those impacted by change and for the vision of change? How are those who disagree treated? What forums are available to give voice to resistance? President Hrabowski talked about the difficulty of program elimination while moving forward on minority achievement in the sciences. He exhibited concern for students by setting high expectations. President Hrabowski talked about the reasons often given for students not doing well in the sciences, that is, poor high school preparation coupled with hours worked while taking a full class load. But he also engaged faculty to express concern for assigning the best faculty to freshman science courses, giving more feedback prior to midterms, and emphasizing the importance of such practices as group study and tutorial sessions. These expressions of concern are excellent examples of building momentum necessary for productive change.

## OPENNESS AND HONESTY

This hardly seems worth our notice. Of course openness and honesty are important for trust. But the evidence tells another story. The evidence of behaviors suggests that during uncertainty, many leaders are open and honest, but only with a very select few people. Perhaps it goes to the notion that leaders are supposed to know what is going to happen or to produce the desired results. During challenging change, results often take a long time. How open and honest are we during the turbulence of change? How do we evaluate our behaviors and institutional practices for a transparency necessary to help generate trust that we are moving toward our desired vision? How can we communicate the necessity for any alternations that must occur along the way? Of course, we have visible numerous recent examples where openness and honesty were obviously not intended. For organizational trust, however, the issue is more often that openness and honesty are limited to an inner circle, which stimulates concern and doubt in the larger community.

## IDENTIFICATION

Evidence abounds that when individuals identify with the values of the institution, there is a strong likelihood that change can occur. President Hrabowski talked about the importance of identification when he discussed his own role of leadership with the Meyerhoff program and in his efforts to identify others on campus with influence and the willingness to commit time and energy to these efforts. The key here is to advance fundamental change in ways that are consistent with the overall values of the institution. In some ways, it is a form of helping constituents understand that to stay the same (support the core) we must change (alter the practices).

Perhaps this notion of organizational trust seems like a lot of work, and it is. But I think that the lack of significant productive change calls for a revised perspective. I am convinced that President Hrabowski was successful because he had a sense that his role was not just to express his support for change but to develop and initiate processes that would build a climate and culture of trust for change. He was responsible for the role of president and the process of the presidency. The passion of the leader may bring near-term results, but I would offer that enduring productive change rests on infusing passion throughout the institution. Perhaps organizational trust is really the trust of many stimulated by the trust of one. It is yet another way to envision the role and process of the presidency.

# CHAPTER

# The Morality of Shared Responsibility: Preserving Quality through Program Elimination

*William E. Kirwan*

In the spring of 1988, the Maryland General Assembly enacted a major piece of legislation restructuring public higher education in the state. For decades, the state had maintained two independent systems of higher education institutions: five degree-granting campuses of the University of Maryland and eight comprehensive campuses of a state college and university system. Each system operated under the authority of a governing board.

As a result of the 1988 legislation, these two systems were merged into a single entity known as the University System of Maryland with a single governing board. The legislature was careful to differentiate the missions of the various campuses in the new system and designated the University of Maryland, College Park, as the state's flagship university mandated to "maintain programs and faculty that are nationally and internationally renowned." The legislation also designated College Park as the state's number one higher education funding priority, calling for it to have a funding level comparable to the best-funded public universities in the nation.

Over the previous two decades, College Park had made steady progress in advancing the quality of its programs, especially its graduate programs. By the end of the 1980s, it could boast of eight to ten programs ranked among the top twenty-five (public and private universities) according to the National Research Council's decennial rankings. It also had a top rated honors program that attracted exceptional students, but its regular admissions programs were not generally seen as a "top choice" by talented high school graduates in Maryland.

As president of the University of Maryland, College Park, at the time, I worked to achieve and enthusiastically greeted the actions of the General Assembly, and the entire campus community looked forward with great excitement as to what we would accomplish. These feelings were reinforced by a generous budget appropriation for the academic year 1989–1990 and by the initial appropriation for 1990–1991. Unprecedented levels of investments were made in core programs. Faculty and student recruiting surged. Morale was high. The future seemed bright. And then something totally unexpected happened.

Early in the fall semester of 1990, a phone call came from the state's budget officer explaining that Maryland's tax receipts were unexpectedly down and the budget was out of balance. Since the state's constitution requires a balanced budget, he explained that funds from the initial 1990–1991 appropriation would have to be withdrawn. We were assured that this preemptive action would fix the problem and things would soon get back to normal. Quite the opposite occurred.

As it turned out, Maryland was at the leading edge of the early 1990s national economic downturn, and the state's economy got worse, not better. Over the course of two years, the university's budget was cut a half dozen times. By the time the "bleeding" stopped, General Fund support had been reduced by 20 percent, or $40 million. The euphoria that ushered in the new legislation was replaced by despair. While budget cuts are always a blow to campus morale, their impact is multiplied when they occur so closely on the heels of generous commitments and heightened expectations.

The university's leadership was faced with a difficult dilemma: how to maintain the university's aspirations and the progress toward its ambitious goals in the face of such a dramatic reversal of fortunes. The moral principles emphasized, the actions taken, and the process followed are the subject of this essay, offered with the hope that there are relevant lessons to be learned for the current economic crises facing so many colleges and universities.

## THE PATH FORWARD

As the cuts mounted, I quickly recognized that we faced both a short-term and a long-term problem: the need to balance the budget by the end of the fiscal year and the need to begin a process to stabilize program budgets, protect our priorities, and restore a sense of momentum to the campus community. For any university, there are few choices available to address the short-term problem—freeze hiring, withdraw vacant lines, recapture uncommitted operating expenses, defer maintenance, and so forth. With the pressing urgency for securing funds, such steps cannot adequately protect programmatic priorities. Funds must be found wherever they exist. (N.B. In those days, universities in Maryland were not permitted to maintain a reserve to address emergency fiscal situations. Fortunately, that operational constraint has now been removed.)

The greater test and challenge was to demonstrate to both the internal and external communities that the university's aspirations for excellence would not be curtailed. Additionally, we needed to demonstrate that even though the state had to suspend its commitment to the enhancement of the university, the university would find a way to maintain its momentum until the state's economy rebounded. Tuition was, of course, one source of revenue that the university could tap—and it did so through larger than normal increases. Compounding the problem, however, was the fact that the university had just begun an enrollment reduction plan, supported by the state in its halcyon budget days, whereby undergraduate enrollment was to be reduced by 20 percent over five years, with the state providing additional funds to offset the loss of tuition revenue. Through a rather transparent "shell game," the state was able to claim that it met this commitment to the enrollment plan throughout the economic downturn. The enrollment reduction plan, though a huge challenge given the resource realities, was extremely important for the university and was a prime example of why we needed to find resources to invest in our strategic priorities.

It was clear both practically and politically that the university could not rely on tuition increases alone to sustain its momentum. We needed to look within our existing resources to determine how we could shift funds from programs of lower priority to those of higher priority. Administrative and service programs were given specific and ambitious targets for reallocation.

Of course, as is the case today, most of a university's budget is in its academic programs and that—both then and now—is a much tougher nut to crack. Unless it is cracked, however, the amount available for reallocation is modestly incremental.

Thus, it was decided that we had to take a comprehensive look at substantial program reductions, closures, and eliminations. Given the shared governance traditions on the campus, it was also clear that this could only occur with the active participation and collaboration of the campus senate.

## THE PROCESS

As we began the reallocation process, two principles became self-evident. First, the Senate leadership would need to be engaged from the start and have substantial input at each major step along the way. Fortunately, the Senate leadership was invested in the high aspirations of the university administration and became an important partner in the reallocation and restructuring effort.

The second overarching principle was that the effort would require extraordinary patience. We could handle the short-term budget issues. It was the long-term planning that we had to get right and make a success through a shared responsibility with the larger campus community.

From the start, there were several objectives in mind. First and foremost, we needed funds to invest so that we could sustain and enhance the quality of our best programs and protect our highest priorities, such as the enrollment reduction plan. Equally important, we needed to demonstrate to the campus community that the administration was serious about continuing the drive for excellence and was willing to make tough-minded decisions to move toward the university's shared aspirations. There was also a third objective. We wanted to send a signal to the state about the depth of our commitment to building excellence, thereby positioning ourselves as a university worthy of renewed investment when the economy rebounded.

The first step was to convene the Senate Executive Committee, review the state of the budget, and impress on committee members the damage that would be done if we allowed our cuts to be across the board. I emphasized the need to take significant actions to reallocate resources among the academic programs, even if this meant eliminating some departments. I explained that major shifts of resources would be done through a careful process of review that would include the Senate as an active participant. I asked the Senate to provide me with a set of criteria to be used in the consideration of major program reductions or eliminations. The Senate was eager to support the effort. The criteria they produced (in record time) proved to be extremely valuable and included the following: the quality of programs as measured by the National Research Council and other reputable ranking studies, the programs' centrality to the university's mission, enrollment demand for programs, and the impact program reductions would have on our service commitments to the state and on minorities and women. The establishment of these criteria before the program review process began gave the process added credibility.

The second step was to create a sixteen-member Academic Planning Advisory Committee (APAC) to advise the provost and me as we began the detailed review of where program reductions should occur. The majority of this group was composed of leading faculty members representing a cross-section of academic programs at the university. It also included two deans, two department chairs, a Senate representative, and two student leaders.

Once the criteria were developed by the Senate, the provost asked each dean to develop a report indicating how they would accommodate permanent budget reductions of up to 10 percent. The deans were instructed that they could not make across-the-board cuts, that their recommendations had to follow the Senate's guidelines, and that their recommendations had to be based on considerable input from the college community.

While the colleges were developing their plans, APAC was reviewing extensive data on the colleges and departments, including quality indicators and enrollment trends. By the time the college reports were submitted, APAC was in a position to give informed advice and counsel to the provost. The provost developed a preliminary set of recommendations and submitted them to me on March 1, 1991, six months after my initial meeting with the Senate Executive Committee and seven months after our first budget cut.

The provost's initial recommendations included the elimination of two dozen degree programs, seven academic departments, and a college. It was made clear that an effort would be made to find all tenured faculty in eliminated departments new tenured homes in related disciplines and that courses in programs recommended for elimination would be continued for a reasonable period of time to allow currently enrolled students to complete their degrees.

Needless to say, the program elimination recommendations were met with mixed feelings on and off the campus. Many applauded the boldness of the decisions while others, including most especially alumni, faculty, and students from the affected programs, raised a howl of complaint. Most will agree in the abstract that program eliminations in the face of budget exigencies are a worthy thing to consider. However, as soon as a specific program is named, detractors abound. Demonstrations, led largely by alumni and students, took place in front of the administration building on several occasions, and letter writing campaigns were launched.

As part of the initial planning process, we had decided that once programs were recommended for elimination and departments were recommended for closure, open hearings would be held so that the affected

units could make their case for continuation. APAC selected faculty review committees for each department recommended for elimination.
These committees continued to study the data on the departments, held
open hearings (to which members of the Senate Committee on Programs
and Curricula were invited), and sought advice from national experts in
the affected disciplines. This phase of the process continued over the
summer and into the fall of 1991.

By December of 1991, roughly fourteen months after the initial budget
cuts, the provost's final report based on recommendations from APAC
was completed and sent to me. This document was given to the Senate
with my strong endorsement and recommendation. Early in the spring
semester of 1992, roughly eighteen months after the initial round of
budget cuts and my first meeting with the Senate Executive Committee,
the Senate took final action on the report. The credibility of the report
and the process was greatly enhanced because of the central role played
by the provost, J. Robert Dorfman, a longtime faculty member at College Park who enjoyed enormous respect across the campus.

## THE RESULT

The Senate voted overwhelmingly to eliminate twenty-nine degree
programs, eight departments, and one college. The closest vote had a 70
percent majority. All others had in excess of an 80 percent majority. Non-
tenured faculty in affected departments were given notice following established procedures. Where appropriate, some tenured faculty in these
departments were relocated to departments in related disciplines. Others
chose to take an early retirement option.

As a result of the program closings and other reallocations, $13 mil-
lion was made available for redirection to programs of higher priority.
This represented nearly one-third of the entire budget cut assigned to the
university by the state. These resources, together with increased tuition
revenue, enabled the university to recapture its momentum.

The overall effort gained considerable praise from state leaders and the
board of regents. It also received favorable editorial comment in the
media. It contributed to a renewed enhancement effort by the state during the latter half of the 1990s and first two years of this decade. Regrettably, some of these gains have been erased by a new round of budget
cuts tied to the current economic downturn.

The university's push for excellence has continued unabated since the
completion of the restructuring effort. In the latest *U.S. News & World
Report* rankings, College Park is tied with the University of Texas at the

top of the second tier of national universities (53rd). Thanks to the enrollment reduction plan and the university's rising reputation, admission to College Park has become highly competitive. The average SAT score for this fall's entering class of roughly 4,000 students is about 1270. Of course, these advances result in significant part from actions subsequent to the reallocation effort, including most especially the leadership of the university's current president, Dan Mote; effective leadership at multiple levels of the university; and the generous budget investments by the state. Nonetheless, I believe the restructuring effort played a critical role by enabling the university to continue with its reenrollment reduction plan and invest in other priorities, thereby sustaining the aspirations and momentum of the university at a critical juncture in its development.

## LESSONS LEARNED

The eighteen-month-long budget restructuring and reallocation process at College Park was all consuming for the campus community. It had a positive outcome, but the gains came at some considerable cost. For most of the participants, decisions had to be made and a process developed without the benefit of prior experience. As a result, mistakes were made along the way. With the passage of time, it is instructive to look back and to list some of the most important lessons learned. These include the following:

1. **Be confident the juice will be worth the squeeze.** The energy and effort required to complete a major reallocation process is enormous. It is difficult for the campus to focus on other initiatives and activities until the process is complete. Unless considerable savings are likely, the effort is not worth the expenditure of physical and emotional energy.

2. **Engage the shared governance bodies from the outset.** Nothing is more sacred to shared governance organizations than their role in faculty rights and curriculum matters. Any hint that the administration has already decided the outcome of a process before the governance organizations are consulted will doom the effort to failure.

3. **Define the process at the beginning.** The credibility of the process is crucial. This can be achieved only if the rules of engagement are established through a collaborative process at the outset, not as the need for decisions arises.

4. **Patience is a virtue, but it comes at a cost.** It is tempting to approach a major restructuring effort with the idea that it is best to make the decisions, get them over, and get on with the real business of the uni-

versity. Given the fundamental nature of the issues at stake, however, such an approach is doomed to failure, as it will create irresolvable tension between the faculty and the administration.

In the College Park effort, the recommendations were discussed in so many forums and over such a period of time that the emotion (as well as the participants) had been exhausted by the time of the final vote of the Senate.

But patience also has its price. Targeted departments were left in a state of limbo for many months. Alumni of those departments were irate, and students and faculty were frustrated, all of which kept the campus in a state of tension for a considerable period of time.

**5. Data rule!** It is to be expected that qualitative judgments will play a role in the final decisions on most important matters. But especially in matters as sensitive as the continuation of programs, the decisions need to be informed by reliable and extensive data gathered in a timely manner. A uniform data set was compiled on all departments, which departments had a chance to review and correct. This proved to be very useful and added to the credibility of the process.

**6. Mind the media.** Perhaps the single biggest mistake we made was a sin of omission. We did not put the same strategic thought into communicating the process and its purpose with the media as we did with the campus community. We assumed, naively, that what we were doing would be of little interest outside the university. We were wrong. We grossly underestimated the interest of the media in the demonstrations and the letter writing campaigns, and this was a mistake. It placed us in a defensive mode in explaining our actions. A perception was created of a university in great distress, not one committed to taking bold steps to preserve its best programs and protect its highest priorities. Although the story eventually got told for what it was, the short-term damage to the university in terms of public perception was regrettable.

**7. Celebrate the accomplishment.** To successfully accomplish a budget reallocation of the magnitude described above requires the physical and emotional energy of a substantial portion of the campus. While it is essential to show sincere compassion and support to those who have lost their departments, it is also important to recognize those who have made the process work. It is equally important to talk about the results of the efforts to the larger community. There can be no doubt that the legislature, the governor, the business community, and the public at large took note of what we had done, and this resulted in long-term benefits to the university.

## FINAL THOUGHTS

With the perspective of hindsight, I can say that the effort undertaken by the university to restructure its academic programs and departments was an important and valuable step. The morality of the process derived from its openness, its predictability, its objectivity, and the sharing of the search for quality outcomes.

Among other things, the process enabled us to eliminate departments that were no longer of significant value to the university. And, as noted above, it had both a real and symbolic impact on our drive to improve the quality of the university. It is not, however, an exercise to be entered into lightly or often. The investment of both physical and mental energy is enormous. It is a nearly all-consuming activity.

The determination of the conditions when such an effort should be undertaken is difficult to define. Obviously, it would be best if institutions had in place an ongoing process to weed out programs no longer central to the university's mission. But that is not the norm in academe. The presence of an economic crisis is certainly a necessary condition for such action, but it is not sufficient. It requires a consensus among the administrative and faculty leadership that dramatic action is required to preserve important institutional priorities and goals. I also believe it is something a president would do only once during his or her tenure and, in any case, not more than once per decade in the life of the university.

# Reflections on Leadership

# CHAPTER

# Leadership and Teaching in the American University

*Thomas K. Hearn Jr.*

In what follows, I will reflect on the culture and organization of the university as a distinct institutional type. I suggest that the university climate militates against the exercise of leadership conceived of as traditional executive authority. This presents a growing problem in a period in which external regulation and demands for accountability are requiring the university to behave more like a traditional "corporate" entity, thus requiring effective and efficient leadership. Legislators, trustees, and stakeholders impose these demands. This central dilemma for the university leader has its own equally distinct solution. I will try to suggest a way, drawn from teaching, that the task of university leadership can be exercised effectively while reflecting the particular organizational character of the university.

In leadership studies, it is common to distinguish between "leadership" and "management." Leadership is required for institutional change—the preserving or alteration of mission and the maintenance of strategic vision. Management addresses the tasks of regular maintenance and repair. While my uses of these terms in this essay will reflect ordinary use that may blur these distinctions, it is leadership, not management, that the university generally resists (though some leaders have managerial wounds as well).

In the university setting, "administration" refers to a group of people as well as to a set of tasks. The term administration can, of course, range over leaders and managers, leadership and management. My concern is directed to the role of leadership in the university.

Another explanatory note: I set out these ideas to present them—I had no idea where or when—for a nonuniversity audience. This conference changed the audience but not the entire scheme of the essay. Some of these observations may be self-evident to academic audiences, but they are worth reviewing.

## THE SUBJECT OF LEADERSHIP

From long observation and experience in groups of every sort and size, I remain convinced that leadership is essential to the success of all forms of collective enterprise. Understood generally as the process by which people unite to achieve common or shared purposes and projects, leadership is a sine qua non of successful collective endeavor. Groups may have good ideas, ample resources, and promising opportunities, but failure threatens unless and until the essential human resources are mobilized by effective leadership.

I came to the subject of leadership years back as the result of a dramatic experience—a literal epiphany. I was a relatively new academic vice president at the University of Alabama at Birmingham. The legislature in Alabama would regularly appropriate funds based on estimated tax income that predictably exceeded actual funds receipted. The politics of this deplorable fiscal practice made it too tempting to avoid. "Proration" was the practice of reducing state budgets during the fiscal year to the level of actual income. During the year in question, proration had been severe and academic budgets had been cut several times. Another round of proration promised to be an administrative ordeal of the first order. The easy reductions already had been taken.

Proration could not be uniformly applied to all schools and departments. Some areas were experiencing enrollment growth and others were in decline. New and strategically important programs required sustained budgetary support. After meeting with the deans, individually and in groups, I gave each dean a target for expense reduction in the various school budgets. As you can imagine, this was a process fraught with conflict and controversy. Trips to professional meetings to present research results were being cancelled. Equipment necessary to scholarly inquiry was not to be purchased. Classes were to be made bigger or teaching loads increased. Each dean knew lots of areas, not in their own schools of course, where these reductions could and should be taken. In this process, a miserable time was had by all.

Late in the afternoon on the day the budget reduction reports were due, my feet were propped up on the desk as I watched the sunset out the window, pondering my woes. My assistant came with the reports, which he had separated into two groups. One group, he said, had done what was necessary, but the other group "would need more work"—that is, had not met their budgeted reductions. Delay, defer, and deny is often a bureaucratic strategy of choice, and most of the deans had far more practice than I. Setting these reports in front of me on the desk, my assistant said "good night" and left.

My feet remained on the desk as I looked at the two stacks of reports before me, dreading the assignment ahead. No one relishes conflict over money. There was thus more pain to mete out, more arm wrestling with deans seeking to protect their cherished programs and their status as defenders of their faculties.

As I reflected on the matters at hand, a thought suddenly struck with the force of revelation. Without looking, I knew which reports were in what stacks—and I knew with certainty. The reason struck with a similar force. Among the group of deans reporting to me, I had good leaders and I had poor leaders. The good leaders had met the requirement, and the poor leaders had not. Leadership sorted the reports.

In this moment of insight, the next thought, which also jolted me, was that no one had mentioned the word "leadership" to me since I was a Boy Scout many years—lifetimes—ago. It was a moment of illumination and clarity that brought utter certainty and conviction.

I knew from that moment that I would be different and that my conception of my responsibilities would change. My job—contrary to what I thought—was not in those reports. My task was the people whose job it was to prepare the reports. My job was not the budget. My challenge was to develop the capacity of those who were responsible for the budget. Despite the fact that I occupied a senior executive position, no one had explained this distinction to me. Leadership was the missing ingredient.

This moment of epiphany was so vivid that I still recall the details of it with clarity. As it felt at the time, it was a moment of transition. As an academic, I, of course, headed to the library and in time discovered James MacGregor Burns' classic work, *Leadership*, a book that became for me, and remains, an essential guide.[1]

Burns' work had a substantial scholarly influence, establishing the subject of leadership as a topic of more than historic interest. When Burns came to Wake Forest in the middle 1980s to lecture, I had a lengthy and unforgettable visit with him. Among other things, he told me that when researching this work in the New York City Public Library, he found no card catalog entry for "leadership." There were listings under "leaders," but the generic subject "leadership" had yet to be recognized as a separate domain of study.

I have continued to engage the subject of leadership, which has brought me further blessings and benefits. When I came to Wake Forest, I learned of the Center for Creative Leadership (CCL) in Greensboro. William Friday, then head of the University of North Carolina and Chairman of CCL's board, invited me to serve. I have done so ever since, and in time I succeeded Bill Friday as chair of the Board of Governors. My opportunity to be a part of an institution where some of the world's most important leadership research and training are conducted has been a constant source of interest and, indeed, inspiration.

## DISTINCTIVE UNIVERSITY CULTURE

One key axiom of CCL research is that leadership is not a generic set of influences to be exercised in the same way in any and every institutional setting. While all organizations have leadership requirements, how those requirements are exercised will differ radically in military, business, charitable, or volunteer institutions. Leadership must reflect the nature and purpose of the institution and be exercised in conformity with the mission and structure being served. There is no such thing as leadership generically effective in every situation. There is only leadership in a specific institutional context.

The American university is a highly specialized—indeed, a unique—institution of great and growing importance to our nation and to the world. In the information economy, the university produces the essential economic resource: the trained intelligence of our people. The research mission of the university, in science and in culture, is a constant source of intellectual experimentation, novelty, and innovation.

While discussion about the "information age" inevitably draws attention to the growing economic impact of the university, we can never lose sight of our larger cultural and public purposes. The university preserves and interprets the best of what human intelligence has created and written. It retains our cultural and intellectual memory and thus the identity not only of the American nation but also of many nations. As such, we preserve and interpret the records of the past while we create the ideas and leaders for the future. The university is a repository of past achievement and the foundation of future innovation.

In America, the university is a uniquely democratic institution where ideas and ideals compete in the free-for-all of the intellectual marketplace. The general public often regards this marketplace with dismay, believing that some of the ideas proffered are outrageous or dangerous. Indeed, they sometimes are. But we are all beneficiaries of the maintenance of this intellectual free-for-all that ensures that no orthodoxy is free from evaluation and criticism. This ferment is essential to the genius of the university and to the democratic genius that is America. The American university is created by and in turn sustains democratic institutions.

It follows, of course, that the leadership needs and challenges of the university must reflect this remarkable and challenging institutional environment, albeit one whose very culture is resistant to the exercise of leadership understood as the exercise of executive authority. Such resistance is a consequence of the ferment required by the democracy of ideas.

In addition, this resistance derives from the highly decentralized systems by which universities are organized and governed. Schools, departments, institutes, centers, and the like form a network of associations that are variously organized, funded, and governed. Despite what an organizational chart might look like, no ordinary organizational structure exists to govern by means of a traditional hierarchy. Inevitably, commitment and identity in the university tend to be directed to the parts rather than the whole. I am reminded of an aphorism attributed to Clark Kerr: "A university is a group of mutually antagonistic fiefdoms held together by a parking problem!"

At the same time, however, the external demand for and requirement of leadership and accountability in the university is growing from public and private agencies. We thus face a growing dilemma. As an organization resistant to the exercise of central authority, we nonetheless confront public requirements for accountability that demand leadership authority—and increasingly so. Indeed, one consequence of the university having moved to the center of the economic order is that oversight and the expectation of effective outcomes have inevitably followed. With growing influence has come growing oversight.

The consumer movement has overtaken American higher education in recent decades. A symptom of the rise of consumerism, as well as a cause of it, is the proliferation of college guides and rankings. These are the "consumer reports" for our "industry," and shoppers compare price, value, and durability as they might when choosing a car or a dishwasher. Consumers demand value and measures of accountability, and consumers serve in the legislature and on university boards.

As the university has gained importance and influence, it has attracted the attention of government regulators of every sort: local, state, and federal. The days when our schools were "society's pets"—places for the youthful gaiety of football games, parties, and fun—are long past. We must meet and pass every standard—legal and regulatory—that other large institutions, public and private, confront. Whether it is the IRS, the FTC, the EPA, HIPPA, OSHA, or any of the other regulatory acronyms, the university must have its regulatory house in order.

Casual, decentralized leadership systems staffed by volunteer committees are inadequate to the challenge this new regulatory environment presents. The university has been required to professionalize its administrative staff to meet these requirements, which has met with criticism on many campuses. The fact remains that regulation from external agencies must be matched and managed by competent professionals. Universities are now sometimes described by faculty, not in praise, as "bureaucratic" or "corporate." So we have become.

It is increasingly common for presidents and chancellors to be called CEOs, an expression never heard a few years ago. "CEO" perhaps embodies this tension I am describing, for this very title suggests a kind and scale of authority that is uncongenial within the culture of the university.

## SHARED AUTHORITY

Given that leadership must inevitably be exercised in a particular institutional context, it is essential to appreciate the unique purposes specific to each setting. The special context of the university as an institution bears this point out.

First of all, universities themselves are remarkably different. While they may all formally do the same or similar things, their missions and cultures are different. I do not mean merely that schools differ according to type—a liberal arts college is different from a technical or community college or a private university is different from a land grant institution. I mean rather that institutions of the same type—be they colleges or public or private universities—have quite different notions of the way in which the work of the institution is to be conducted. Universities form unique cultural environments. One fallacy of college rankings is the assumption that because universities all grant degrees, they are alike in what they do and can be compared as differing instances of the same enterprise. While similar in what they do, colleges and universities are substantially different in how they regard their purposes. Knowledge is infinite, but education is finite. Therefore, schools are inevitably specialized.

Thus, the first and most obvious task for any institutional leader is to know his or her own institution intimately and thoroughly. The need to know an institution and its people well poses a particular difficulty for a newly chosen leader, especially one coming from outside that university. In its simplest terms, the dilemma for the new leader is that the first thing a university community wants to know is what this person proposes to do. Without knowing the institution thoroughly, however, it is impossible, even dangerous, to render specific decisions except in the case of some immediate problem or crisis.

The essential strategy for the newcomer is to conduct a careful institutional audit, listening rather than speaking, and to postpone any substantive decisions until such time as the institution, its problems, and people are thoroughly consulted and understood. In this instance, the new leader is the pupil and the university is the teacher, helping the leader come to understand the culture and the people of this place and the challenges being faced.

What most characterizes the university as an organizational type is its radical decentralization. Sometimes centralization/decentralization is discussed as a matter of optional organizational style, some managers preferring greater or lesser autonomy in subunits. I mean something stronger. A university by its nature and purpose must be a decentralized organization and must be administered as such. Crucially, the work of the faculty, which is the work of the university, is organized through departments, schools, and centers. That work, conducted in these organizations, is the structure on which the entire work of the university rests.

The academic expertise gathered at the departmental level is of the highest order. That expertise, together with the traditional entitlements of academic freedom, means that academic organizations must be given broad latitude in determining what they do and how they do it. Curriculum, faculty selection and development, and student advising are of necessity under departmental authority. There can often be planning that attempts to coordinate and strengthen the work of various academic centers. But what has been called the "tyranny of departments" is a way of life and an essential feature of the university at work. The expertise determining the work of teaching and scholarship can be "coordinated," but it cannot be "managed" without reference to its own specialized academic function.

Nor is it just the faculty and the academic organization that is the source of the decentralized influences in the university. A university is a complex set of overlapping constituencies, all of which are complexly organized and all of which have legitimate roles to play, depending on the issues involved, in the life and work of the university. In addition to the faculty, there are students, staff, alumni, parents, the donor publics, athletic associations, legislatures, trustees, educational organizations and associations, accrediting bodies, and civic partners. This list is by no means exhaustive. Each of these groups exercises a centrifugal force, distributing the sources of influence and rendering the exercise of hierarchical executive authority impossible over a broad range of subjects.

This decentralized character of the university has accelerated in recent decades by the professionalization of the faculty. A generation ago, it was common for aspiring scholars following graduate school to serve a single institution for an entire career. There was such a figure in my own family, a person who occupied heroic status in my family. My grandmother's cousin, Gleason Bean, had earned a PhD—at Harvard, no less. To my family in a small Alabama town, that was a singular achievement. Following graduate school, Professor Bean joined the faculty at Washington and Lee and became an essential part of the life and work of that school for his entire career. He was—I knew him in his retirement years—wedded to that school and its people. His first and only loyalty was to Washington and Lee.

Faculty members now regard their primary professional peers as colleagues in the same fields in other universities as well as their own departments. Academic careers are more likely to be mobile, and institutional loyalty has been compromised by this change in the structure and organization of American intellectual life. Faculty do not simply serve a university but a scholarly discipline. The university is a location for the practice of a profession defined by colleagues and professional organizations across the country and increasingly around the world.

As well, the Cultural Revolution of the 1960s and 1970s had a greater impact on the university than on most other institutions in society. Many themes of the Cultural Revolution emerged on America's campuses. An anti-institutional and antiauthoritarian attitude ("Never trust anyone over thirty!") was an essential part of that climate and culture. Of course, the graduates of that era now serve in positions of academic importance across America. This general distrust of authority further conditions the way in which leadership is regarded, especially as the external requirements of accountability are being ever more exercised toward the academy.

The substantive work of the academic environment, as well as this highly decentralized organizational setting, contributes to the atmosphere of criticism and dissent in the university. Faculty members spend their lives working to expose existing intellectual problems to critical scrutiny with the hope that new and more adequate answers to questions in their disciplines can be found. The quest for the new, the novel, the unrecognized, or even the revolutionary is the work of teaching and scholarship. No one ever won a Nobel Prize, not even a summer research grant, by claiming that the status quo is right and adequate. The academic mind lives to question existing orthodoxy, and that habit of mind is prone to extend to the administrative environment of the university. There is thus an academic basis for the general concern with which faculty regard the organization and administration of the university. In the university, the old slogan is reversed: "Those who can teach, do. Those who cannot, go into administration."

Even though in various university departments the skills and work of administration, leadership, and organizational development are taught, there is general disregard for the special and specific exercise of those very same skills in the university setting. The central administration of the university represents a constant imposition of central authority that the academic community is constitutionally disposed to resist.

University leadership thus is caught between a climate and culture that resist the imposition of external standards and the demands from various public agencies that these standards be applied, and applied rigorously. Perhaps in some past era, universities were generally left alone to do their own thing on the basis of a public consensus that universities were good places doing good things. The combined influence of tax revolts, consumerism, and the strength of regulatory agencies means that such a happy time is gone for good. When tax revenues decline, higher education is often high on the list of things to cut.

The university and those who exercise leadership there must find new ways to address this environment of accountability, all while preserving the special genius of the university as a place devoted to the process of discovery and to the preparation of our citizens for lives of service and accomplishment.

## THE POOL OF FUTURE LEADERS

Other obstacles to leadership bear mentioning, other institutional characteristics that have the effect of limiting the leadership function in the context of the university.

First, the character of the academic mind and preparation for service in the academy obviously determines the likely pool of leadership talent. To pursue a terminal degree is a formidable challenge in time, effort, and money. Such an undertaking will often require five years or more with all of the attendant sacrifices of foregone income and extended student status. Those who choose this project are a special breed. They are, first and foremost, intellectually gifted, the best and brightest products of our undergraduate programs. Their talent and academic motivation have generally attracted the attention of faculty mentors, and they have received consistent academic encouragement and support. Such people have a clear academic motivation and are drawn to the domain of ideas and discovery. Those of academic inclination, when they discover that they can be paid to read, study, and write about their interests, want no other life and can imagine no other vocation so ideal and rewarding. The last thing such people as a group have in mind for their lives is to "push paper." There is a general disdain or disregard for the work of administration—given the primacy of the academic ambitions for which they were prepared. Thus, the pool of individuals likely to be interested in and talented at administrative leadership is inevitably small, and the motivation in the academic environment for administrative work is often absent, especially in the earliest years of an academic career.

Various programs at universities and at the American Council on Education address the problem of university leadership. But the absence of a sizeable pool of academically trained and successful scholars who are interested in careers in educational leadership is a chronic problem for leadership in the academy.

Unlike businesses where talented young executives are put on a fast track, the academic organization generally operates according to a fixed seniority system. The position of department chair, for instance, tends to rotate among the senior staff in an academic department. This system militates against the possibility that a reasonably young academic, early in his or her career, might occupy a department chairmanship. Thus, very few young scholars are given the opportunity for the position of departmental chair to be an early formative experience for a career in educational administration.

The department chair is a critical position. Indeed, one could argue that it is the single most important administrative position in the university. In departments, members of the faculty are hired, curricula established, students advised, and, critically, promotion and tenure decided. While these decisions are reviewed outside departments, the departmental outcome is presumptively determinative. Thus, this position of chair is especially critical in understanding the work of the university at its basic level, and it provides a vitally important learning experience for potential academic leaders.

In addition, the decision of the university community in recent decades to make department chairs a rotating position has been a mixed blessing. In an earlier day when department chairs were appointed for indefinite terms, they exercised a great deal of authority, and that authority was immediately adjacent to the work of the faculty. Now that the position rotates, faculty members are often reluctant to make difficult decisions that might adversely affect their colleagues, knowing that one or the other of those colleagues will be the occupant of the chair in just a year or two.

The selection process for leadership positions in the academy, based primarily on committees representing the decentralized centers of influence in the academy, also has a limiting potential on leadership in the university. Each committee member acts to protect and support the special interests and concerns of the separate represented domains. Successful candidates must, therefore, impress the committee that nothing adverse will happen to the interests of any of the assorted programs represented by the committee.

Search committees take on a kind of corporate personality, each member typically posing to each candidate the same set of questions arising from that committee member's domain of concern. These committees also work to limit the internal contention that might result from the conflicts among and between their various interests. This effort at consensus effectively means that any committee member who objects vigorously to the candidacy of any particular individual can effectively veto that candidate. Search committees generally operate with a de facto blackball system.

Candidates with forceful and passionately held views on relevant subjects, assuming the interview process surfaces those opinions, are not likely to survive committee selection. Nordo candidates survive who are idiosyncratic or eccentric in any respect. All of us have known talented candidates whose personality cannot be chosen in a process of selection where committees are the primary vehicle.

This search process frequently works to the disadvantage of internal candidates who have been involved in local decision making, inevitably controversial, and are regarded as problematic by disadvantaged interests. This is not always the case, of course. Knowing the personalities on the committee, internal candidates can sometimes navigate these conflicts with better information and diplomatic skills.

Fixed academic attitudes are also at work in university executive searches. A typical faculty opinion is that there is no specific and unique talent or requirement for the work of educational administration. Thus, excessive attention is given to the academic qualifications of candidates, and not enough attention, if any, is given to the talents and competencies of effective leadership. A frustrated trustee serving on such a committee once remarked to me, "The committee acts as if they are hiring a faculty colleague or a research professor, not a leader." That frustration is often legitimate. Faculty committee members are looking naturally for people like themselves, not necessarily those with the talent of leaders.

The selection process can resemble a human demolition derby, a car race in which jalopies crash into each other until only one remaining car is moving. That car, of course, is also damaged, but it is at least running. The search process often amounts to such a process of candidate demolition and sacrifices the characteristics of a meritocratic process. It is, however, a process that often serves to protect and secure the decentralized academic interests of the committee members.

The transition period into a new position of responsibility within the university is fraught with leadership risks. The question to which everyone wants an answer is, "What is this new leader going to do?" People reasonably expect the new officer to have something substantive to say. The dilemma, of course, especially for a new person coming from the outside, is that he or she does not know what is required. Thus, new university officers go through a very difficult and challenging process of trying to establish credibility while taking a period of time—as long as possible or necessary—to ascertain what steps would be most constructive.

The old adage about having a single chance to make a first impression bears particular attention during periods of transition. A new officer must solicit advice and assistance from as many seasoned veterans as possible. Early presentations to important constituencies must be carefully crafted, with special attention to the interests and concerns of the audience. As soon as I was named president of Wake Forest, I began to get, as you can imagine, large amounts of mail and publications from all segments of the university. I noticed immediately that no two pieces of correspondence and no two publications looked alike. There was no standard institutional signature, no standard graphic identity.

This struck me at once as a problem needing a quick solution. So shortly after I arrived, with the help of design consultants, and with the involvement of a fairly small—clearly too small—group of participants, the new administration promulgated a new logo and graphic design requirements. The result was what I did not know then to expect but should have. The new design requirements were interpreted as everything from an invasion of territorial prerogatives to an attempt to abolish the historic seal and diminish the motto of the university. We held firm, and the new design standards were in time accepted. For a period I was dubbed the "logo cop" since people would get from me copies of documents and publications marked and noted that had not meet the new design criteria.

A much broader and better process was needed. I made a mistake of some importance in a period of transition. People care, rightly so, about their own graphic identity, and control over such matters as publications is often a matter of contention. I learned from the experience.

Lastly, tenure in the executive offices of universities tends to be relatively brief. These numbers fluctuate over time. In good economic times, tenures are longer. To make fundamental changes in educational programs or organizations is not of weeks or months but of years and may often take longer than an administrator has years in office. To conceive plans, to win support for those plans, to garner the resources such plans might require, and then to put those plans in place requires a time cycle likely to meet or exceed the expected terms of senior officials. These frequent transitions in office are themselves an adverse factor on the leadership structure of universities. Leadership changes are disruptive, and shorter terms in office will inevitably mean reduced influence and authority in such offices.

## LEADERS AS TEACHERS

Three general separate but related subjects fall under the broad interdisciplinary subject of leadership. The first involves personality: what are leaders like? This question has its origins in the charismatic or "great man" view of leadership that regards leadership as a particular form of human genius, akin to musical or artistic genius. Though more or less discredited, there still is necessary interest in the personal qualities and characteristics of those who are successful leaders.

The second general topic is the function of leadership: what is it that leaders do? This involves a general analysis of the leadership role in organization. The functions identified range broadly from generic values and mission to strategy and planning. What leaders do is a distinct question from what leaders are like.

A third more general subject involves performance: how does leadership render organizations effective? What are the requirements, including leadership and organizational relationships, that cause groups and organizations to be maximally effective or "high performing"? Leadership is one feature among others of organizations that achieve their goals.

I will focus on just the first of these questions: the qualities required of persons to lead effectively in the setting of the university.

There is, indeed, a social paradox when we consider the matter of leadership in America. American universities produce the finest graduates in the world. And while universities may conspire against the active creation of leadership within its ranks, other organizations and institutions do not. Indeed, business and military organizations, for example, are specifically and continually focused on leadership and leadership development. Organizations like CCL assist groups of every size and description in putting in place systems that will facilitate the development of the leadership capacity for the future. There is a great deal of public initiative and effort on this subject with the best-trained talent pool in the world.

Yet when it comes time to fill a critical position in a place of great leadership importance, there are never enough talented applicants. In the key positions within the hierarchy of American organizational life, executives seldom report that there were ample highly qualified candidates from which to choose. All of us who do executive selection—in the university or in our other associations—can testify to this talent deficit.

Of course, many candidates are functionally qualified, having the background and experience that the position would seem to require. What is often missing, however, are those personal qualities that are always more critical than qualifications. Thus, the question of the personal as well as the functional talent of potential leaders remains central.

I wish to pose the idea that pedagogy is the process that most helpfully guides the conduct of leadership in the university. Given the university setting as it has been described, the work of leadership is best regarded as a kind of teaching, with policies and proposals being regarded as pedagogical exercises calculated to inform, explain, and, in the best cases, persuade.

Teaching is a collective process involving and requiring leadership. A teacher in a classroom occupies a leadership position. At one level a deliberative rather than a practical process aimed at outcomes, teaching involves the presentation of problems for common and collective consideration, the discussion of proposed solutions to those problems, and often the selection of the solution that seems optimal after evaluation.

Teaching also presupposes a structure of authority, the definition and control of the pedagogical process being under the leadership and guidance of the teacher. However, the authority of the teacher rests in the deliberative process itself, in the mastery of the content being considered. The process of teaching generates outcomes, as all of us who have been given grades are acutely aware, so the process involves purposeful choices.

What set of personal qualities should we seek in leaders appropriate to the climate and culture of the university?

The first personal requirement for leadership as a form of teaching is a passion for ideas, a love of learning. A university leader must, above all, love the university as a place of learning and discovery. This does not mean that university leaders should be in every case professional academics, though that qualification will be generally desirable. It is necessary, however, that the university mission be embraced with passion and dedication.

That is a vital requirement, of course, because universities are, from the perspective of a corporate leadership culture, entirely maddening. (Business leaders who become business school deans regularly report this.) As an organization, the university is, as a result of its decentralized character, generally inefficient in its decision making. Leaders in the university need a teacher's passion for learning and the consequent acceptance of the environment for leadership in this unique organizational context.

A second personal requirement is a high tolerance for process. In a decentralized organization with overlapping and sometimes conflicting mechanisms of governance, there is seldom a simple path from a proposed change, large or small, to its actual implementation. It is necessary to regard this process of deliberation and exploration as one in which every opportunity for instruction and the exchange of views is exploited. A university leader cannot control this process, complex and often controversial, as a business executive might. Rather, the process must inevitably be seen as one in which better ideas and better outcomes are presented and advocated, and in which disagreements and conflicts of opinion are aired.

Essential to good teaching is effectiveness at communication. The essence of teaching is communication. No duty of the university leader can be regarded as more important than communication in directing processes of deliberation and in being the spokesperson and advocate for the university to its vast array of internal and external constituencies. In this present media age, an essential requirement of university leaders is that they be confident and competent communicators when a microphone or a television camera is in their face.

The communication requirement, in pedagogy and leadership, is of supreme importance. In the process of leadership selection in the university, communication looms large, even paramount, in the minds of selection committees. What a selection committee will certainly know after an extensive interview is whether a candidate is a good communicator. What will inevitably be less certain is the quality of the ideas being put forth. Thus, effective communication is a necessary requirement but does not guarantee the success of the university leader. Long and effective engagement with ideas as a teacher and researcher helps ensure that candidates are substantive and not merely glib.

Lastly, teachers as leaders of deliberative processes must have a high tolerance for criticism and dissent, for when ideas are advanced, they will likely provoke criticism, including personal criticism. Whatever an individual may say about the thickness of his or her skin, no one likes to be criticized and held up to public disregard. However, in a decentralized institution, populated by brilliant people who are armed with the weapons of academic freedom and great intellect, leaders may often find themselves the subject of intense, even bitter, criticism. The typical teacher–researcher has few experiences of being in the cross fire. The ability to face criticism and still render outcomes without regard to conflict is a major test of whether a teacher has the capacity to be a leader of the academic enterprise.

In the end, the personal requirements for leadership in the university correlate closely with a range of talents particular to effective practitioners of the art of pedagogy.

## CONCLUSION

Let me present an illustration of what this notion of leadership as pedagogy looks like in operation. The leader in this case was our conference chair, Dave Brown, then provost at Wake Forest.

In the early 1990s, Wake Forest faced a number of important questions. As we evolved from a teaching institution to a teaching and research institution, the faculty required more time for research. Without compromising our instructional programs, this required hiring additional faculty. In addition, our student academic casualties were overwhelmingly in the first year. Since our admissions are selective, our guiding assumption is that we should graduate everyone we admit. We needed major changes in the first-year experience for students. Technology was presenting us, like schools everywhere, with major challenges. Uniformity and universality would be required to have a robust environment available to everyone, with the result that our academic program could realize the full benefits of technology. We were moving at different speeds in different directions in information technology across the institution.

As provost, Dave chaired a program-planning group that he charged with the task of dealing comprehensively with these and other issues. Over the course of almost two years, the committee held town meetings and put forward report drafts and revisions of drafts. Since curricular charges were involved, proposals had to pass the undergraduate faculty. We had a full-blown campus discussion, complete with student demonstrations.

Since these plans required a large proposed tuition increase, for an entire year the board of trustees discussed these proposals and their financial implications. This was a period of rising concern about hikes in tuition—a quite specific concern of the trustees—and we had to be certain that we could afford to implement whatever plans might be adopted. Thus, an educational or pedagogical process for the trustees went on in tandem with the planning group.

In 1996, the committee proposed, the faculty passed, and the trustees adopted what we then called the Plan for the Class of 2000. (This plan took four years to implement fully.) It involved major changes to the first-year experience, new faculty positions with no enrollment increase, and uniform universal technology. Each student would be given a personal computer as part of the cost of tuition. The trustees approved a graduated increase in tuition of $3,000 per year. This plan brought substantial and important changes across our university.

What is notable about this effort, in retrospect, is not just its successful outcomes (there were particular concerns about the board's willingness to raise tuition so dramatically), but how thorough were the processes of deliberation, discussion, and conferral. Of course, there was dissent throughout the process and at the end. But there were opportunities throughout the study for the university community to be involved in the discussion. Dave Brown did a masterful job as our teacher, assisted by many members of the faculty and the administration.

Though the problems and outcomes were much less significant, I would contrast the Plan for 2000 with the process referred to earlier regarding our graphic identity. That process was flawed, and in a certain sense failed, because it did not provide the community the deliberation and consultation that might have engaged the community in the problem and the solution. Had our process been more deliberative, our implementation would have been more effective and timely.

In short, our challenge then may have succeeded better had we approached this policy change as an exercise in learning that stressed, to carry the metaphor, not just lectures but discussion, with participation encouraged from each and every member of the class. Expecting—and I dare say even welcoming—the atmosphere of criticism and dissent would have produced the results characteristic of the teaching process itself: new and more adequate solutions to the issue at hand.

Ultimately, the leadership challenges presented by the unique culture and organization of the university are best addressed by the very skills— what I have called the "genius"—that most inform these distinct characteristics. These talents are, I have said, the quest for the new, the novel, and the unrecognized. All are the bedrock and foundation of the process of critical inquiry. Importantly, they are also key aspects of leadership.

The teaching that informs this notion of leadership is not "be still while I instill." The teaching I refer to is deliberative and interactive, involving mutual give and take. Administrative leadership in a university is likely to be effective if policy development and change is conceived as an exercise in teaching and learning aimed at deliberation, clarification, and selection.

And though the proposition may sound anathema to university faculty, good teachers do effective university leaders make.

## NOTE

1. James MacGregor Burns, *Leadership* (New York: Harper and Row, 1979).

# CHAPTER 22

## Models for Moral Leadership: From Wile E. Coyote to Homer
### A Response to President Hearn's Essay

*Larry E. Penley*

In reading President Hearn's essay about presidential leadership, I found myself considering my own view of leadership and, particularly, the issue of culture and its impact on leadership. That consideration led me to try to answer four questions: (1) How does one lead? (2) What does a leader do? (3) To what end does one lead? and (4) Under what constraints does one lead?

In answering these questions, I connected each with a separate person or character. First, how does one lead? I connected that question with Homer. What does one do? I connected this question with Michelangelo. The third was to what end does one lead? I connected this question with Father Wojtyla. Finally, I connected the question of under what constraints one leads with Wile E. Coyote, the cartoon character.

### UNDER THE CONSTRAINT OF CULTURAL VALUES

I'll start with Wile E. Coyote—under what constraints does one lead? Wile E. Coyote's behavior can be thought of in terms of leadership. He has vision. He has focus. And he is really persistent at going after that Roadrunner. And usually we think of leadership in terms of vision, persistence, and focus. So, there is a certain obvious connection between Wile E. Coyote and leadership.

Of course, equally significant is understanding the constraints that Wile E. Coyote faces. The constraints are extremely important in understanding what the Wile E. Coyote cartoon has to say about leadership as well as the cartoon itself. He never succeeds. He uses outrageously in-novative approaches to capture the Roadrunner, and it is always enter-taining. Indeed, in this environment one does not expect the Roadrunner to lose. Neither does one expect Wile E. Coyote to win. If the Road-runner were to lose and Wile E. Coyote were to win, we would not watch the cartoon any more. It would no longer be entertaining.

So, the constraints under which the characters are drawn are really im-portant in making this a successful cartoon. Those same constraints of an organization remind me of the impact of organizational culture on leadership; culture always trumps strategy. When I think about strategy, I try to remind myself that, indeed, it is the culture that will allow me as a leader to succeed, and it is that same culture that has the potential for inhibiting success. Strategies are very much a sidelight to culture. In Chapter 6, Greg Farrington says, "After all, you are a community, and the community has values" reminding me once again that it is the cul-ture with its values that is so important to leadership. The constraints of working within the culture and the impact of its values are the backdrop for the leader's fomenting change and accomplishing something. I use Wile E. to remind myself of the constraints of culture, the power of cul-ture over strategy, and how a leader has to use culture to lead.

## BRIDGING THE CHASM BETWEEN WHAT WE ARE AND CAN BE

To what end does leadership intend? I connect this question with Fa-ther Wojtyla, otherwise known as Pope John Paul II. As a Catholic, I have found myself having a great deal of trouble understanding this pope. The mystery of this individual goes back to the very first day of John Paul II's election as pope—when Yolanda (my wife) and I were in Venezuela. I was a much younger visiting professor at the Universidad de Carabobo. On the day of John Paul II's election, we were taking the day off to go to the beach. We were on one of those ubiquitous microbuses when we heard on the radio that John Paul I had died. Everyone on the bus was quite upset. But very quickly for these sort of elections, a new pope was chosen who took the same name of John Paul. This particular pope seemed, however, an enigma to me from his very election as Holy Fa-ther: Why did this Polish pope behave the way he behaved?

Only gradually I began to understand that he did not behave as most popes behaved. He was, after all, fundamentally a priest. But in behav-ing as a priest, he has to be understood as a particular kind of priest. Al-though of the Roman Church, he comes more out of the Eastern tradition. As I sought to understand him, I found that seeing him as Eastern and as a contemplative helped considerably in understanding him. I saw him as one who believes that the priest stands between us and the unknown, between us and God. As a priest, he bridges the chasm between what we are and what we can be. He acts as a means of revelation. This seemed to be central to his conception of self and of what a good priest does; at least this was my means for understanding him and his behavior. Father Wojtyla—as priest rather than pope—represents for me the answer to the question of "To what end?" for a leader.

One must have a prescient view, I believe, of what institutional opportunities there are for a university if one is a good president and leader. Developing this view requires that the leader define the institution's future in light of what the leader believes lies ahead. There is in a good leader of a university a responsibility to employ revelation to build a culture that reaches forward toward the future, that bridges from what we know now to what could be known, or from where we are to an end result we would like to have for the institution. Victor Hugo said, "Good government consists of knowing how much future to introduce into the present." Leadership as well, I suspect, consists of knowing how much of the future to introduce into the present, but, perhaps more important, also of recognizing that good leadership necessitates introducing some of the future into the present.

## TAKING ACTION

The third question was "What does one do as a leader?" I relate this question to Michelangelo as sculptor. I suppose that is because I have always taken the story that was once told to me about Michelangelo so very seriously. That story remains a reminder to me of the behavior of a leader. According to the story, Michelangelo was asked by an observer of his work, "How do you create such beauty?" He replied so simply, "The beauty is already in the stone. All that I do is remove the ugly parts." When I think of leadership, I think of Michelangelo's story. Real leadership is not in the envisioning part. It is the active part of leadership described by Michelangelo. In a university, one encounters so many faculty members who are very bright, intellectually capable people, but all are not leaders. These very bright faculty members are quite capable of great vision, but many of them are not leaders. Like so many nonfaculty who are not leaders, many faculty members do not understand what a leader does, that is, the action of revealing beauty through the very hard work of a stonecutter.

Jim Barker comments in Chapter 7 that he has found himself doing a lot more rowing than steering as a president. To me, that is what Michelangelo was talking about. When Freeman Hrabowski was depicting himself walking around campus, talking with those on campus, and interacting with students, he was talking about Michelangelo's action as stonecutter. Whenever leadership is described as something abstract and intellectual, I find myself thinking instead of the hard work that leadership really requires—the step-by-step work of using a hammer and a chisel to remove the ugly parts. In the end, the activity of the leader demands the humility of the stonecutter to reveal the beauty of the vision.

## HIGHLIGHTING IMAGES AND NARRATIVES

The fourth question is "How does one do it?" That is, how does one lead? I connect this question with Homer, because the leader necessarily must exercise a Homeric responsibility. Because all of us still read *The Odyssey*, we all know the great stories that Homer told. In those stories, Homer developed a mythology, filled with symbolic images via narratives that still speak to the human experience today. *The Odyssey* still speaks to us in the twenty-first century because it speaks about culture—about human culture.

What a leader must do, then, is exercise a Homeric responsibility to bring to life, through symbols and metaphor, what we cannot easily express for ourselves. This is a leader's teaching responsibility. It is a teaching responsibility that creates for us meaning in the present about the envisioned future through the symbolization process. The Homeric responsibility must be carried out step by step through communication, discourse, dialogue, and debate—the very fundamental processes that we appreciate in universities.

What the leader does is teach, and in doing so the leader captures for us a reasonable vision about the future. With metaphor and symbol, the leader uses the existing culture to bridge from where we are to where we might be.

## SUMMARY

In summary, Tom Hearn has led me to consider a president's leadership as described by the following. Under the constraints of an institutional culture, the leader stands between us and a possible future, providing for us a perception of a possible end state via the hard work of symbolizing the dreams and hopes for the future of the faculty, staff, and students of the university. In other words, the leader exercises a Homeric responsibility as a stonecutter, like Michelangelo, to do the priestly duty of revealing the future under the constraints of what we hope is not the digital world of Wile E. Coyote.

# CHAPTER

# Searches and Succession Planning
## A Response to President Hearn's Essay

*Graham B. Spanier*

I have been in higher education administration for twenty-seven years. I was a young, assistant professor, maybe something of a troublemaker. No one took actions on my reports. I got frustrated. At twenty-eight I became a "professor in charge" of something like the equivalent of a department chair. Back then I believed that leadership was not something one could train for. I tended to learn from the mistakes of others.

Over the years, I have changed my mind about succession planning. Because university administration has become so complex (legal, legislative relations, etc.), it will be increasingly important to consciously prepare leaders for their roles in higher education.

In addition, I think we are doing ourselves a disservice when we are so narrowly focused on process that we forget that there are people around us who are phenomenally good. There are several persons at Penn State who would make wonderful presidents. We must balance process and cultivating new presidential talent.

I also think there are different personality types. I may not myself have been a candidate for a training program, but there are many others who would be.

I hope that my academic training contributes to my being a better administrator—for example, that I have an intense curiosity about people. I cannot honestly recall making direct connections between my own discipline and leadership.

There is a lot of talent around us. One's particular discipline or background may not mean too much in the end. It is a shame when too much weight is given to one's discipline in the presidential search process.

## CAVEATS AND CHARACTERISTICS

At Penn State we identify at least three rising stars at the university, and they spend a year with a vice president. This is an internal program. Here are some of the things I point out:

**1. No one should move into administration unless he or she respects the role of an administrator.** When an individual agrees to do an administrative job only as a self-sacrificing service to the institution, this is a disservice to everyone. We need administrators who care about what they are doing.

**2. Do not even consider administration if you cannot tolerate disagreement and anger.** Not only will your picture be in the paper from time to time, but the student paper may also feature you with unflattering cartoons. Petitions and letter writing campaigns are all destined to make you feel bad. One must be prepared to feel bad, survive it, and bounce back quickly. People must be prepared to be blamed for things that are not their fault. As one's arena broadens, the more one gets credit as well as criticized. If one has the need for constant reinforcement, administration is not the thing.

**3. An administrator should not accept a position unless he or she is ready to make every decision on the basis on what is in the best interest of the institution.** A lot of people fail by asking what is in their best interest, or how do they hold on to this job longer. People should not move into administration if they are afraid to lose their job. There has to be a certain level of integrity, of principle.

# CHAPTER

# The Contrarian's Guide to University Leadership

*Steven B. Sample*

## INTRODUCTION

Few institutions last as long as universities—and precious few are as difficult to lead. The long-term leader of a university succeeds not because he follows a formulaic approach to academic leadership; rather, such a leader follows what I call a *contrarian* approach.

Clark Kerr observed that since the year 1520 only about eighty-five institutions have remained continuously in existence. They include several Swiss cantons, the Roman Catholic Church, and the parliaments of the Isle of Man, Iceland, and Great Britain. But some seventy of the eighty-five institutions that have survived continuously for the past half millennium are universities.[1]

The very things that make a university so stable—its myriad traditions and entrenched and tenured constituencies—are what make it so hard to govern. Many excellent academicians felt equipped to lead a university but crashed and burned within a few years' time. Most brought with them a lot of conventional wisdom about academic leadership. And even when such conventional wisdom was billed as unorthodox or new and improved, it typically reflected a set of false assumptions about how universities and human beings work.

The contrarian academic leader works hard to see things through the

Editor's note: Portions excerpted from Steven B. Sample, *The Contrarian's Guide to Leadership* (San Francisco: Jossey-Bass, 2002).

eyes of others while at the same time assiduously cultivating her intellectual independence. That allows her to bring her own approach to making decisions, breaking new ground, and handling what I shall call the less prestigious aspects of university leadership.

## UNIVERSITY LEADERSHIP: IS IT IN YOU?

The first step along the path of contrarian academic leadership requires brutal self-honesty: *Am I meant to be a university leader?*

One of the shrewdest insights about leadership I ever heard came from a man who—although outstanding in his academic field—wanted nothing to do with being a leader himself.

In the spring of 1970, when I was 29, I learned I had won a fellowship from the American Council on Education that would allow me to serve an administrative internship with Purdue University President Fred Hovde for the 1970–1971 academic year. I was elated by the opportunity. Despite having only recently been awarded tenure and promoted to associate professor of electrical engineering at Purdue, I was already leaning toward a career in administration. With the ACE fellowship, I would be able to spend a considerable amount of time learning about university governance without having to give up my research grants or my graduate students.

Soon after the award was announced, I happened to bump into a colleague, Vern Newhouse, who was a highly respected senior member of the electrical engineering faculty.

"So, Sample," Newhouse said, "I see you've won some sort of administrative fellowship in the president's office."

"Yes, that's true," I said.

"And you'll be learning how to become an administrator?"

"I suppose so."

"And then you'll probably want to be president of a university somewhere down the road?"

"Well, I don't know. I guess I've thought about it now and then," I said, somewhat disingenuously.

He smiled and said, "Personally, I've never had any ambition whatsoever to be an administrator. I am totally inept at managing things. Why, as you may know, I can't even manage my secretary or my graduate students. But I've been a careful observer of ambitious men all my life. And here, for what it's worth, is what I've learned: Many men want to *be* president, but very few want to *do* president." And with that he wished me well and walked away.

My experience over the last third of a century tells me that Professor Newhouse was absolutely right. Leadership is a peculiar kind of calling. University leadership roles, particularly at the level of a president or chancellor, are not necessarily appropriate for those who have achieved distinction in academic positions that may be, in a formal sense, lower on the totem pole. Nor should such persons, however gifted they may be, necessarily want to take on positions of leadership in the institutions of which they are a part.

## THE CONTRARIAN'S APPROACH TO SUBSTANCE VERSUS TRIVIA

University leaders must frequently subordinate the things they are most interested in, or which they feel are most important, to the urgent (but often ephemeral) and sometimes trivial demands of others. These others may include lieutenants, the media, politicians, protesters, board members, parents, employees, financial analysts, faculty committees, and organizers of black-tie dinners. As I always tell those who aspire to academic leadership, "Along with helping to guide and shape one of the most noble and important institutions in society, a university president must also kiss a lot of frogs!"

In this regard, I have deduced Sample's 70/30 Formula for Top Leadership—to wit: Under ideal conditions, up to 30 percent of a top leader's time can be spent on really substantive matters, and no more than 70 percent of his time should be spent reacting to or presiding over trivial, routine, or ephemeral matters. In one sense, this formula is very counterintuitive. In an age in which management literature always focuses on vision, most people assume big-picture things should dominate a CEO's agenda.

Freshman presidents often enter the fray determined to spend most of their time as true leaders (i.e., working on issues that really count), while delegating all the seemingly unimportant parts of their job to staff. Such naïfs are generally gone in a year or two, victims of a dragon born of minutiae, which could have been easily slain in its infancy but suddenly grew to man-eating proportions. In other words, most of a top leader's time must necessarily be spent dealing with trivia and ephemera if he wants to survive and maintain his effectiveness as a leader over the long haul.

The real danger implicit in Sample's 70/30 Formula is that the 30 percent of a top leader's effort devoted to important matters (such as independent thinking and inspiring his followers) may shrink to 20 percent, and then to 10 percent, and then to 5 percent, and finally to nothing, as the press of routine and relatively trivial matters ultimately consumes all of his time and energy. I know scores of university presidents who find themselves in this position and who feel impotent and unhappy as a result. It requires enormous discipline for the top leader in an organization to maintain the substantive component of his job near the 30 percent level.

Thus, the person who wants to *do* president (as opposed to simply *be* president) should be delighted with a 70/30 split in favor of trivia over substance. By contrast, people who need a higher percentage of substance in their lives should stay away from top leadership positions altogether.

## CONTRARIAN RECRUITING

If you have decided you are equipped and eager for both the trivia and the substance of academic leadership, and you have been given the opportunity to exercise your ability in this arena, your next step is to assemble a leadership team.

Teddy Roosevelt once observed, "The best executive is the one who recruits the most competent men around, tells them what he wants done, and then gets out of their way so they can do it." I buy that (if we include women as well as men), with the qualification that a university leader should not merely get out of the way of his lieutenants, but actively assist them and forge them into an effective team.

As we walked across the Purdue campus one day in the spring of 1971, President Fred Hovde explained to me how he was agonizing over whether to appoint a particular person to fill a key vacancy in his administration. I naively asked him if he thought this candidate was "the right man for the job." Hovde stopped and said, "Steve, that's the wrong question to ask. There's no such thing as 'the right man for the job.' The appropriate question to ask is, 'Is he the best man available for the job within the time frame in which I must fill the position?'"

Hovde went on to note that a near superstar is the wrong person for a particular job if someone better is available. And conversely, a truly mediocre candidate may be the right person for the job if he is better than anyone else who is available and if you absolutely must fill the position right away.

This illustrates one of the trickiest parts of major-league university leadership—the inevitable trade-off between whom you would like to have as a lieutenant and who can actually be recruited within the time that is available for making the appointment.

## CONTRARIAN MANAGEMENT: WORK FOR THOSE WHO WORK FOR YOU

Once the contrarian academic leader has a team in place, she must again go against conventional wisdom if she is to forge them into an effective unit.

One of the most important lessons I learned in this area occurred in 1971 when I was named the deputy director for academic affairs of the Illinois Board of Higher Education. There I learned a great deal from the board's chairman, George Clements, who had made a name for himself as the man who built the Chicago-based Jewel Tea Company into a major national grocery chain.

When I first arrived at my post, Mr. Clements gave me some basic advice about leadership. "Steve," he said, "you should spend a small amount of your time hiring your direct reports, evaluating them, exhorting them, setting their compensation, praising them, kicking their butts, and, when necessary, firing them. When you add all that up, it should come out to about 10 percent of your time. For the remaining 90 percent of your time you should be doing *everything you can* to help your direct reports succeed. You should be the first assistant to the people who work for you."

This is powerful contrarian advice—and is rarely followed. Even a university head who subscribes to the contemporary democratic theories being taught in the business school finds it difficult to think of his lieutenants as his equals, much less as his bosses. But that is exactly what Mr. Clements was saying: "Work for those who work for you!" If you are not in the process of getting rid of a lieutenant, bend over backward to help him get his job done. That means returning his phone calls promptly, listening carefully to his plans and problems, calling on others at his request, and helping him formulate his goals and develop strategies for achieving those goals. It is not that you should simply be your lieutenant's staff person; you should be his best staff person.

Virtually all leadership experts, whether they subscribe to traditional or au courant theories, depict leadership as a glamorous and majestic calling. But the contrarian university president is not fooled. She knows that effective day-to-day leadership is not so much about herself, as it is about the men and women she chooses to be her chief lieutenants. She knows that a lot of the things on her own plate will be minutiae and silliness, while her lieutenants will get to do the fun and important things.

## DECISION MAKING FOR THE CONTRARIAN ACADEMIC LEADER

A contrarian university president does not make decisions before he needs to and does not make more decisions than he has to. In particular, he never makes a decision that can reasonably be delegated to a provost, vice president, or other lieutenant.

Even in small colleges and universities, there are compelling reasons why a leader should consistently delegate most decisions to selected lieutenants. The first has to do with time constraints. Making a good decision is hard, time-consuming work, and no leader can make many good decisions in a month's time, much less in a day or a week. So he needs to carefully reserve for himself only the most important decisions and to cheerfully delegate the rest.

A second major factor in favor of delegation is that it helps develop and nurture strong lieutenants. A leader cannot expect his lieutenants to grow and grow up unless he gives them the opportunity to make real decisions that will have real consequences for the institution, without their being constantly second-guessed by the leader.

Finally, the contrarian leader who is willing to delegate almost all decisions to lieutenants has an opportunity to build a much stronger and more coherent university than does the leader who tries to make all the decisions himself.

Within the art of delegating decisions, there is the need on occasion for a university leader to appear to be making decisions when in fact he is not. In April 1992, the city of Los Angeles became engulfed in a horrific and bloody riot, triggered by a jury's acquittal of several police officers who had beaten an arrested motorist named Rodney King. In actual fact, the rioters left the University of Southern California untouched, but at the height of the disturbances (which surrounded the university's campus) we fully expected to suffer widespread arson, looting, beatings, and even murder.

Fortunately, the university had a well-developed emergency plan for dealing with a catastrophic earthquake. One of our vice presidents, surveying the growing mayhem from the top of a university building during the early hours of the riot, said to himself, "This looks like an earthquake to me!" and forthwith ordered the implementation of the earthquake emergency plan. With that, students from outlying housing were brought in to temporary quarters in the central campus, every university police officer and all physical plant staff were called back to active duty, the perimeter of the campus was secured, observers with radios were placed atop strategic buildings, phone banks were set up to deal with tens of thousands of calls from parents of students and families of staff, and a centralized command-and-control post was opened to coordinate the entire business.

What was the president's role during the three days of rioting? I walked around and showed the flag, so to speak. I shook hands, chatted with students and staff, asked questions, listened to people tell their stories, and gave out copious compliments and reassurances. Everyone thought I was in charge, making seventeen decisions a minute, but I really was not. Instead, all the decisions were being made by people who had been trained for months in the handling of a catastrophic emergency.

Was my presence on campus useful? Yes, very. The fact that the president of the university was highly visible night and day during the riots gave everyone a sense of security, which probably helped reduce panic and improve cooperation among students and staff. But in terms of decision making, I was careful to delegate everything to lieutenants while taking full responsibility for whatever might go wrong.

A leader should also be careful not to rush into making decisions that lie beyond the scope of his authority. In the late 1980s, when I was president of SUNY-Buffalo, our law school faculty decided to ban representatives of the judge advocate general corps from recruiting in the law school building because of the federal government's policy prohibiting homosexuals from serving in the armed forces. The matter was quickly appealed to me. Rather than jump precipitously into the hornet's nest of gays in the military, I decided first to find out who actually had the authority to ban various persons from using a particular university building. Was it the faculty for whom that building was home? The president? The SUNY-Buffalo Governing Council? The chancellor of the SUNY system? The SUNY System Board of Trustees?

Eventually everyone, including even the law school faculty, agreed that the authority to prohibit certain persons or groups from using university facilities lay exclusively with the president. This process of pinpointing the locus of authority automatically transformed the law faculty's action from an actual banning of the JAG corps to a simple recommendation to the president that the JAG corps should be banned. This transformation in turn changed the nature of the decision I had to make, because in academic circles it is one thing for a university president to decline to approve a faculty recommendation and quite another for him to overturn a decision that the faculty feel is legitimately theirs to make.

Moreover, if it had turned out that the authority for banning people from the law school building lay exclusively with the law faculty and not with the president, then I would have been absolved from making any decision at all. I might have publicly expressed agreement or disagreement with the faculty's decision, but I would not have had to take responsibility for it.

The foregoing example is instructive as to why a university leader should avoid, whenever possible, engaging in a two-front war when it comes to decision making—that is, quarrelling simultaneously over who has the authority to make a particular decision and what the decision should be.

## THE CONTRARIAN'S GUIDE TO INNOVATION

At the heart of contrarian academic leadership is a certain intellectual and creative independence that allows the leader to find new horizons of opportunity and novel solutions for seemingly intractable problems. Toward this end the leader must work assiduously to cultivate in herself and in her advisors the capacity to *think free*—free, that is, from all prior restraints. It is popular these days to talk about thinking out of the box or brainstorming, but thinking free takes that process to the next level, staying in a mode of inventiveness long after one has left one's bounds of comfort.

Thinking free was the secret to many of my successes as an inventor of electrical devices and very naturally translated into an effective tool for university leadership. The key to thinking free is first to allow your mind to contemplate really outrageous ideas and only subsequently to apply the constraints of practicality, practicability, legality, cost, time, and ethics. Thinking free is an unnatural act; not one person in a thousand can do it without enormous effort.

It is well known among engineers that the most important inventions in a particular field are often made by people who are new to that field— people who are too naive and ignorant to know all the reasons why something cannot be done and who are therefore able to think more freely about seemingly intractable problems. The same is true of the leadership of universities: it is often fresh blood and a fresh perspective from the outside that can turn an ailing organization around.

When my wife and I were interviewing in the early 1980s for the presidency of the State University of New York at Buffalo (a.k.a. the University at Buffalo, or simply UB), we saw a university with great underlying strengths and numerous superficial problems. Unfortunately, the problematic surface was all that was perceived by most of UB's constituencies at the time.

Never in our lives had we encountered a university that was so down on itself or that was held in such low esteem by so many of its own faculty, students, administrators, townspeople, and alumni. The body politic of the university seemed to be bruised all over—whenever we touched it, no matter how gently, it seemed to quiver and shrink back a bit. There were also formidable economic and political obstacles blocking UB's development.

However, from my wife's and my perspective, we saw that the inner core, the infrastructure if you will, of the University at Buffalo was in exceedingly good health and that the possibilities for advancing the university were much greater than many realized. The next nine years more than justified Kathryn's and my seemingly unfounded optimism. By the end of that period, UB had been elected to the prestigious Association of American Universities (only 61 of the more than 3,500 colleges and universities in America are members of the AAU; UB was the first public university in New York or New England to have been elected), sponsored research funding had tripled, applications for admission had doubled, we had completed or begun construction of more than two million gross square feet of new buildings at a cost of more than $400 million, UB was raising more private funds each year than all the other SUNY campuses combined, and *U.S. News & World Report* had named UB as one of the five most rapidly rising universities in the country.

Was it a miracle? No. Was the president a genius? No. It was just that my wife and I, coming from our experiences at the University of Nebraska, Purdue University, and the University of Illinois, were able to see UB and its surrounding community from a very different perspective. In other words, our thinking about UB was freer and less constrained than that of our colleagues and peers in Western New York.

## CONCLUSION: THE NEED FOR CONTRARIAN ACADEMIC LEADERSHIP

Studies of leadership are often unduly influenced by nostalgia and the benefit of hindsight. During a crucial juncture in the American Revolution, members of Congress openly doubted the abilities of the Continental Army's commander-in-chief, George Washington. Historian

Norman Gelb notes that John Adams, at a dark hour of the war, wrote in his diary: "Oh, Heaven! grant Us one great Soul! . . . One leading mind would extricate the best Cause, from that Ruin which seems to await it."[2]

Washington obviously carried with him no mystical blueprint for unlimited success, no formula or checklist that worked miracles in every situation. He did, however, bring a contrarian's approach to leadership, combining deliberate and effective decision making with imagination, courage, and grueling hard work.

Today's academic leaders need that same contrarian approach. They cannot copy anyone else's approach on the way to excellence; in fact, they often cannot even maintain their existing position without doing things in new ways. The playing field of academic leadership is being reshaped dramatically by economic and social forces. The ongoing commercialization of education is both a threat and an opportunity, and university leaders will need enormous amounts of creativity and self-discipline to balance the traditional values of the academy against the potential benefits of the marketplace.

Within this realm of uncertainty and possibility, the contrarian leader recognizes that her calling is an art, not a science. Effective management may be a science—although I have my doubts—but effective leadership is purely an art. In this sense, leadership is more akin to music, painting, and poetry than it is to more routinized endeavors. And just as there is no one true theory of art, there is no one true theory of leadership.

This makes the contrarian academic leader's experience at times more exhilarating than that of other leaders, and at times more excruciating. But it will always be *his* experience—one for which he willingly takes responsibility. And what could be a greater or more meaningful adventure in leadership than that?

## NOTES

1. Clark Kerr, *The Uses of the University*, 4th ed. (Cambridge, MA: Harvard University Press, 1995), p. 115.

2. Quoted in Norman Gelb, "Winter of Discontent," *Smithsonian*, May 2003.

# CHAPTER 25

## Sample's Golden Mean and Thoughts about Thought
### A Response to President Sample's Essay

*Larry R. Faulkner*

It is a pleasure to have the opportunity to comment on Steve Sample's essay, which is really an appetizer for his marvelous book, *The Contrarian's Guide to Leadership*. I commend it to everyone here. There is no academic leader in America whom I admire more than Steve. What he has accomplished is remarkable, and through it all he has remained both humane and largely in good humor. His essay here and his book highlight favorite methods of his that might actually be practiced and learned by others. Of course, Steve's success also rests in large measure on sheer talent, and there is no way for any one of us to better ourselves in that direction. But we can better our methods, and Steve has put forward some useful ideas for this forum.

I admire Sample's Golden Mean, which is the abbreviated name I give to his rule of 70/30. Steve makes the point that a large part of a presidency is inevitably consumed with the countless small tasks, events, and acts that are required to maintain both momentum and the community of the university. A president or chancellor who resents these things and attempts to delegate his or her share of them will indeed soon trade away both momentum and community. Sample's Golden Mean places the ideal fraction of the time dedicated to them at 70 percent, a sound figure, I believe. That leaves 30 percent of the time, in the ideal, for what Steve calls "substance," by which he means engagement with that much smaller number of matters that will shape the future of the institution in a significant way. He goes on to highlight what we have all experienced, which is the tendency for time for substance to be traded away, so that the 70 percent becomes 80 percent, 90 percent, or even 100 percent. By setting out the rule of 70/30, Steve provides a really valuable guideline against which all of us can, and should, continually evaluate our use of time.

In his writings on leadership, Steve Sample places tremendous emphasis on "thinking gray" and "thinking free." But for now, I want to just stress the thinking itself. Time to think evaporates so easily for a president, chancellor, or provost; yet, without serious thinking there is no real chance that an institution will do other than drift in the winds of fashion and passion. All of us, if we are honest, will admit to having seen a great deal of that kind of drift in the American academic world during our careers. I believe that the lack of time committed to serious, independent, creative thinking is one of the reasons for the surprising homogeneity of structure, identity, and approach to mission that we see across America today. We rightly celebrate the diversity among America's institutions of higher education, but among those institutions the approaches to curriculum, finance, admissions, intellectual scope, and interface with the public do not vary so much, despite tremendously varied missions. Perhaps we would be a lot more effective in addressing the enormous challenges before us if we took more time to think and innovate, rather than being so prone to mimic our peers.

Central to Steve Sample's philosophy is a concept of conversation, which shows up in this very principle of trying to preserve 30 percent of the time for substance. But he also says something else in his essay related to this idea:

> Making a good decision is hard, time-consuming work, and no leader can make many good decisions in a month's time, much less in a day or a week. So he needs to carefully reserve for himself only the most important decisions and to cheerfully delegate the rest.

What strikes me about this passage is not the admonition for us to delegate. All of us have heard that many, many times. The important idea is the way Steve sets out decision making as a process, involving not just the ability to decide, but also the time required for careful study, for listening, for evaluation. There is only so much capacity for all that, and it needs to be expended carefully, almost according to a budget. This is an important concept that most of us disregard pretty regularly.

Finally, let me comment on the situational effectiveness of a leader, simply because I believe that there is a make-or-break aspect to it. Steve makes his point on this topic with his doubts about how the great Washington would fare in the political or military scenes of this day. The success of every leader is critically dependent on the match between that leader and the culture of the organization or society to be led. If the leader does not understand the culture intimately and is not fundamentally resonant with it, sheer leadership talent and superb technique rarely count for much. Substantial risks always attend both the decision by an institution to appoint a new leader and the decision of the leader to accept. Most factors that will ultimately determine success or failure can, at the time of appointment, be discerned darkly or not at all. But resonance with the culture is a factor that does lend itself to fair evaluation by both sides even in the stage of courtship, and it merits great weight in the decisions reached by all parties.

# CHAPTER

## Innovation and Focus
### A Response to President Sample's Essay

*Marye Anne Fox*

Steve Sample's "The Contrarian's Guide to University Leadership" emphasizes the need for team work achieved by identifying highly capable associates with whom to work and then striving to work for them. It emphasizes thinking free and the need for artful listening to others' views. It stresses that basic moral principles and organizational missions must guide fundamental decision making. Perhaps above all, it gives advice in determining "which hill you're willing to die on."

### A NEW HOME FOR TECHNOLOGY TRANSFER

Through North Carolina State University, the state of North Carolina was creating a new model for private–public partnerships for effective technology transfer. A decade before I became chancellor (in 1998), then-Governor Jim Hunt had arranged for the transfer to the university of a parcel of 1,000 acres of undeveloped state land immediately adjacent to NC State University's main campus. His vision was that this land would be converted to an oasis for nourishing effective partnerships that would take innovative ideas from a basic research stage through to commercializable products and, hence, would yield jobs for North Carolinians.

This was not to be a typical university research park, where intellectual connection to university research can be tenuous and where the main advantage to the university would be income derived from land lease fees paid by companies that chose to locate on the campus. No, companies would in fact be forbidden from building or leasing space at all unless there was a direct and ongoing relationship with one of NC State's academic or research units. This relationship could involve collaborative research or commercialization, sponsored research contracts or grants, graduate fellowships or scholarships for students working in allied disciplines, consulting agreements with individual faculty members, joint sponsorship of seminars or lecture series, or employee appointments as adjunct professors, among others. These required partnerships were also clearly distinguished from those undertaken solely to benefit private sector firms.

Hunt's premise in proposing this generous land transfer was a twenty-first-century update of the land grant (a consequence of the Morrill Act of 1862) that led to the founding of NC State in 1887. In parallel with this historical connection, this land transfer was to be used for the benefit of the average North Carolinian. Originally, this mission centered on agriculture, and then later on "mechanic arts." The current version was to focus on emerging technologies, on the inventions created by NC State students and faculty, spawning new businesses either through venture capital investment or through collaboration with their partners. By providing a completely green field approach, we believed we could together revolutionize the way technology transfer might be accomplished. In recognition of the evolution in this thinking over the first century of the university's life, this campus was designated as the "Centennial Campus."

In addition to the research space per se, the master plan would provide on-site access to facilities needed for full success in a knowledge-based society. Among the services to be provided were high-speed broadband connections, quality restaurants, on-campus condominiums, a golf course to be constructed on otherwise unbuildable flood plain land, a hotel, and a conference center.

By the start of Fall 2000 classes, the number of private partners had grown to fifty-eight, achieving a growth rate that was five times faster than in the previous two-year period. In addition, a University and Community College Bond Referendum was passed in November 2000, providing NC State with $468 million for capital construction, in which two major academic engineering buildings would be located on Centennial Campus. The North Carolina legislature also approved our request to allow development of underutilized pasture land adjacent to the College of Veterinary Medicine according to the Centennial Campus model, with an IAMS Imaging partnership to represent the first collaboration. And in his last days of his fourth term in office, Governor Hunt responded favorably to our request for the transfer of an additional 200 acres adjacent to the Centennial Campus, expanding our options for further build-out.

Clearly, a threshold for a critical census on the Centennial Campus had been attained so that full community service build-out could begin. There were now about 1,500 private sector employees, 350 faculty, and 1,500 students present each day on the Centennial Campus. Accordingly, contracts were signed with a private sector partner to begin condominium construction, and a detailed business plan for the hotel, golf course, and conference center prepared by an external expert consultant was reviewed positively by both the board of trustees and the UNC Board of Governors.

## A SUDDEN SHIFT

Then the terrorist attack of September 11, 2001, took place. Seemingly overnight, the economy softened, venture capital dried up, and tourism declined.

Of significance to the Centennial Campus master plan, and to our conference complex in particular, troubles in the tourism industry led to a profound weakening of support of the North Carolina Hotel and Motel Association (HMA) for the hotel, golf course, and conference center. Unexpectedly, the HMA, which had been an early supporter of the Centennial Campus concept, began vociferously to invoke concerns about the university's fiduciary responsibility for public funds. A substantial concern of the HMA was that the hotel/conference center model, if successful, might also be extended to other universities, as our research collaboration model had been.

The HMA also expressed reservations about what they called unfair competition that allegedly favored the complex over private sector developers. (The Centennial Campus concept was based on special legislation exempting universities from the Umstead Act, which prohibited competition with the private sector. This exemption permitted public universities to create new spin-off businesses and allowed retention and reinvestment of lease revenue streams.) Suddenly, it seemed that our success had become a threat to those with whom we wanted to collaborate.

Indeed, the HMA hired two well-known lobbyists to lead opposition to the project, even to the point of proposing legislative revocation of the Umstead exemption for existing Centennial Campus buildings. Although several studies specially commissioned by the UNC Board of Governors had reaffirmed the wisdom of proceeding, the real lobbying pressure began as the Council of State considered whether to allow the use of state land for the project. Rather than persisting in asking elected officials to incur political risk, with a potentially larger long-term cost to the university, we chose instead to back away, for a time, from the project.

## LESSONS LEARNED

One of a university's most cherished traditions is the willingness to learn from experience. As we explore viable routes to overcome the financial and political obstacles facing further development of support services on our Centennial Campus, we do well to reflect on lessons learned.

The clearest lesson is that partnerships, even if successful for the greater community, can be threatening to interested parties in related fields unless a clear benefit is convincingly anticipated by everyone. Fiscal responsibility and alignment with university mission are not enough to assure full community support. We should have sought actively, at each stage of our master planning, proactive involvement of the HMA in designing this project, rather than only exhibiting an openness to listening to their position. Perhaps then our decision-making process would have been more understandable to them, and progress toward our educational goals might have felt more collaborative. Without clear illustrations of how their association would benefit from our mutual progress, we assumed too much in expecting shared appreciation of the anticipated positive effect on our university programs.

A second lesson is that change of an accepted paradigm is always difficult. In this project, we clearly encountered strongly held perceptions that universities should focus narrowly on teaching, research, and service directed to their own students. We had not yet effectively convinced all of our partner communities of the importance of university-based economic development or that auxiliary support services can enhance these traditional missions without major state financial investment if university administrations are granted operational flexibility. Innovative ideas, which are the lifeblood of a university, can be inherently threatening to those who have enjoyed great success in implementing other models.

And perhaps the most important lesson we have learned is patience, patience, patience, even when success seems to be absolutely assured by action. Recalling Sample's advice that leadership is about ideas and values, I determined that this was not a hill I was willing to die on—at least not until we have achieved a broader appreciation for actions needed if the university is to function as a true engine for innovative economic growth.

In the end, it is essential to sustain and preserve the core mission of the university, even when the full realization of the university's potential must be deferred.

# CHAPTER

## Personal Qualities for University Leadership
### A Response to President Sample's Essay

*Timothy J. Sullivan*

The organizers of the Smith-Richardson Foundation Forums on Presidential Leadership have chosen to tackle a tough subject. Great leaders are hard to find. Great leadership is even harder to explain. This is true despite what seems to be the perpetual production of books about leadership and the exponential growth of self-described experts who make a fine living telling the less well-informed what leadership really means.

What nearly all of these experts and authors produce is a kind of white noise—full of catch words, half-clever phrases, and seven, or ten, or twenty steps that guarantee that doing the footwork will make you the leader of your dreams.

Where can we turn for better thinking? To an unlikely source. Of obscenity, the late Justice Potter Stewart famously wrote, "I can't define it, but I know it when I see it." Substitute "leadership" for "obscenity" in Justice Stewart's formulation—and we have the beginning of wisdom that trumps just about any highly hyped book on leadership that I know.

Why do I say that? Because I believe that Emerson was right when he wrote, "There is properly no history—only biography." To my mind, leadership—at least the real thing—is the unique expression of a singular person operating in a "one of" environment. Under these circumstances, the chances of drawing repeatable lessons about leadership are slim to none. Of course, it is possible to study leaders and to discern something at least marginally useful about which to talk or to write. We know the drill. We have heard most of it a thousand times. It goes like this: Great leaders must be both tactically and strategically gifted. Great leaders must have the confidence to choose good people and give them room. Great leaders must have the power to dissemble—that is, to make marginal people or irrelevant ideas seem important if the larger needs of the organization are thought so to dictate. You will find this latter point listed in every encyclopedia of leadership. Just look under the entry titled "justifiable hypocrisy."

Forgive me if I suggest that such lessons tell us little about the critical qualities that make great leaders in the university or in any other context. What lies at the heart of the mystery of great leadership is what lies in the heart of a great leader. And penetrating the secrets of the human heart is among life's most daunting tasks. Which is why I think the literature of leadership focuses far too much on delineating rules of conduct and far too little on examining traits of character of individual leaders. It should be the other way around. The study of character should be the starting place for any serious examination of leadership.

I know that I was not asked to write this essay to expound at length on my personal theory of leadership. That is good, because I do not have one. I do want to offer some brief thoughts about just a few of the personal qualities without which great leadership is not possible. Some of what I say will be thought trite. It probably is, but what is trite is often true and conceals something significant that we tend to overlook, or at least not connect properly to a larger and more important insight.

Integrity—Without a powerful sense of personal honor, leadership is impossible. Brains, beauty, wit, soaring eloquence, or a single-digit handicap add up to nothing without an honesty that compels moral choice even under the hardest circumstances. Another great judge, Elbert Tuttle, said it very well: "For what is a share of a man worth?" he asked. "If he does not contain the quality of integrity, he is worthless. If he does, he is priceless. The value is either nothing or is infinite."[1]

Love—The power of love is like none other. The context of leadership, transforming inspiration, comes when the leader loves his or her institution—its people and its values. Mere affection will not do. There must be a passionately felt union of values between the leader and the institution he or she leads, a union that has been made impregnable by love.

Will and Focus—The distractions of the moment are numberless. We all know them. We need not name them. Some of those distractions must claim our time. Steve Sample's essay makes that very clear. Yet through all the trivia and the insistent selfish agendas of the perennially self-obsessed, true leaders must see with unfailing clarity the larger objectives they not merely seek to achieve—but which they must achieve.

Let me quote another thought from another one in my judicial pantheon. Justice Holmes wrote, "If you want to hit a bird on the wing, you must have all your will in a focus. You must not be thinking about yourself—you must be living with your eye on that bird. Every great achievement is a bird on the wing."

**Perspective**—Great leaders are ambitious. I suppose that goes without saying. But ambitious for what? Success comes in many varieties. Winston Churchill identified two. "There are two kinds of success," he said, "initial and ultimate." What he did not say is that most of us settle for initial success and hope that the ultimate takes care of itself. That is a mistake, although an understandable one. The great leader needs the ability consistently to turn away form the sweet sound of applause earned by short-term victories if such victories diminish, as they often do, the chance for ultimate triumph. This is hard to do, because it requires the suppression of ego and the nearly universal appetite for personal commendation. It means we must tolerate the misunderstandings or the criticisms of others whose abilities or responsibilities are smaller. The president's perspective must be unique—it must run deeper and extend further than that of anyone else. That is why the president must be steady in his or her will to ultimate success.

**Self-Denial**—When a president of Washington College (soon to be Washington and Lee), General Lee was asked by a young mother what she should teach her son. "Madame," Lee replied, "teach him to deny himself." No leader dares ever forget that. Leadership in the end is the act of inspiration taken to its highest level. Leadership that is magical has a magical effect on others. We may all hope for moments of magic in our lives as leaders. Some of us will never be so lucky; others will. We enhance our chances greatly if we see ourselves truly as the servant of others. It is not enough to support and encourage our subordinates; we must believe and act on the belief that the success of those who work with us is not merely important, but is more important than our own success—which is another way of saying that the fate of the institutions we lead must always matter more than what happens to us. We will find incredible strength in turning away from praise and glory if we do so because we love our institutions more than we love our own ambitions.

This list of virtues is not exhaustive, but it is critical. Each of the qualities I described is a necessary condition for leadership whose legacy will last. And as Emerson said, or at least almost said, we will find more useful insights into the secrets of leadership by studying great lives rather than great events. The trick is to work inside out; that is, from the study of the leader within acting on the challenges and the circumstances he or she encounters without. Even doing this, of course, we may fail in our quest to understand the true nature of the special gifts of a great leader. We should not be surprised. So often in life we discover that what is supremely important is also supremely mysterious.

## NOTE

1. Elbert F. Tuttle, "Heroism in War and Peace," 13 *Emory University Quarterly* 129 (1957): 138–159.

# CHAPTER 28

# Leading in the Unique
# Character of Academe: What It
# Takes

*Kathleen M. Ponder and Cynthia D. McCauley*

B eing a faculty member at the Center for Creative Leadership requires a passion for understanding what leadership is and how to
effectively practice "it." No practice of leadership, no type of leader,
escapes our interest. So you can imagine how eagerly we leapt upon
the invitation from Dr. Thomas Hearn to attend the three Smith-
Richardson Forums on Presidential Leadership and hear prominent and
successful university presidents discuss how leadership takes form in the
world of academe. After listening intently to the rich discussions and
studying the powerful essays, we began a process of inquiry directed at
relating their leadership lessons and strategies for learning to two of CCL's
leadership frameworks: the Model of Leader Competencies and the
framework of Learning Tactics.

## LEADERSHIP LESSONS

Many times during our conversations with CCL clients, talk turns to
what it is like leading in their particular industry. This discussion usually
begins with a protestation that "you can't possible understand the very
unique demands faced by *our* organization's leaders." Yet, once novel surface descriptors of the requirements are removed, what remains is not so
unique. In fact, the leadership challenges associated with organizations
of all kinds remain fairly constant. And the competencies needed to meet
these challenges do not vary either. Leaders everywhere need to be vi-
sionary, take risks, innovate, manage change, make decisions, influence

**Figure 1**
**Model of Leader Competencies**

LEADING OTHERS
Maintaining Effective Teams and Work Groups
Building and Maintaining Relationships
Valuing Diversity and Difference
Developing Others
Communicating Effectively

LEADING THE ORGANIZATION
Managing Change
Solving Problems and Making Decisions
Managing Politics and Influencing Others
Taking Risk and Innovating
Setting Vision and Strategy
Managing the Work
Enhancing Business Skills and Knowledge
Understanding and Navigating the Organization

LEADING YOURSELF
Demonstrating Ethics and Integrity
Displaying Drive and Purpose
Exhibiting Leadership Stature
Increasing Your Capacity to Learn
Managing Yourself
Increasing Self-Awareness
Developing Adaptability

others, communicate effectively, build relationships with diverse individuals and groups, and possess drive to get the job done.

CCL's Model of Leader Competencies (Figure 1), based both on research and conversations with leaders, organizes the knowledge, skill, and attitudinal assets possessed by effective leaders into twenty groupings and further clusters these competencies into three broad categories: those used to respond to broad organizational challenges ("Leading the Organization"), those used during interactions with constituents and stakeholders ("Leading Others"), and those competencies that speak to the internal constitution of the leader ("Leading Yourself").

As we listened to the forum participants discuss how they worked their way through a complex web of challenges and crisis, we heard how they, too, relied on this set of competencies to survive and succeed. But how they expressed these competencies and the relative importance each had to their success was significantly altered by the unique nature of university life. Forum participants described three defining features of university life that shape the president's exercise of the leadership competencies identified by CCL.

First, the president must lead in a culture built around a resistance to authoritarian, hierarchical leadership—a necessary resistance designed to allow ideological ferment associated with democracy. Throughout all forum discussions, we heard vivid descriptions of academe's highly volatile, free-thinking context. Leading an American university was described as leading an "intellectual free-for-all" with a radically decentralized culture shaped by the "tyranny of departments" (Thomas Hearn). Departmental units were described as operating as loose confederations of academicians with fierce allegiance first to their field and only secondarily exhibiting loyalty to their university.

We were told that the position of president does not come with much power and that while "some presidents and chancellors are being called CEOs, the title suggests a kind and scale of authority that is uncongenial within the culture of the university" (Thomas Hearn). Trying to centrally manage and control departments and faculty runs counter to a cornerstone of university life: academic freedom. In academic circles, a president can decline a faculty recommendation, but it is not acceptable for the president to overturn a decision that faculty feel legitimately belongs to them (Steve Sample). In fact, presidents are cautioned not to rush into making decisions that may lie beyond the scope of their authority. Faculty expect to be a part of the decision-making process, and a university relying only on it's president for good ideas is a university in trouble (Lawrence Bacow). The whole notion of faculty working as a team driving toward attainment of the president's agenda runs counter to the academic culture in which faculty prize academic freedom, autonomy, and choice. Hearn reminds new presidents that the work of teaching and scholarship can be "coordinated," but it cannot be "managed."

Second, the president must lead an organization with an extraordinary purpose. While businesses strive to make a profit, military organizations work to win wars, and nonprofit organizations pursue social good, universities exist to promote and sustain democracy by providing bright minds with an unfettered intellectual marketplace. Hearn describes the university as an important and constant source of intellectual experimentation and innovation, preserving and interpreting the best of what human intelligence has created and, thus, holding a sacred responsibility for the identity not only of America but of many other nations as well. Forum participants described the university as "society's conscience" (Al Yates), a place responsible for furthering the ideals of democracy (Mary Sue Coleman), and a utopian experiment holding up humanistic ideals (Steve Sample). And they spoke of an awesome leadership responsibility: to not only protect the right of all members of the university community to self-expression, but also to just as strenuously guard the right and hold others accountable to reply and to debate (Gregory Farrington).

Forum participants described this lofty mission as placing an exceptional responsibility on the shoulders of its leaders, since it must be carried out in an environment seeking to commercialize education (Steve Sample). The successful president must operate with fiscal shrewdness and scrupulous accountability but at the same time stay true to the university's mission (Thomas Hearn). University leaders need enormous amounts of creativity and self-discipline to balance the traditional values of the academy against the potential benefits and pressures of the marketplace (Steve Sample).

Third, the president must contend with a university culture not hospitable to leadership recruitment and development because of its faculty's focus on the life of the mind and career paths firmly rooted in academic disciplines. While executives scramble for top leadership positions in other organizations, most university faculty do not eagerly pursue organizational leadership roles. The university model of leadership placement is not a capacity-building, development, or succession-planning model. Rather, it is either a replacement model that works to find volunteers to fill necessary slots in order to keep the university moving. Or it is a prestige-seeking model in which recruitment efforts focus on finding a scholar to bring distinction or cache to the university because of scholarly achievements—not because of demonstrated leadership abilities.

Forum participants write of faculty viewing with disdain the role of department chair, seeing it as a temporary rotation out of more worthy work in the world of ideas, even though presidents view the chair position as the most important leadership role in the university (Thomas Hearn). Given this faculty preference for idea work over leadership, faculty spend little energy and resource developing the skills, attitudes, and knowledge of management and leadership, causing many forum participants to question the appropriateness of having faculty in leadership roles. Further, they question whether the job of leading fits the interests and passions

of those who have achieved academic distinction, some forum participants suggesting that giving too much weight to a candidate's discipline
in the presidential search process is a mistake (Graham Spanier). A practicing president (or provost or chair) finds that few in the university community aspire to her job, and even fewer think it requires any special
kind of skill. This dearth of interest in and understanding of leading, either as president or chair, profoundly impacts the president's exercise of
leadership and leader selection and significantly shapes the leader–fol-
lower relationship.

So, given this unique culture, how do forum presidents contend with
the major responsibilities of leadership? In what unique ways do these
presidents practice the leader competencies outlined in the CCL model?
Among the twenty CCL leader competencies, the patterns of discourse
among the presidents at this forum suggest that successful presidents require extraordinary skill in practicing eight of the competencies:

- Understanding and navigating the organization
- Building and maintaining relationships
- Valuing diversity and difference
- Managing yourself
- Managing politics and influencing others
- Demonstrating ethics and purpose
- Self-awareness
- Developing others

## COLLABORATING, NOT COMMANDING

While CCL's research indicates that problems with interpersonal relationships can and do derail the careers of promising executives in the
corporate world (Van Velsor & Leslie, 1995), there is a mitigating factor
tempering the impact of their relationship skills: these top leaders can
exercise positional and hierarchical power. Their ability to hire, fire, re-
assign, and demote employees creates a climate that is more accepting of
idiosyncrasies and even bad behavior. The same holds true in the
branches of the U.S. military. From their first days in boot camp, those
serving in the military know that rank deserves respect and deference,
regardless of the personal characteristics of the person holding that rank.

But at the university, forum participants reported that tenure, academic freedom, and academic experts from a broad array of fields all me-
diate presidential power and militate against the exercise of hierarchical

authority. Schools and departments each exercise centrifugal force and distribute sources of influence, rendering the exercise of hierarchical executive authority impossible (Thomas Hearn). Presidents, like most leaders, also must influence multiple constituencies (e.g., boards of trustees, legislators, alumni and donors, accreditation agencies, faculty groups) over whom they have no positional power. How do you lead a university without much positional power, without reliance on the authority to command policies and procedures? An authoritarian approach in the hands of a university leader is guaranteed to fail.

## UNDERSTANDING AND NAVIGATING THE ORGANIZATION

First, forum participants talked about developing a deep understanding of their institution—its history, culture, core strengths, influential voices, and inner workings. This knowledge allows presidents to see the living system that makes up their institution, navigate within that system to get things accomplished, and ultimately become a part of that system. As Larry Faulkner noted, "If the leader does not understand the culture intimately and is not fundamentally resonant with it, sheer leadership talent and superb technique rarely count for much."

Understanding the organization was particularly emphasized in descriptions of transitions to a new presidency. Although educational institutions have some common dynamics, they also have their unique identities, cultures, and social systems. Already having this understanding of the institution was seen as one of the benefits of promoting an individual from within the university to the top leadership role (Father Edward Malloy, Charles Steger). However, outsiders can sometimes see aspects of the organization that insiders have become blind to, as Steve Sample illustrated in his story of becoming president of the State University of New York at Buffalo: "My wife and I . . . saw a university with great underlying strengths and numerous superficial problems. Unfortunately, the problematic surface was all that was perceived by most of [the university's] constituencies at the time." For those who do move into the role of president from outside the university, a key strategy for getting to know the new institution is to spend considerable time out talking to faculty and staff (Dale Knobel, Albert Yates).

Change initiatives also require strong competence at understanding and navigating the organization. The process William Kirwan led to eliminate programs at the University of Maryland was built on his deep understanding of the institution and how the system could best deal with severe budget reductions. Instead of responding simply with a short-term, decentralized approach to cutting budgets, the university undertook a comprehensive look at program reductions and eliminations. Kirwan knew what would be important in this process to the internal and external constituents and how to involve the campus community in getting this hard work accomplished together. In relating his own experiences of downsizing, John DeGioia shared this lesson: "When preparing to cut, you need to achieve as deep a grasp as possible of the impacts of the proposed cuts. These are fragile ecosystems. You need to understand the key points in those systems when making reductions."

## BUILDING AND MAINTAINING RELATIONSHIPS

Forum participants also explained how they moved their university agenda forward within and outside the university community by cultivating relationships strong enough to get consensus around particular ideas and issues. Through these relationships, they empower their presidency.

Accounts of forum presidents skillfully handling their challenges cite their *relational skill*—their ability to inspire, influence, and sustain trust-filled relationships with all kinds of people—as a potent source of power. No matter what the challenge or crisis, forum presidents rely on coalitions and networks to move their agenda and the university forward (e.g., Mary Sue Coleman's long-term, transparent consultative process involving regents, faculty, administration, and key community groups, enabling her to enact necessary budget cuts; Philip Dubois' use of standing campus and community committees to assist the community in its grieving process over the death of a gay man, Matthew Shepherd; Gregory Farrington's ongoing solicitation of help from faculty experts with differing viewpoints; Freeman Hrabowski's development of strong relationships with institutions and organizations that could support the Meyerhoff scholars).

Forum participants humbly acknowledged the limitations of their positional power and stressed the importance of relying on relational power to sway events in the direction they favor. Rather than fight against the decentralized university culture, they embrace it. Rather than despair at the fundamentally contentious nature of faculty, they harness their skepticism and capacity for criticism to create solutions and the "most noble achievements and enduring changes" (David Hardesty).

## VALUING DIVERSITY AND DIFFERENCE

But strategically building coalitions and collaboratives within academe is a uniquely dicey and often dangerous undertaking. Employees holding diverse worldviews and values working in business or the military find their personal preferences subjugated to the mission of business and military organizations. Human Resources policies and cultural protocol manage the expression of personal differences so that the work of the organization gets done. Employees are instructed in how to not give offense.

But not so in academe, where the central purpose of academe is promoting workplace diversity. Faculty exercise and prize academic freedom, a freedom that often entails a war of hotly contested ideas (Thomas Hearn). And the student body spends its time encountering and being instructed in critical analysis of a wide variety of worldviews and values.

To preserve this free exchange of ideas, presidents facilitate rather than minimize dissent, while at the same time deftly orchestrating debates to allow at least tolerance and, hopefully, mutual understanding. The president's unique challenge is to champion the free expression and exploration of diverse ideas and ways of being, while avoiding the eruption of destructive behaviors by people whose deepest, most cherished beliefs are being challenged.

They must maintain a fierce commitment to free expression, ensuring that all sides of issues at stake are heard (Mary Sue Coleman). For university presidents to possess competence in "Valuing Diversity and Difference" requires that they express more than mere tolerance for difference. It demands an authentic and deep commitment to unfettered intellectual debate, enabling them to dispassionately and respectfully hear, and give hearing to, all in the university community.

## MANAGING YOURSELF

Sometimes the president's relationship challenge entails keeping open dialogue with warring groups, each fervently committed to fundamentally different beliefs and courses of action, some that the president may find personally offensive. Philip Dubois contended with gay rights groups and religious fundamentalists. E. Gordon Gee encountered the United Daughters of the Confederacy and an angry multiracial student body, both espousing opposing perspectives about the name of a campus building, Confederacy Hall. Mary Sue Coleman hosted the Palestinian Solidarity Conference and encountered firestorms of criticism and outrage from community groups.

Because of the core purpose of academe, forum participants suggested that the university president must be invitational to all, "expecting and even welcoming the atmosphere of critics and dissent" (Thomas Hearn). The university leader must work assiduously to cultivate the capacity to think free, "to contemplate really outrageous ideas and only subsequently to apply the constraints of practicality, practicability, legality, cost, time, and ethics" (Steve Sample). An unintended slip in presidential voice or demeanor can disturb the fragile atmosphere of openness. Graham Spanier warns that if you cannot tolerate disagreement, anger, and un-flattering interviews and cartoons, then the life of the university presi-dent is not for you.

Like leaders of religious organizations, the leader of academe stands as a moral model, a model whose every behavior is closely watched. Even small gestures take on significance: "Mr. Quayle, then sitting vice presi-dent, came back to his alma mater and gave a rousing anti-affirmative action speech. On the platform with Mr. Quayle, I was very visible. Yet it was more than I could do to clap politely because he really worked the students into a frenzy. Later, I learned that the black community noticed that I did not quite clap, and they did see that as a political statement" (Robert Bottoms).

## MANAGING POLITICS AND INFLUENCING OTHERS

Forum participants suggested that their survival depends on their abil-ity to manage the unique political environment of the university—to nurture coalitions among groups with disparate agendas, to talk and be-have in ways that encourage the discovery of commonalities as well as differences. Especially in times of crisis, the president's voice matters (Philip Dubois). To encourage disparate interest groups to come together, the president must be able to inspire confidence and be confident (Charles Steger) in a course of action. At other times, he or she must be "priest" and coalesce the community in grieving and healing (Philip Dubois; Charles Steger).

Competence in building coalitions to support an organization's forward movement and mission stands as a crucial capability for leaders of all kinds of organizations. But the underlying motivation driving university leaders to forge collaboratives springs from a different place. Leaders from many other sectors pursue relationships to attain personal power and prestige, and the drive to forge partnerships emanates from a desire for financial gain, for competitive advantage, or to feed a competitive spirit (Al Yates).

But forum participants suggested that successful university presidents cultivate relationships with others not for self-aggrandizement but for a fundamentally different reason relating to the unique mission of the university. Institutions of higher education value human development over monetary gain. Their primary purpose is to educate all bright minds and to provide society with an unfettered marketplace of ideas; they are not in the business of producing goods and services for profit. And so their motivation for collaborating and partnering comes from a deeply felt commitment to this purpose (Al Yates, Thomas Hearn). While on the surface the act of coalition building may appear similar to the politicking engaged in by other leaders, effective university presidents firmly anchor these relationships in the ethical standards, values, and mission of their university.

The successful university president described by forum participants engages others in relationships not to seek power and position but to seek truth, integrity, competence, and compassion (Al Yates, Philip Dubois). While displaying a commitment to open dialogue and engagement, university presidents also stand ready to adopt principled, value-driven stands when necessary, willingly accepting personal discomfort and danger because their personal values passionately align with the values of their institution (Gregory Farrington, Al Yates, Tim Sullivan).

## DEMONSTRATING ETHICS AND PURPOSE

The most effective leaders of all kinds of organizations demonstrate behaviors that show a valuing of the collective good; they demonstrate self-sacrifice to reach organizational goals, display responsible idealism, and inhibit behaviors associated with self-protection and self-interest (Bales, 1999). But forum participants pointed to a distinctive set of core values possessed by effective university presidents. People look to college presidents to provide moral leadership every day (Scott Cowen).

When E. Gordon Gee faced dissension over the naming of a university hall, he let us see a core value of his, human dignity, in action. Taking his position angered wealthy university alumni. Gee might have framed the dilemma quite differently, analyzing the varying merits of each course of action from a financial vantage point. But he did not. And he might have considered which alternative posed the least threat to him physically and professionally. But he did not.

Because university leaders are charged with achieving two "bottom lines"—one the achievement of a higher order mission and the other financial stability—the nature and maturity of their personal character are critical. Unlike their business counterparts, university presidents must meet financial targets while pursuing a mission that includes unprofitable pursuits (e.g., philosophy, religion, social work departments). Individuals entrusted with the advancement of a university, a place dedicated to human development and betterment, must be in charge of their ego and be in passionate pursuit of a purpose much larger than themselves.

Throughout their writings, forum participants describe the special virtuosity and character required of the president: for example, Farrington and Graham Spanier suggesting that successfully leading a university requires good character and values and a high level of integrity and principle; Al Yates indicating that good leaders must first be good people that we can trust in and be assured of their virtue and know they will do the right thing; Julianne Thrift describing the special responsibility of the president to use crisis to reemphasize basic values and fundamental societal values; Lawrence Bacow's exhorting presidents to "tell them what makes you tick, what you care about, what your values are"; Freeman Hrabowski reminding leaders of the importance of focusing on substance and being passionate about your beliefs; Graham Spanier saying that people should not move into administration if they are afraid of losing their job but that they have to show a certain level of integrity and principle.

There is a prescriptive aspect to the leader competency "demonstrating ethics and purpose" when applied to the leader of an institution of higher education. The president must be an individual struggling to live at the highest stage of human development, propelled by a valuing of service, human dignity, interdependence, and global harmony rather than self-protection, personal competence, and control (Hall, 1995). Personal qualities trump academic and business qualifications when your job is sustaining an organization whose purpose is to further the ideals of democracy and human development (Al Yates, Thomas Hearn). Philip Dubois reminds university presidents that "your stakeholders . . . are measuring your conduct during the crisis. They know that a crisis does not *make* character—it *reveals* character."

## SELF-AWARENESS

Like senior leaders everywhere, university presidents find it hard to get a realistic appraisal of their impact on the people they lead. Are they seen as demonstrating unwavering commitment to the university's higher purpose? Senior positional power generally prevents honest assessment. As Al Yates reminds us:

There are not very many people who are willing to tell a CEO that he is "full of it," so leaders who seek balance must also seek ways to encourage their trusted lieutenants to summon the courage and will to be candid and truthful about such delicate but crucial matters. Our lives balance, at times, on precariously high wires, and we need to cherish those people who consistently help guide us back to the safety of solid ground.

Like other senior leaders, university presidents must find a way to get candid feedback. Are the perceptions of others in line with how they hope to be seen? They have got to nurture skills, abilities, and perspectives reflective of a willingness to understand and improve themselves by seeking feedback. Intentionally and routinely, they must solicit anonymous feedback from a wide array of constituents (e.g., developmental 360 assessment) and take the pulse of the community's culture. They must be conscious of the behaviors they value—those mental concepts of desirable and undesirable behavior existing in the mind as a network of priorities of different kinds of behavior (Koenig, 1981). They also need a keen awareness of the content of their soul.

## DEVELOPING OTHERS

All organizations recognize the value of ongoing training and development for their employees. However, in academe, field-specific development assumes a central role. The very mission of the university—producing trained intellects—is jeopardized unless faculty members continually push the limits of their understanding in their field of study. Throughout their career, faculty see development of field expertise as paramount, and they expect the university to support them in their efforts to stay current and contributory.

University presidents nurture the intellectual prowess of their faculty. They find resources to support key faculty learning activities: academic sabbaticals, research, attendance at professional meetings and conferences. But ordinarily, they do not groom faculty to assume senior leadership roles. University culture is not very hospitable to leadership recruitment and development. Unlike other business and military organizations that specifically and continually focus on leadership and leadership development, universities conspire against the active creation of leadership within its ranks (Thomas Hearn). Some leaders in higher education even take the position that a sitting president does not need to accept the job of succession planning (Andrew Benton).

Hearn warns of the dilemma of succession planning in a world where faculties do not chase leadership posts but, instead, follow career paths in their academic discipline. He explains the difficulty of preparing faculty for senior leadership when potential candidates come from a life of academic focus and scorn for "paper pushing." Rather than being sought after, most professors see the job of leading others as disdainful. The critical role of department chair is viewed as an unpleasant rotational duty requiring everybody to "take their turn" after three years (Dale Knobel). Many university chairs even resist the notion that they are management.

Developing faculty to assume the role of provost, chancellor, or president of their institution is so incompatible with faculty interests that some forum participants seriously questioned whether the job of top leadership is even appropriate for those achieving distinction in academic positions (E. Gordon Gee, Steve Sample). Many excellent academicians who did feel equipped to lead a university crashed and burned within a few years because they lacked leadership expertise (Steve Sample). Like their counterparts in business, having a narrow academic orientation and resisting changing from the role of academician to leader caused their career as leader to derail (Van Velsor & Leslie, 1995).

Despite an inhospitable culture, forum participants take seriously the task of identifying future leaders from within the university community. They recognize the need to create a robust and ready leadership pipeline because of the increasing complexities of leading an American university community. Tim Sullivan reminded his forum colleagues that effective day-to-day leadership is not so much about the president as it is about the men and women he chooses to be his chief lieutenants. And Andrew Benton writes that it is incumbent upon him to "keep an eye out for those who may succeed me."

Because the academic community values academic prowess and not leadership expertise, some forum participants recommend a "back door" approach to developing the leadership skill of potential successors. They intentionally shape the job experiences of those working for them, teaching them as they work together running the university. The success of this strategy is born out by CCL research (McCall, Lombardo, & Morrison, 1988). By example and by actively teaching them how to work more effectively, they provide a good dose of on-the-job training. Thomas Hearn takes seriously his role as teacher of his administrators and frames his job not as being reports or budgets but as developing the capacity of those who are responsible for these reports or budgets. Steve Sample reports adopting advice he received to

> spend a small amount of your time hiring your direct reports, evaluating them, exhorting them, setting their compensation, praising them, kicking their butts, and, when necessary, firing them. . . . It

should come out to about 10 percent of your time. For the remaining 90 percent of your time you should be doing *everything you can* to help your direct reports succeed. You should be the first assistant to the people who work for you.

## STRATEGIES FOR LEARNING

In addition to what they learned, the forum participants also shared stories and insights about how they learned—and continue to learn. Their examples of learning practices represent all four sets of tactics in CCL's learning-from-experience framework: Action Tactics (learning by doing), Thinking Tactics (learning by reflecting), Accessing-Others Tactics (learning from others), and Feeling Tactics (learning by tapping into emotions). Leaders use these tactics to learn from their own experiences, which are the primary vehicle for learning to lead. Stating what we have heard from many leaders across organizations and sectors, Al Yates reminds his colleagues that "so much of what we can learn about the true nature of leadership must come from the pain and risks of personal experience." Our research indicates that leaders maximize the learning they take away from these challenging personal experiences when they utilize multiple learning tactics (Bunker & Webb, 1992; Dalton, 1998).

### Action Tactics

When people are using action tactics, they immerse themselves in challenging situations, figure things out by trial and error, and allow their own experience to be their guide. This volume is full of stories of university presidents who had to respond quickly to confront challenges. This is most strongly illustrated in the case of crisis, such as the Matthew Shepard murder or the riots in Los Angeles. Decisions are made and actions are taken as events unfold in real time and sometimes before reactions to those events are known. The subsequent consequences of those decisions and actions are fodder for learning and growth.

Learning by trial and error is also prominent when presidents and their universities forge into new territory or undertake agendas beyond the routine work of academe. Take, for instance, the development of the Centennial Campus at North Carolina State University. Although there was a long-term plan for this public–private initiative, Marye Anne Fox describes navigating through developers, financing options, shifts in the economy, and political processes. The same is true for the University of Michigan's journey through the legal system. At each step of the way, plans could be made for various potential scenarios, but improvisation and reacting in the moment yielded additional insights.

To deal with the new or the unexpected, leaders often pull learning forward from past experiences and adapt them to the new context. Mary Sue Coleman illustrated this as she related experiences at the University of New Mexico and at the University of Iowa that prepared her to address the complicated issues she faced in her first year at Michigan. Another example comes from the University of Southern California where one of the vice presidents used the university's plan for dealing with earthquakes to organize a response to rioting near the campus.

## Thinking Tactics

When people use thinking tactics, they reflect on their past experiences, imagine the future and how different options might play out, and regularly access knowledge already accumulated and articulated by others. The forum format—the presentation of essays followed by thoughtful responses—is a prime example of using reflective thinking as a learning tool. The act of writing the essays forced forum presidents to dissect their dilemma, dig deep into the facts and feelings of the situation, and formulate what wisdom would become theirs as a result of the experience. Their essays not only talk of what happened, but include reflections on "what if . . ." and "what I would do differently."

But it did not take this forum to get the participants to recognize the importance of reflective learning. It seemed obvious to us that participants had already reflected on a number of the events and situations that they described. And Al Yates may deserve the "reflective learner" award for keeping notes for ten years on what he has learned from personal experience about the nature of leadership. Another tactic was highlighted by Scott Cowen: Always do a post-audit of a crisis with your team to articulate lessons learned and how you could do it better the next time.

Tapping into existing knowledge is another thinking tactic. There was considerable evidence throughout the forum essays of this tactic also being readily used. References are made to favorite books, authors, philosophers, and former university presidents. And accessing best practice information from other universities played an important role in helping several participants deal successfully with a challenge.

Perhaps thinking tactics stand out as the most comfortable for those in academe. Most academics enjoy reading, writing, and thinking about the world. With academe's reverence for these activities, this joy is allowed free reign. Academics, more than any other group, reflect thoroughly on all sides of an issue, dig deeper into implications and assumptions, and critique more vociferously in order to get to a learning.

## Accessing-Others Tactics

When people access others for learning, they regularly seek the advice of those around them, seek out people who have more experience than they do, and look for role models as a source of learning. Andrew Benton articulated an accessing-others tactic (which was repeated by others): "I have purposely surrounded myself with a senior team that, for the most part, approaches problem solving in different ways than I do." Gregory Farrington teased, "At Lehigh there is a group of us who work together. I'm, of course, the president. But I need help to avoid making major mistakes." This tactic of seeking the advice of others is also used more broadly in the university community. James Barker asked faculty for help in deciding how to respond to the request for removal of the South Carolina Confederate flag. He stressed the "wisdom in the counsel of many," and "found that asking those not normally asked is particularly helpful and significant."

Sometimes particular expertise is sought out to provide coaching. Mary Sue Coleman relied on others to educate and prepare her to deal with legal questions and with the media. Robert Bottoms called on a journalism professor to coach him in preparation for a *Today Show* appearance.

And finally, participants talked about learning as they worked for and with other leaders. Steve Sample participated in an ACE fellowship program that allowed him to work closely with the president of Purdue University for an entire year. Father Edward Malloy had the benefit of working closely with his predecessor and "legend" at Notre Dame, Father Hesburgh. Several participants highlighted the role of mentors in their development as leaders.

## Feeling Tactics

When people use feeling tactics, they carefully consider how they feel and how others feel in the various situations they confront, and they learn to trust their gut instincts. The importance of *emotional intelligence*—an awareness of your own emotional responses and those of others and the ability to manage yours—is now recognized as a key differentiator between average and exceptional leaders. Leaders must seek to understand an issue by its feelings as well as cold facts.

Emotional language colored each of the forum essays. Some presidents spoke of their own struggle to deal with personal emotional responses to the issues they faced. Philip Dubois spoke poignantly of his need to rely on his family to help him sort through his personal emotional response to the killing of a gay man and the hateful responses of some community members. Emotions also often accompany moments of personal insight, as Tom Hearn noted being "jolted" by a sudden revelation.

Others spoke of the emotional impact on others. In describing the reactions of different members of the university community to removing "Confederate" from the name of Confederate Memorial Hall, Gordon Gee spoke of weighing "one type of hurt over the other." Mary Sue Coleman related her realization of how the University of Michigan victory in the Supreme Court cases was a source of deep pride in the African American community but did not remove their deep pain of the past—two contradictory emotions allowed to coexist. Emotions trigger learning, they accompany learning, and they help embed important lessons deep into the student's memory.

## SUMMARY

University presidents—like CEOs in many types of organizations—face the challenges of creating change, balancing the demands of multiple constituencies, dealing with unexpected crises, and adapting to changes in the external environment. However, universities do hold a unique position in American society and maintain a distinctive character, creating different constraints for the university leader. Likewise, the same competencies and learning strategies needed for effective leadership in other settings are also needed in the university setting. However, the university setting appears to put particular demand on relational competencies—those skills, abilities, and mindsets that enable leaders to build trust, confidence, and fairness in their relationships with a diverse set of individuals and communities, or, as Albert Yates put it, "developing a special resonance with each of the many people and groups important to the success of the organization."

## REFERENCES

Bales, R. F. 1999. *Social Interaction Systems: Theory and Measurement.* New Brunswick, NJ: Transaction Publishers.

Bunker, K. A., and A. D. Webb. 1992. *Learning How to Learn from Experience: Impact of Stress and Coping.* Greensboro, NC: Center for Creative Leadership.

Dalton, M. A. 1998. *Becoming a More Versatile Learner.* Greensboro, NC: Center for Creative Leadership.

Denison, D. R. 1997. *Corporate Culture and Organizational Effectiveness.* Ann Arbor, MI: Denison Consulting.

Hall, B. P. 1995. *Values Shift: A Guide to Personal and Organizational Transformation.* Rockport, MA: Twin Lights Publishers.

Koenig, L. W. 1981. *The Chief Executive.* New York: Harcourt Brace Jovanovich.

Kotter, J. P., and J. L. Heskett. 1992. *Corporate Culture and Performance.* New York: Free Press.

McCall, M. W., Jr., M. M. Lombardo, and A. M. Morrison. 1988. *The Lessons of Experience: How Successful Executives Develop on the Job.* San Francisco: New Lexington Press.

Schein, E. H. 1992. *Organizational Culture and Leadership.* San Francisco: Jossey-Bass.

Van Velsor, E., and J. B. Leslie. 1995. "Why Executives Derail: Perspectives across Time and Cultures." *Academy of Management Executive* 9(4), 62–72.

# CHAPTER

# Lessons Learned

*David G. Brown*

From these essays and the discussions that followed, a few common and consistent themes emerged. As the chronicler of these forums, I have attempted to summarize the themes that emerged most often. Each of the eight themes is illustrated by quotes from the participants or by responsible paraphrases.

These themes represent the "lessons learned" by a group of highly successful presidents who have willingly shared their time and expertise so that other leaders, both within the academy and beyond, can themselves be even more effective.

Because these themes and lessons have grown from specific incidents in the leadership lives of specific individuals, the editor has chosen to present them in the collective "we." Hopefully, this will make the lessons more real and motivate more people to take them to heart.

**1. Advance University Values.** *We are the voice, chief implementer, and the lead advocate for the fundamental values of the university. Apply them to the big decisions! Use the bully pulpit both within and beyond the university!*

> "Leadership must reflect the nature and purpose of the institution and be exercised in conformity with the mission and structure being served."
>
> Tom Hearn, Wake Forest

> "Tie your programmatic aspirations with the university's highest goal."
>
> Wayne Clough, Georgia Tech

"[T]he difficult decisions we had to make needed to be based on widely accepted principles reflecting the university's mission and values. . . . The institution must clearly understand its mission, its strategic strengths and programmatic niches, its capacity, the broader community's needs, and the interdependent environment in which it operates."

Freeman Hrabowski, Maryland, Baltimore County

"A key role of the institutional leader is to keep alive a sense of oneness."

Phil Clay, MIT

"Compassion for people should be demonstrated after fair and objective decisions are made. The order of these two imperatives is critical."

Al Yates, Colorado State

"In order to create a realistic institutional vision, that vision in some way must reflect the values of that institution and its people."

Bill Gordon, Wake Forest

"The central task of the leader is the creation of an environment of common understandings."

Al Yates, Colorado State

"It is advisable to take every opportunity you can to tell your institution's own story in your own words."

Phil Dubois, Wyoming

"Each president has the responsibility to tell the story of her college's mission, repeatedly. We need to tell the story again and again, with passion. . . . The president has a special responsibility to use crisis-opportunities to reemphasize the basic mission in the minds of all constituencies."

Julianne Thrift, Salem

"Symbols matter, and so does substance."

Phil Dubois, Wyoming

"Culture always trumps strategy. The leader can only accomplish something within the context of the culture and its values which act as constraints on the leader."

Larry Penley, Colorado State

"[T]hese cases were going to continue to provide us with the opportunity to educate our campus and educate the public on the issues at stake and begin to heal some of the rifts that had developed on both sides of this important national issue."

Mary Sue Coleman, Michigan

"A basic value and priority for me has been to create and then support the very best leadership team possible, recognizing the axiom that people do not stay with good organizations, they stay with good leaders. My favorite quote is one that has been ascribed to John Gardner. I do not know if he said it or not, but he should have if he did not: 'The first and last job of a leader is to keep hope alive.' I have used this many times in speaking with our own leadership team, urging them to spend more time and give more attention to their best people, rather than worrying about what cannot be fixed. I think our biggest job as CEOs is finding the right leadership, people who not only know their job, but have the people skills to make omelets without breaking eggs. That is how you create a culture of excellence, where people actually take satisfaction from the accomplishments of others."

James Moeser, North Carolina—Chapel Hill

"When major events occur, it is very important that the president lead in setting the tone and articulating clearly the principles that are involved. A president's absence or silence can be so noticeable that it can be perceived as a statement in itself. The tactics of dealing with a situation flow from the values and principles involved. If they are not clear, then the tactics are likely to seem hollow and out of context."

Greg Farrington, Lehigh

"Transforming inspiration comes when the leader loves his institution, its people, and its values."

Tim Sullivan, William and Mary

"[You need to have a] genuine desire to serve an institution and to serve other people rather than serving yourself."

Bill Gordon, Wake Forest

"An administrator should not accept a position unless he or she is ready to make every decision on the basis on what is in the best interest of the institution."

Graham Spanier, Penn State

"Be willing to take clear positions on issues of fundamental principle. . . . Ultimately the level of respect that society has for colleges and universities is going to be in direct proportion to their willingness to stand for humane values."

Greg Farrington, Lehigh

"People look to presidents of [academic] institutions to take a [moral] stand."

Scott Cowen, Tulane

"It is a very sad commentary that the pain of acting to align our actions with the values of the university is frequently greater than the pain of doing nothing."

Molly Broad, North Carolina System

**2. Honor Personal Convictions.** *On a few critical occasions we have acted because we, personally, thought it was the right thing to do. Have the courage of your convictions!*

"In order to weather forces that would have your job—or even your life—you need the courage that grounds you in the sense that what you are doing is right."

Gordon Gee, Vanderbilt

"To have the courage of one's convictions is a prerequisite for effective leadership."

Al Yates, Colorado State

"Without a powerful sense of personal honor, an honesty that compels moral choice even under the hardest circumstances, leadership is impossible."

Tim Sullivan, William and Mary

"[Effective leaders] possess a clear set of ethical standards that can be communicated and understood."

Charles Steger, Virginia Tech

"Because we inevitably find ourselves involved in controversy, often regarding basic principles, it is essential that we own and understand a set of basic values that we act to preserve and enhance."

Bob Bottoms, DePauw

"Good leadership is almost always dependent upon personal qualities and characteristics, personal values, even character."

Bill Gordon, Wake Forest

"Do not let the crisis override your principles, but do not let abstract principles get in the way either."

Phil Dubois, Wyoming

"[What's important in a crisis] is consistency, candor, honesty, a bit of humility, visibility, and speed."

Greg Farrington, Lehigh

"It is important to be transparent—absolutely clear—about what you value and what you expect."

David Hardesty, West Virginia

"Openness, transparency, and candor are key attributes at the time of crisis."

Scott Cowen, Tulane

"Since people are going to be reading entrails, trying to decide who you are, tell them and tell them right from the beginning."

Larry Bacow, Tufts

"We enhance our chances [for success] greatly if we see ourselves truly as the servant of others."

Tim Sullivan, William and Mary

"Leadership is service."

Jim Barker, Clemson

"We want to trust our leaders, to be assured of their virtue, and know they will make the right choices. Virtue, it can be asserted, is really the basis of trust—and thus, of leadership."

Al Yates, Colorado State

"Build trust and confidence."

Freeman Hrabowski, Maryland, Baltimore County

"Prepare to lead in your own way and in your own style."

Andy Benton, Pepperdine

"Draw your own conclusions based upon what you see."

Larry Bacow, Tufts

"The first personal requirement for leadership as a form of teaching is a passion for ideas, a love of learning."

Tom Hearn, Wake Forest

"Passion gives us stamina."

David Hardesty, West Virginia

"True passion, as conveyed through thoughtful language and behaviors, is a critical aspect of leadership."

Al Yates, Colorado State

"If you are going to make a difference, you must have passion. A lot of people talk, but change will not occur if one does not have passion."

Wayne Clough, Georgia Tech

"You have to want to be involved, to have a passion, to be excited."

John Ryan, SUNY–Maritime College

"Genuine humility ... understanding our own inability to control all the forces around us, is important to good leadership."
                                                      Al Yates, Colorado State

"[Focusing on ultimate goals] requires the suppression of ego and the nearly universal appetite for personal commendation."
                                                 Tim Sullivan, William and Mary

"I knew that I had to have ... sufficient humility to acknowledge when I made mistakes and attend to the aftermath."
                                                   Edward Malloy, Notre Dame

"I try not to take myself as seriously as others take me."
                                                        Jim Barker, Clemson

"Do not even consider administration if you cannot tolerate disagreement, anger."
                                                    Graham Spanier, Penn State

"Teachers as leaders of deliberative processes must have a high tolerance for criticism and dissent."
                                                     Tom Hearn, Wake Forest

"A little integrity is better than any career."
Ralph Waldo Emerson, as quoted by Molly Broad, North Carolina
                                                                      System

"The leader must work assiduously to cultivate in herself and in her advisors the capacity to *think free*."
                                           Steve Sample, Southern California

**3. Plan and Make Decisions.** *We must plan for the future and patiently guide others toward it. Have a process and a plan! Make decisions!*

"If the issue is vital, stand up and take whatever heat that comes."
                                                        Jim Barker, Clemson

"The real action is what leadership is about: it is not the visioning. . . . Good leadership is knowing how much future to introduce into the present."
                                                  Larry Penley, Colorado State

"Many men want to *be* president, but very few want to *do* president."
                                           Steve Sample, Southern California

"Leaders both steer and row."
                                                        Jim Barker, Clemson

"An important strategy for progress is to take away all excuses that people give for making bad choices."
                                                      Al Yates, Colorado State

"We are responsible for creating messages for the future."

        Pam Shockley-Zalabak, Colorado—Colorado Springs

"Take the lead in talking about the issue."

        Freeman Hrabowski, Maryland, Baltimore County

"What administrators have to do in a situation such as this, ideally, is to weigh one type of hurt over the other and figure out which loss is the least costly to the university's spirit and to its ideals."

        Gordon Gee, Vanderbilt

"Avoid appointing commissions, task forces, committees, and the like unless there is a clear and important objective in mind. Before embarking on any major initiative, be confident the juice is worth the squeeze."

        William Kirwan, Maryland System

"True leaders must see with unfailing clarity the larger objectives they not merely seek to achieve—but which they must achieve."

        Tim Sullivan, William and Mary

"Make your presence felt. Walk around and show the flag."

        Steve Sample, Southern California

"Summon the courage to make difficult choices; respect and a clear conscience are more important than popularity."

        Al Yates, Colorado State

"Under ideal conditions, up to 30 percent of a top leader's time can be spent on really substantive matters, and no more than 70 percent of his time should be spent reacting to or presiding over trivial, routine, or ephemeral matters."

        Steve Sample, Southern California

"Obtain a clear vision for where you want to go and how you want to get there."

        Andy Benton, Pepperdine

"During my time as president, I have made every effort to bring other Holy Cross religious into positions of leadership and responsibility so that they could constitute a core group of potential successors."

        Edward Malloy, Notre Dame

"You cannot be prepared for every crisis, but you can be prepared."

        Phil Dubois, Wyoming

"Have a well developed emergency plan."

        Steve Sample, Southern California

"[My media advisors'] relentless demands to think in advance about our reactions to various outcomes allowed me to learn how to shape

our public presence on the substance of the cases. . . . Our most grueling discussions focused on the scenario of a possible defeat."

                                        Mary Sue Coleman, Michigan

"[We] called together our crisis management team, a standing body
that had existed for some time at our institution."

                                        Philip Dubois, Wyoming

"Define the process from the beginning. The credibility of the process is crucial. This can be achieved only if the rules of engagement
are established through a collaborative process at the outset, not as
the need for decisions arises."

                                        William Kirwan, Maryland System

"We had established clear consultative procedures, and we put them
to good use."

                                        Mary Sue Coleman, Michigan

"Avoid . . . whenever possible . . . quarrelling simultaneously over
who has the authority to make a particular decision and what the
decision should be."

                                        Steve Sample, Southern California

"When confronted by crisis, seek ways to ensure that your institution is not defined by the crisis itself, but by your response to it."

                                        Phil Dubois, Wyoming

"I thought I could do things quickly, but not substantively. I found
that I could do things substantively, but not quickly."

                                        Jim Barker, Clemson

"Great institutions are seldom built by giant leaps, but rather by
small steps taken consistently in the same direction."

                                        Al Yates, Colorado State

"The most important lesson we have learned is patience, patience, patience, even when success seems to be absolutely assured by action."

                                        Marye Anne Fox, North Carolina State

"Patience is a virtue, but it comes at a cost."

                                        William Kirwan, Maryland System

"Time is a real ally if you can use it, in terms of minimizing disruption to the organization."

                                        John DeGioia, Georgetown

"Time pressures push presidents to avoid mistakes rather than make
courageous moves."

                                        Dale Knobel, Denison

**4. Maintain Institutional Morale.** *We must lead in tranquil times and times of crisis. Be as positive as possible! Recognize that leaders are needed most in times of crisis!*

> "It is the responsibility of the president to engender an expectation of excellence, to create a culture of high expectations."
>
> Harold Martin, Winston-Salem State

> "Leaders must forego the luxuries of pessimism, cynicism, negativism, irresponsibility, and, at times, independence. . . . Seek always to turn adversity to advantage; look for the silver lining, the ray of hope and opportunity."
>
> Al Yates, Colorado State

> "Be confident and inspire confidence."
>
> Andy Benton, Pepperdine

> "My most important objective during these stressful times was to maintain morale throughout the university community, and I worked toward that goal every day."
>
> Mary Sue Coleman, Michigan

> "In times of crisis, especially financial crisis, the role of the president is to protect the institution's priorities and sustain its sense of momentum."
>
> William Kirwan, Maryland System

> "In times of severe crisis, the president's voice matters, and it may be the only one that does."
>
> Phil Dubois, Wyoming

> "Consistency in decision making breeds comfort and confidence. Ambiguity should be avoided."
>
> Al Yates, Colorado State

**5. Consult and Involve.** *We must accomplish most of our objectives through others. Build a quality team and give its members room to succeed! Consult widely!*

> "The essential strategy for the newcomer is to conduct a careful institutional audit, listen rather than speaking, and to postpone any substantive decisions until such time as the institution, its problems and people, are thoroughly consulted and understood. . . . A new officer must solicit advice and assistance from as many seasoned veterans as possible."
>
> Tom Hearn, Wake Forest

"In contemplating any significant institutional change, engage the shared governance bodies at the outset."

William Kirwan, Maryland System

"[I continue to] meet individually with a cross-section of faculty each year and get around to the various student residences for informal discussions."

Edward Malloy, Notre Dame

"Consensus should always be sought, but the 'buck has to stop someplace.'"

Al Yates, Colorado State

"Ask experts for advice. They are very wise and they want to be involved. . . . There is wisdom in the counsel of many."

Jim Barker, Clemson

"Especially in times of crises, presidents must involve and acknowledge all members of the college community."

Julianne Thrift, Salem

"Get out and visit faculty in their offices."

Dale Knobel, Denison

Listen to and understand students. They are "coming to us today with a popular culture that is at odds with civility and community."

Phil Clay, MIT

"Everyone—faculty, staff, and students—needs to hear from students firsthand."

Freeman Hrabowski, Maryland, Baltimore County

"A leader has to be sympathetic to [an opposing view], even if he is not sympathetic to its particular manifestation."

Gordon Gee, Vanderbilt

"We should have sought actively, at each stage of our master planning, specific engagement and proactive involvement [of the community] in designing this project, rather than only exhibiting an openness to listening to their position."

Marye Anne Fox, North Carolina State

"Few of us have so many friends that we can afford to sacrifice even one of them. . . . [Leaders should] make the effort to develop empathy with all affected stakeholders, to walk in their shoes as you would your own."

Al Yates, Colorado State

"I felt it refreshing to get so much feedback from all constituencies . . . even have people tell me that I was completely wrong."
                                                                                John Ryan, SUNY–Maritime College

"The contrarian academic leader works hard to see things through the eyes of others while at the same time assiduously cultivating her intellectual independence."
                                                                                Steve Sample, Southern California

"A second personal requirement [for leadership] is a high tolerance for process."
                                                                                Tom Hearn, Wake Forest

"Encourage . . . trusted lieutenants to summon the courage and will to be candid and truthful," especially when the CEO is "full of it."
                                                                                Al Yates, Colorado State

"Communication must be open, honest, direct, and often. Versatility in communication is a skill worth developing. . . . Successful leadership involves seizing every opportunity to teach, to listen, and to learn from those with whom we interact."
                                                                                Al Yates, Colorado State

Communicate "priorities through deliberate use of both time and language."
                                                                                Freeman Hrabowski, Maryland, Baltimore County

"The best executive is the one who recruits the most competent men around, tells them what he wants done, and then gets out of their way so they can do it."
                                                                                Teddy Roosevelt, as quoted by Steve Sample, Southern California

"Hire good people. Support them well and let them excel. It works."
                                                                                Al Yates, Colorado State

"Diversity in people and ideas is a cornerstone of effective leadership."
                                                                                Al Yates, Colorado State

"Build a team with diverse skills."
                                                                                Andy Benton, Pepperdine

"We found that we need all of our distinct 'voices' [perspectives] in the room to best address critical issues. . . . [As presidents] we cannot 'fix' everything and must rely on the contributions of others."
                                                                                David Hardesty, West Virginia

"My most important role was to identify others on campus with influence and with the willingness to commit time and energy to these efforts. . . . Identify allies among leading faculty and influential administrators who can be supportive of change."

Freeman Hrabowski, Maryland, Baltimore County

"Building the team and sharing the message is critically important."

James Moeser, North Carolina—Chapel Hill

"Work for those who work for you. . . . You should be doing *everything you can* to help your direct reports succeed. . . . It is not that you should simply be your lieutenant's staff person; you should be his best staff person."

Steve Sample, Southern California

"My challenge was to develop the capacity of those who were responsible . . . not to do their job."

Tom Hearn, Wake Forest

"Never make a decision that can be reasonably delegated."

Steve Sample, Southern California

"As president, one must work hard to create a system of colleagues that supports the institution as a whole."

Scott Cowen, Tulane

"To change the culture within an institution, one must involve and transform some of the faculty leadership."

Harold Martin, Winston-Salem State

"[Do not] underestimate the significance of the direct assistance necessary to perform the [president's] task effectively."

Edward Malloy, Notre Dame

"I learned that lawsuits come with the terrain and that having expertise and good judgment in the Office of the General Counsel is extremely important."

Mary Sue Coleman, Michigan

"Any academic institution that has to rely upon its president for all its good ideas is a university in trouble."

Larry Bacow, Tufts

"Provide advance notice to affected constituencies."

Gordon Gee, Vanderbilt

"[Recognize] the importance of distributing information from the university to the public on an ongoing basis during each crisis."

Phil Dubois, Wyoming

"Many media representatives are lazy: just plan for it."

Phil Dubois, Wyoming

"Mind the media."

William Kirwan, Maryland System

"Learning how to deal with the press is an essential lesson for college presidents."

Bob Bottoms, DePauw

"In this present media age, an essential requirement of university leaders is that they be confident and competent communicators when a microphone or a television camera is in their face."

Tom Hearn, Wake Forest

**6. Mind the Data.** *We have found that data trump hunches, opinions, and even instincts. Collect diverse opinions! Get the numbers!*

"Data rule."

William Kirwan, Maryland System

"Take time for careful study prior to each major decision."

Larry Faulkner, Texas

"The time of transition between election and assuming the responsibility is a prime opportunity for putting together one's leadership team, soliciting advice from experienced presidents, interacting with the members of the board of trustees and other major constituencies, and reading in the literature about presidential leadership and about higher education."

Edward Malloy, Notre Dame

"The first and most obvious task for any institutional leader is to know his or her own institution intimately and thoroughly."

Tom Hearn, Wake Forest

"Visit other campuses to learn from other effective models."

Freeman Hrabowski, Maryland, Baltimore County

"When preparing to cut [or to make any major decision], you need to achieve as deep a grasp as possible of the impacts of the proposed cuts. These are fragile ecosystems. You need to understand the key points in those systems when making reductions."

John DeGioia, Georgetown

"When facing a crisis, look to the institutions that have been there and done that, and when possible, learn best practices before you need them."

Phil Dubois, Wyoming

**7. Exercise Our Priestly and Teaching Roles.** *As presidents we are responsible for both an institution and a community. Accept your responsibility for counseling! Coach!*

"Our primary consideration in the management of each crisis was to provide maximum institutional support to the families of the victims."

Philip Dubois, Wyoming

Tend to people first. "If we did not tend to people and treat them well, we could lose forever our most precious asset, and any physical recovery [from a Fort Collins flood] would be a hollow victory."

Al Yates, Colorado State

Show "appreciation for the efforts and accomplishments of colleagues and students."

Freeman Hrabowski, Maryland, Baltimore County

"We must build organizational trust, a trust that is dependent on but extends beyond personal credibility." Key elements in organization trust are competence, consistency, concern, openness, and honesty and an understanding of the value of change.

Pam Shockley-Zalabak, Colorado—Colorado Springs

"[A true leader] exercises a Homeric responsibility to bring to life through narrative and metaphor what we cannot easily express for ourselves. It is a teaching responsibility, one that creates meaning about the future through the symbolization process."

Larry Penley, Colorado State

"Be certain to celebrate individual and organizational accomplishment coming from all areas of the institution."

William Kirwan, Maryland System

**8. Do Not Ignore Self-renewal.** *The presidency draws on a broad spectrum of skills and provides many opportunities to be with very interesting people. Take advantage of these learning opportunities! Keep healthy!*

"It seems to me that we need a lot more time to think, write, teach, and reflect."

Scott Cowen, Tulane

"Save time to think."

Larry Faulkner, Texas

"A final consideration that became clear during the first year of my presidency was the importance of a sense of balance in my personal life with regard to prayer, recreation, reading and scholarly engagement, and sufficient rest and relaxation."

Edward Malloy, Notre Dame

"You're not a superhero. . . . Pay attention to your own health."

Phil Dubois, Wyoming

"Have a mentor outside your institution, especially if you are a president who came to office from within."

Charles Steger, Virginia Tech

"If you do make a mistake, do not run away from it and do not ever repeat it again."

Scott Cowen, Tulane

"It is okay to make mistakes as long as you learn from them."

Larry Bacow, Tufts

"Always do a post-audit of a crisis and make sure you articulate lessons learned. After it is over, it is important to sit down and analyze how you could do it better the next time."

Scott Cowen, Tulane

"Encourage self-examination by yourself and others."

Freeman Hrabowski, Maryland, Baltimore County

## MORAL LEADERS IN ACTION

Leaders are most influential—and most visible—in times of crisis. Crises reveal the fundamental convictions, styles, and strengths of leaders. The picture painted by the incidents reported in this volume, and the lessons derived from them, highlights a group of leaders with strong personal convictions about the welfare of others and society as a whole.

University presidents honor most the values of their institutions, even when those values are unpopular in the larger society. Decisions are informed by multiple perspectives and made in the context of well-understood personal convictions about right and wrong. The vignettes chronicled in this volume reveal that university presidents put the interests of others above self-interest. They pursue enduring and future benefits over immediate gratification. They listen to others, eschew profitability for its own sake, and examine conventional wisdom. They act. They are indeed moral leaders.

I am in awe at the quantity and quality of time so many talented and busy moral leaders gave to the forum and this book as a commitment to the profession. Our hope is that leaders who read this volume will select at least five or ten of the lesson quotes that are most meaningful to them. Our hope is that they will contemplate the opportunities in their own situations and that they will act with more knowledge, more anticipation, more confidence, more conviction, and with the morality of each decision paramount in their thinking.

# INDEX

# ABOUT THE EDITOR
# AND CONTRIBUTORS

Contributors are identified by the position they held when the essays in this volume were presented. Philip L. Dubois now holds the position of Chancellor at the University of North Carolina at Charlotte. Marye Anne Fox is now Chancellor at San Diego State University. Presidents Thomas K. Hearn, Father Edward S. Malloy, and Timothy J. Sullivan have since retired.

LAWRENCE S. BACOW, President, Tufts University

JAMES F. BARKER, President, Clemson University

ANDREW K. BENTON, President, Pepperdine University

ROBERT G. BOTTOMS, President, DePauw University

DAVID G. BROWN, Provost Emeritus, Wake Forest University

MARY SUE COLEMAN, President, University of Michigan

SCOTT S. COWEN, President, Tulane University

PHILIP L. DUBOIS, President, University of Wyoming

GREGORY C. FARRINGTON, President, Lehigh University

LARRY R. FAULKNER, President, University of Texas at Austin

MARYE ANNE FOX, Chancellor, North Carolina State University

PAMELA B. GANN, President, Claremont McKenna College

E. GORDON GEE, Chancellor, Vanderbilt University

WILLIAM C. GORDON, Provost, Wake Forest University

DAVID C. HARDESTY, President, West Virginia University

THOMAS K. HEARN JR., President, Wake Forest University

FREEMAN H. HRABOWSKI III, President, University of Maryland, Baltimore County

WILLIAM E. KIRWAN, Chancellor, University System of Maryland

DALE T. KNOBEL, President, Denison University

EDWARD S. MALLOY, President, University of Notre Dame

CYNTHIA D. McCAULEY, Faculty, Center for Creative Leadership

LARRY E. PENLEY, President, Colorado State University

KATHLEEN M. PONDER, Faculty, Center for Creative Leadership

STEVEN B. SAMPLE, President, University of Southern California

PAMELA SHOCKLEY-ZALABAK, Chancellor, University of Colorado at Colorado Springs

GRAHAM B. SPANIER, President, Pennsylvania State University

CHARLES W. STEGER, President, Virginia Polytechnic Institute and State University

TIMOTHY J. SULLIVAN, President, The College of William and Mary

ALBERT C. YATES, President Emeritus, Colorado State University